D0462951

THE BEST LITTLE ARMY IN THE WORLD

THE BEST LITTLE ARMY IN THE WORLD:

The Canadians in Northwest Europe, 1944–1945

J. L. Granatstein

PATRICK CREAN EDITIONS

An imprint of HarperCollins*PublishersLtd*

By the end of the war, having paid a steep price in blood for the peace-time neglect of military professionalism, [First Canadian Army] was probably the best little army in the world. Certainly in the performance of the Canadian Army overseas the government of Canada got much more than it deserved.

—LCol (ret.) Dr. John A. English, *Lament for an Army: The Decline of Canadian Military Professionalism*

Contents

CANADIAN LANDINGS ON D-DAY

June 6, 1944

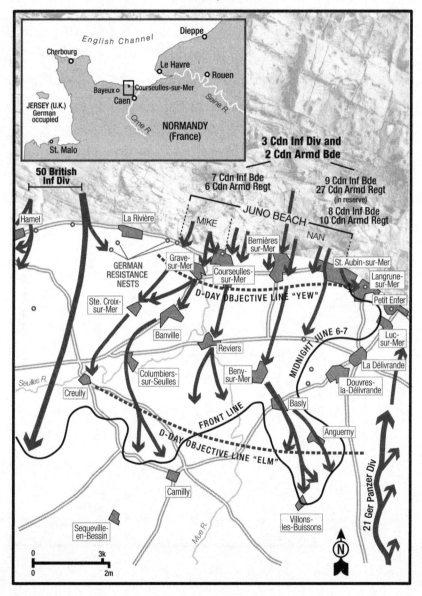

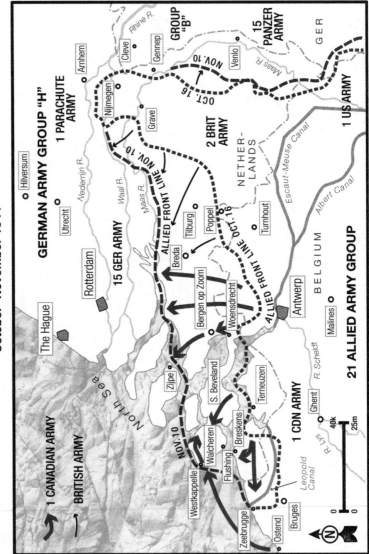

THE NORTHERN FRONT
October–November 1944

GERMAN ARMY GROUP "H"

GROUP "B"

15 PANZER ARMY

GER

1 PARACHUTE ARMY

Arnhem

Cleve

Gennep

Venlo

Rhine R.

NOV. 10

OCT. 16

Nijmegen

Grave

2 BRIT ARMY

NETHER-LANDS

1 US ARMY

NOV. 10

ALLIED FRONT LINE

ALLIED FRONT LINE OCT. 16

Hilversum

Utrecht

Nederrijn R.

Waal R.

Maas R.

Maas R.

15 GER ARMY

Tilburg

Poppel

Turnhout

Escaut-Meuse Canal

Albert Canal

Rotterdam

Breda

Bergen op Zoom

Woensdrecht

Antwerp

BELGIUM

Malines

The Hague

North Sea

Zijpe

S. Beveland

Terneuzen

R. Scheldt

Ghent

21 ALLIED ARMY GROUP

1 CANADIAN ARMY

BRITISH ARMY

NOV. 10

Walcheren

Breskens

1 CDN ARMY

40k

25m

R. LYS

Westkappelle

Flushing

Leopold Canal

Zeebrugge

Bruges

Ostend

N

0

0

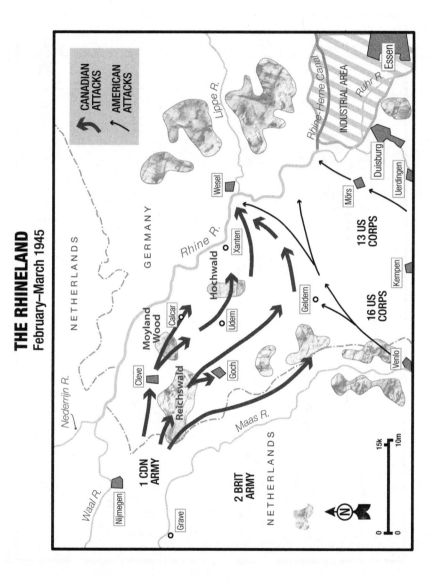

THE RHINELAND
February–March 1945

CANADIAN ATTACKS
AMERICAN ATTACKS

NETHERLANDS

GERMANY

Nederrijn R.

Waal R.

Nijmegen

Grave

Cleve

Moyland Wood

Calcar

Reichswald

Goch

Udem

Hochwald

Rhine R.

Xanten

Wesel

Lippe R.

Rhine-Herne Canal

Ruhr R.

Essen

INDUSTRIAL AREA

Duisburg

Uerdingen

Mörs

Kempen

13 US CORPS

16 US CORPS

Geldern

Venlo

Maas R.

NETHERLANDS

1 CDN ARMY

2 BRIT ARMY

15k

10m

0

0

N

THE FINAL PHASE
March–May 1945

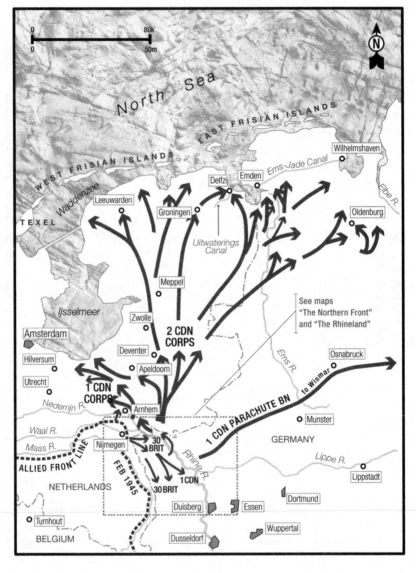

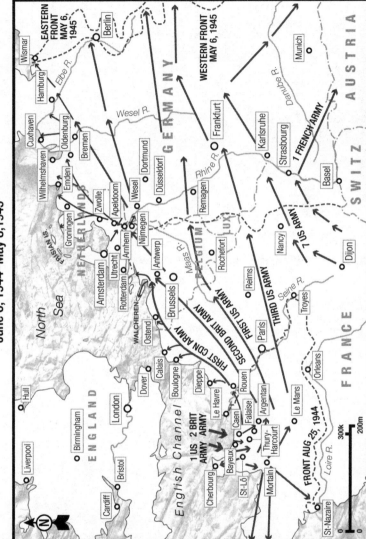

VICTORY IN EUROPE
June 6, 1944–May 8, 1945

EASTERN FRONT MAY 6, 1945

WESTERN FRONT MAY 1945

GERMANY

AUSTRIA

SWITZ

North Sea

NETHERLANDS

BELGIUM

LUX

FRANCE

ENGLAND

English Channel

Wismar
Hamburg
Berlin
Cuxhaven
Oldenburg
Bremen
Wilhelmshaven
Emden
Groningen
Zwolle
Apeldoorn
Arnhem
Nijmegen
Wesel
Dortmund
Düsseldorf
Remagen
Frankfurt
Karlsruhe
Strasbourg
Munich
Basel
Dijon
Nancy
Rochefort
Reims
Paris
Troyes
Orleans
Le Mans
Argentan
Falaise
Rouen
Le Havre
Dieppe
Boulogne
Calais
Dover
Ostend
Antwerp
Brussels
Walcheren
Rotterdam
Amsterdam
Utrecht
Frisian Is.
Hull
Liverpool
Birmingham
London
Bristol
Cardiff
Caen
Bayeux
St-Lô
Cherbourg
Thury-Harcourt
Mortain
St-Nazaire

1 FRENCH ARMY
7 US ARMY
THIRD US ARMY
FIRST US ARMY
SECOND BRIT ARMY
FIRST CDN ARMY
1 US 2 BRIT ARMY ARMY

FRONT AUG 25, 1944

Elbe R.
Wesel R.
Rhine R.
Danube R.
Maas R.
Seine R.
Loire R.

300k
200m
0
0

N

INTRODUCTION

I t is now more than seventy-five years since the Second World War began and Canada went to war on September 10, 1939. The nation had been mired in a long economic depression, hundreds of thousands of men and women were unemployed, and there was no great enthusiasm for going to war. The memories of the casualties and losses of the Great War of 1914–18 remained fresh, but there was in Canada—still very much a British dominion—the certainty that the United Kingdom was right in all circumstances, and that if England felt compelled to do so, London was right to fight Hitler. Then, if Britain was at war, Canada had to be at her side. Independent in law she may have been since the Statute of Westminster of 1931, but in practice Canada remained a psychological colony.

The next six years can only be characterized as a mixed blessing for Canadians. The national economy boomed, there were jobs for everyone, and living standards improved even after rationing and controls were put in place by Ottawa. The nation mobilized a huge military force—10 percent of the 11 million total Canadian population.

The Royal Canadian Air Force (RCAF) went from effectively nothing to 250,000 men, manning a full bomber group and countless fighter, fighter-bomber, and transport squadrons in Europe, Asia, and at home. The Royal Canadian Navy (RCN), again from a standing start, increased its strength to 100,000, and by war's end had convoyed across the North Atlantic half of the merchant vessels that supplied Britain. In addition, the RCN crewed aircraft carriers, cruisers, Tribal destroyers, minesweepers, and dozens of corvettes. These were amazing achievements.

The Canadian Army expanded by even more. In all, 750,000 men enlisted in the Army, almost all of them volunteers for service anywhere. The troops had to learn their new trade on the job, and there were very few competent instructors in the tiny Permanent Force (PM), or the "Saturday-night soldiers," of the militia. Initially, there weren't even boots or helmets for all the men, let alone rifles, tanks, artillery, or Bren guns. But as the war went on, battalions, brigades, divisions, and corps took shape, and the Canadian Army built up a large force in England, initially to defend the British Isles but then to prepare for the invasion of Northwest Europe.

There was a disastrous deployment of a two-battalion brigade to Hong Kong, lost entirely to a Japanese attack in December 1941. There was the disastrous raid on Dieppe in August 1942, when few men made it off the beaches and few who got ashore at all made it back to England. And in mid-1943, soon after the creation of First Canadian Army in England, with five divisions and two armoured brigades, there was the dispatch of the 1st Canadian Division and the 1st Armoured Brigade to fight in the invasion of Sicily as part of the British Eighth Army. That deployment had, by the end of 1943, expanded into a two-division corps, splitting the Army, and leaving three divisions and an armoured brigade under its direct command in England. First Canadian Army would not be reunited until March 1945.

The costly Italian Campaign was, sadly, something of a sideshow, especially so after D-Day, the invasion of Normandy by the British, Americans, and Canadians. The 3rd Canadian Division, supported by the 2nd Armoured Brigade, distinguished itself on D-Day, and it fought long and hard through the Norman villages and the cities of Carpiquet and Caen. The 2nd Canadian Infantry and 4th Canadian Armoured divisions joined it in France in July, and in August First Canadian Army played a major role in closing the Falaise Gap in the face of fierce opposition from the best German panzer divisions.

But there was much criticism, then and since, that the Canadians were slow in sewing the Falaise Pocket closed, and that they were laggard in taking the Channel ports in September. Even the Canadians' stellar, gruelling performance in clearing the Scheldt estuary, thus opening Antwerp to the shipping that the Allies desperately needed, won few kudos. Nor did the Canadians' role in the Rhineland, in crossing the Rhine, and in liberating the Netherlands win much praise (except from the ever-grateful Dutch). First Canadian Army was the Cinderella army, spattered with mud but with no gallant prince to sweep it off to glory.

The argument of this book is that First Canadian Army, with its 185,000 soldiers, backed up by many more in the lines of communication and in England and Canada, became the best little army in the world in 1944–45. There were no Canadians with field marshals' batons in their knapsacks, only officers without battle experience who learned how to fight and defeat a skilful, determined enemy. Few soldiers would win the Victoria Cross, but there was enough gallantry and courage to go around, enough brave men to lead their platoons, companies, and battalions to victory. There were even public relations officers who somehow failed at the task of convincing the world that First Canadian Army truly mattered.

This was unfortunate because in the First World War, the Canadian Corps had earned and established an extraordinary reputation as the shock troops of the British Expeditionary Force. Under Lieutenant-General Sir Arthur Currie, the Corps defeated a quarter of the German army in the final Hundred Days offensive. Its lustre remains undiminished, even for usually critical historians in Britain and Australia.

There is no such renown for First Canadian Army, but there should be. Its unblooded divisions fought much better in Normandy than the critics concede, and it faced tough opposition in the fortified ports on the English Channel. But the soldiers learned how to defeat a formidable enemy, and the Canadians proved themselves on the Scheldt, where, in the most miserable muddy, cold conditions imaginable, they opened the great river to the port of Antwerp while paying a terrible price in blood. It took the Canadians time—and a great conscription crisis at home—to fill their ranks again, but in the Rhineland, in crossing the Rhine, and in the Netherlands and northern Germany, the Army performed with dash, courage, and great skill. General Harry Crerar, the General Officer Commanding-in-Chief of First Canadian Army, was no Currie in battlefield smarts, but he provided competent and sound leadership. The commander of II Canadian Corps, Lieutenant-General Guy Simonds, was arguably the best, most imaginative Allied corps commander, and division commanders like Bert Hoffmeister and Bruce Matthews, as well as brigade commanders such as Robert Moncel, James Roberts, and John Rockingham, were as good as or better than any in the British or U.S. armies. All five of those last mentioned were militiamen, not professional soldiers; all five learned under fire, on the job, how to beat the enemy.

And the Canadian soldiers they led were first-rate. They served in an all-volunteer army (until the very last months of the war), the only one in the Allied ranks. They received good training once their commanders realized that war was a serious business, and they developed an extraordinary esprit de corps—they believed that their platoon in their regiment was the very best one in the best little army in the world. Their equipment, much of it produced in Canada, was good, and it was available in huge quantities. The soldiers fought the Germans hard. Backed by their artillery, armour, engineers, signallers, and logistical expertise, they played a huge role in winning the war—the greatest role of any nation outside the Great Powers of the United States, Britain, and the Soviet Union. The riflemen and their corporals and sergeants became highly skilled fighters, and when casualties inevitably cut down section and platoon leaders, ordinary men stepped forward to lead in extraordinary times.

The best little army in the world? Canadians are not a military people, not ones to pay much attention to their soldiers in peacetime. But Canadians, as historian Charles Stacey wrote, can be fierce and warlike when they are called on to fight in a just cause. The Second World War was a good war, perhaps the last truly good war, and Canadian soldiers rose to the challenge. They paid a high price in blood for their government's neglect of the Army for the two decades after 1919, but they absorbed the lessons of the battlefield, and in Northwest Europe First Canadian Army became a splendid, hard-hitting fighting formation. Their performance in action was superb, and Canadians and others need to know this story.

CHAPTER 1

Going to War Again: 1939–43

The best little army in the world did not exist on September 10, 1939, when Canada declared war on Adolf Hitler's Germany. The Non-Permanent Active Militia (NPAM), the nation's part-time soldiers, numbered some 50,000 men scattered across the land, from Prince Edward Island to British Columbia. Many of the militiamen were veterans of the 1914–18 war; others had joined because their friends and neighbours belonged to the local regiment; still others enlisted for something to do in the dreary years of the Great Depression. Jobs were scarce all across the country, the world seemed to be threatened by fascism and communism, and many men craved a sense of stability and some social status. Even in hard times, the militia provided an anchor. But in many of these understrength units, the soldiers were merely names on a list; most active participants had received only basic training in their local armoury, though they could at least march and fire a rifle. Very few had ever participated in serious (or even non-serious) military exercises during their annual two weeks of summer training, and in any case, there was literally no modern military equipment—no tanks, no armoured cars other than a handful of already obsolete models, few trucks, nothing but Great War–vintage artillery, no modern light machine guns, and frequently little or no ammunition. There were not even enough Great War steel helmets to equip more than a single division, something fewer than 20,000 soldiers. It was all a far cry from the great Canadian Corps that had smashed the German army during the Hundred Days of 1918, demonstrable proof that complete governmental neglect could reduce the military to obsolescence in two decades. Without up-to-date equipment, there was no army.

Without hard training, there were no soldiers either. Summer training was run along the lines of "bang-bang, you're dead," and "no, I'm not; clank-clank, I'm a tank" at Sarcee Camp or Valcartier or Petawawa or others. The federal government, grappling with the crippling Great Depression and the widespread antipathy to the military that had developed out of Canadian isolationism and out of the shock and revulsion at the casualties and losses in "the war to end war," had starved the militia. The Army budgets in the last years before the start of the Second World War were only $18.7 million in 1937–38, $16.7 million in 1938–39, and $21.4 million in 1939–40. This, however, was a big improvement over 1930–31, when the militia budget had been all of $11 million. In current 2015 dollars, we might multiply these numbers by sixteen or seventeen.

Those pathetically small militia budgets included the sums for Canada's professional soldiers, the Permanent Force (PF). The PF in 1939 numbered some 4,261 all told, with 450 of those being officers. The able commanders of battalions and brigades who had remained in the Army after the Great War were now mostly in their fifties; many were older, in ill health, or hopelessly out of date in their thinking. Junior officers were recent graduates from the Royal Military College or direct-entry young men. None of the PF officers had ever seen full-strength units on exercise. There were no full-strength units to see: the country's three PF infantry battalions and its two cavalry regiments, three field artillery batteries, transport companies, and other units were all sadly under-strength. Units were scattered across the country—the Princess Patricia's Canadian Light Infantry had one company in Winnipeg and its other one in Esquimalt, British Columbia. Only once after 1929 had there been a large Permanent Force training exercise—and that exercise, in the summer of 1938, was deemed a fiasco. "Simply put," wrote historian Brian Reid, "the regular army, which was responsible for training the militia in the science of war, did not have a clue." "The Canadian military were not soldiers," Lieutenant-General Maurice Pope later remarked of the PF, "although we had many experts on the King's dress regulations." In effect, there were almost no generals able to lead troops—if Canada had had any trained troops!—on operations.

And yet, and yet, there were some glimmers of hope. Many militia officers were truly dedicated to their hometown regiments. Even though they had to pay for their own uniforms, the officers in many units donated their pay in the 1930s to buy boots for their soldiers— boots the Quartermasters' Stores could not provide. Others, officers and non-commissioned officers (NCOs) alike, devotedly turned up two nights a week to train and tried to keep up with the military literature, especially the *Canadian Defence Quarterly*, published from 1929 by the Department of National Defence. The most ambitious captains and majors applied for the Militia Staff Course (MSC), which trained them for staff posts with lectures and a two-week summer stint of TEWTs, or Tactical Exercises Without Troops. The MSC and the Advanced Militia Staff Course for majors brought militia and PF officers together; so too did the examinations for militia colonels. As a result, at the outbreak of war, there were a few hundred staff-trained officers among the 5,000 officers in the Non-Permanent Active Militia. None of these men were truly ready to take on staff posts in wartime operations, but at least they had the basic rudiments.

The best Permanent Force officers also sought out staff training in the United Kingdom, Canada having no staff college of its own. The British Army operated two staff colleges, one at Camberley, southeast of London, and the other in northern India, at Quetta. Entry to the two-year program was by competition and was open to captains with at least six years' service across the British Empire. The PF ran a prepa-ratory course at the Royal Military College in Kingston, Ontario, and insisted that those sitting the British examinations also pass the Mili-tia Staff Course. Ordinarily, four Canadian officers a year went to the staff colleges, three to Camberley and one to Quetta; in all, between the world wars, sixty-three PF officers earned the coveted "psc," the post-nominal denoting that they had passed the rigorous course. The first year of the course focused on staff work at the brigade and divi-sion levels, the second on work at division, corps, and army headquar-ters. For Canadians, none of whom had seen large-scale units in the field, the course was difficult, although it did provide the opportunity to observe—and for some, like Captain Guy Simonds, to participate in—large British exercises. Some of the Canadians, officers such as Simonds and Major E.L.M. Burns, enjoyed their time of freewheeling discussion and learned much; these two officers intelligently debated the best ways to use armour in the pages of the *Canadian Defence Quarterly* in 1938.

There was also the Imperial Defence College (IDC) in London, a one-year course, usually reserved for brigadiers, that was devoted to high strategy and international relations. Canada sent thirteen officers to the IDC between the world wars, giving its rising stars the opportunity to see how the world appeared to Chiefs of the Imperial General Staff and senior British politicians. Among the Canadian graduates were A.G.L. McNaughton, Harry Crerar, E.L.M. Burns, and Maurice Pope, all officers who would hold high rank in the wartime Canadian Army. There were some perks on these important courses—Harry Crerar's daughter remembered that they had a batman/groom, a cook/general housekeeper, and a parlourmaid; in Ottawa, they had only a cook.

This staff training marked some progress for the tiny Permanent Force and the larger, but still small, militia. Some, but not much. An army of two corps with five divisions and fifteen brigades—the force Canada put into the field overseas in the Second World War—needed staff officers of skill at every level, and, for health or other reasons, not every psc or graduate of the Militia Staff Course was available for overseas service. Staff officers were needed to fill posts in Ottawa, in home defence formations, and in the Military Districts across the country. At the minimum, the headquarters of First Canadian Army required 241 staff officers in ranks from captain to brigadier; the two corps headquarters each needed 68 staff officers, the five divisions had slots for from 13 to 19 staff officers each, and the fifteen brigades needed from 3 to 5 staff officers apiece, depending on whether they were infantry or tank brigades. The pre-war production from staff colleges and courses met some, but hardly all, of the required number of more than 500, without allowing for postings, illness, or battle casualties. There was, for example, such a shortage of trained staff officers that the creation of II Canadian Corps, originally planned for July 1, 1942, had to be delayed for six months. Good staff work, good training, and battle planning made the difference between amateur night and professionalism. The trained and experienced officers necessary for this could not be conjured up overnight.

There had, of course, been interwar planning under way in the army's Directorate of Military Operations and Planning at National Defence Headquarters, notably the preparation of contingency plans. Defence Scheme No. 1, drawn up by Colonel J. Sutherland "Buster" Brown in the 1920s, laid out the Canadian plan in the event of war between the United States and Britain, not a totally impossible eventuality. What was unreal, however, was Sutherland Brown's intent to send spoiling attacks into the United States "and [to] occupy the strategic points," including Spokane, Seattle, Portland, Fargo, Minneapolis, and St. Paul. How the untrained, ill-equipped militia could have accomplished this Herculean feat was left unsaid.

More to the point was Sutherland Brown's Defence Scheme No. 3, the plan that his directorate first prepared in the late 1920s for a large expeditionary force to fight at Britain's side. The Chief of the General Staff, Major-General Andrew McNaughton, sent out the first draft of No. 3 in 1934; privately, he had even pencilled in the names of senior commanders, a clear attempt to ensure that a meddling defence minister could not again do as Sam Hughes had done in 1914 and throw away carefully prepared mobilization plans.

The Army could plan all it wished, but it was the politicians who would decide when and if Canada went to war, and what if anything Canada would contribute to the fight. The Liberal government of Mackenzie King had been returned to power in the general election of 1935, and the prime minister, if he was not wholly isolationist in attitude, was acutely sensitive to the dangers that participation in war would pose to Canadian unity. The memories of the bitter political conflict concerning overseas conscription in the Great War remained fresh in his mind, and in French Canada's. Francophone Canada was anti-British, anti-imperialist, anti-war, and deeply suspicious of the Anglo-Canadian majority. The Liberals depended on electoral support in Quebec, and King would do nothing to jeopardize this. That helped to explain the pathetic defence budgets of the late 1930s; moreover, King correctly believed that the primary task for Canada's military was to defend the homeland, not to fight abroad, and such funding as the military received was directed mainly to the Royal Canadian Navy and the Royal Canadian Air Force.

The government did agree that the militia should be reorganized and re-equipped when resources permitted—unfortunately, that seemed to mean never. And in 1937, King made clear that Army planning was not to be based on an expeditionary force. Defence Scheme No. 3 was duly revised into a home defence plan, but in fact it retained a "field force" of two divisions for overseas service. King's defence minister, Ian Mackenzie, a Great War veteran from British Columbia, collaborated in the subterfuge, even closing his eyes when the Army staff exaggerated the possible scale of attacks on Canada to bolster the case for new equipment (not that this produced much of anything). And after the Munich Crisis of September 1938, the army's senior leadership actively but secretly began planning to dispatch overseas a huge expeditionary force of seven divisions, efforts about which it did not tell the government. Engaged in the excruciating exercise of trying to bring a united Canada into a war that he could see coming as clearly as the soldiers, Mackenzie King would have been furious had he known of these plans.

But he didn't know, and both King and Conservative leader Dr. R.J. Manion publicly promised in March 1939 that they would not countenance conscription for overseas service in any war. King added in Parliament that "the days of great expeditionary forces of infantry crossing the oceans are not likely to recur." That comment did not stop the Army planners, and Brigadier Harry Crerar was charged with putting the finishing touches on the expeditionary force scheme. Smart and able as Crerar was, his plan called for Canada to mobilize six infantry divisions capable of fighting in a temperate climate against a "civilized enemy." No one knew if King and his Cabinet would ever agree to such a force, but Crerar counted on majority English Canadian public opinion, still always ready to back Britain, to demand that at least one and perhaps two divisions be dispatched overseas as a minimum.

Crerar was right in his belief that opinion in English Canada was pro-British, and it scarcely mattered whether Prime Minister Neville Chamberlain's London was in favour of appeasement, as it was until Hitler swallowed all of Czechoslovakia in March 1939, or if it was beginning to believe in the need for war to check Hitler, as it was when the Nazis threatened Poland. The memory of the casualties and political strife of the Great War remained, however. And although there was scant enthusiasm except in the English-language newspapers after Canada's declaration of war against Germany on September 10, pressure on the government to send troops overseas began at once. The government had already, on September 1, ordered Defence Scheme No. 3 put into effect, authorizing the mobilization of two infantry divisions and a corps headquarters. Militia and PF units were called up and guards posted at vital points such as power plants, canals, and key bridges. Thinking of a very limited war effort, King had still hoped to avoid sending infantry overseas, but his Cabinet insisted on this as early as September 7. Still, the finance minister said, there was no money, and on September 19, the ministers agreed to send a single division "when required and trained in Canada." A second division was to be kept available in Canada, but, King added, "It was apparent that a third division could not be thought of at this time, if we were not to occasion protest across the country itself and even more to impair the credit of Canada." War had begun, but the Depression mentality decreeing that spending be limited persisted. It would do so until June 1940 and the fall of France.

The prime minister had wanted the Royal Canadian Air Force to be Canada's major contribution to the war effort, and within days of the announcement that a division would go overseas, Britain asked that Canada lead—and largely pay for—a major air training scheme. The eventual result of this overture was the British Commonwealth Air Training Plan, a massive effort that produced in all 131,000 aircrew. If the idea had reached Canada before the decision to send infantry overseas, that commitment might not have been made. As it was, the RCAF eventually reached a strength of 250,000, a very substantial force that enlisted many of the cream of the crop. With the Royal Canadian Navy taking in another 100,000 men, many of the best-educated recruits were lost for the Army. This certainly had implications down the road.

The 1st Canadian Division nonetheless began to take form. It was to consist of three brigades, each with three infantry battalions, artillery, transport, signals, engineers, and other units. Each brigade would number approximately 5,000 men, each battalion just under 1,000, and the division's strength in all would be some 20,000 officers and men. The three Permanent Force battalions—the Royal Canadian Regiment, the Royal 22e Régiment, and the Princess Patricia's Canadian Light Infantry—were included, one per brigade, and the militia units deemed by the regulars in Ottawa to be the best provided the remainder—the Hastings and Prince Edward Regiment from eastern Ontario, the 48th Highlanders from Toronto, the Edmonton Regiment, the Seaforth Highlanders from Vancouver, the Carleton and York Regiment from New Brunswick, and the West Nova Scotia Regiment. Two of the brigade commanders were militiamen: one a Montreal dairy owner, the other the proprietor of the E.D. Smith jam company. The third was Brigadier George Pearkes, VC, from the PF.

Permanent Force officers were not happy that militiamen were so prominent. Christopher Vokes, a captain at the time, later wrote that "what was mobilized was a mob ... an organized mob, in uniform. The militia officers and sergeants had a vague notion what to do ... They could probably lead a parade down the street ... but that was about the size of it. When it came down to training soldiers for war they knew absolutely nothing." W.A.B. Anderson, a PF artillery captain in 1939 and postwar a lieutenant-general, remembered that the tension between the militia and the regulars was very real. There was little mutual respect in 1939, though this diffused over six years of war. The PF culture was strong, and some, like militiaman Brigadier Stanley Todd, who became a superb wartime artillery commander, were aware they'd got where they did without PF help. Anderson remembered the unpleasantness of hearing people talk in the Camp Petawawa mess about "goddamn PF know-it-alls." The tension existed, as did the amateurishness. In truth, though, all the Canadians were amateurs in September 1939.

King had selected, as commander of the 1st Canadian Division, Major-General Andrew McNaughton, who had served as a brilliant, innovative artillery commander in the Great War, as Chief of the General Staff from 1929 to 1935, and as head of the National Research Council (NRC), Prime Minister R.B. Bennett appointing him to that post after McNaughton ran the army's Depression relief camps. The relief camps had taken unemployed men off the streets and paid them 20 cents a day to build infrastructure or cut trees, but the scheme stirred enough controversy that McNaughton had been shunted to the NRC. But the general was a force, and Prime Minister King knew it. McNaughton might have had Tory connections, but he was a "scientific soldier," one who believed in using weapons to minimize casualties, and this greatly appealed to Mackenzie King. Anderson recalled that McNaughton had an aura about him, a flamboyance without trying for it, and that he could come into any group and liven it up; he was "bright as all Hell."

Still, the prime minister worried about McNaughton because the general did not always seem to understand that he was subordinate to civilian authority. The soldiers, in the general's view, took priority; McNaughton had teared up as he spoke to King about his responsibility for the lives of his men. And in early December, when the prime minister talked to McNaughton just before he left for Britain, King wrote in his diary, "I felt a little concern about his being able to see this war through without a breakdown. I felt he was too far on in years to be taking on so great a job." McNaughton was only fifty-two, but King was right.

Nonetheless, Andy McNaughton was a first-class mind with a scientific bent, a nationalist, a commander who had the affection and trust of his division. He was happiest looking under a truck to fix the transmission or checking the hydraulics on guns. But he was no great trainer of troops, as it turned out, and his judgment of his senior officers was not always the best. In the autumn of 1939, however, McNaughton was almost certainly the best available man for his job.

His division, on the other hand, was far from ready for battle. Some units had only Great War uniforms; others still had no boots. There was almost no heavy equipment—Ottawa was counting on Britain to provide this once the troops went overseas. Nonetheless, in early December 1939, the largely untrained men of the 1st Canadian Division embarked for Britain in high spirits. Matthew Halton, the *Toronto Daily Star*'s foreign correspondent, was there to welcome them: "Seldom have I been more moved and thrilled when, in last Sunday's gray mists, I saw the vanguard of the Canadian army—sons and brothers of the men of Vimy Ridge— land on British soil," he wrote. *The Times* of London caught the spirit too: "The first of freedom's fighters from the Empire overseas are here."

At home, Mackenzie King knew he had to call an election, and he seized on a motion that the Ontario legislature had passed condemning the government's war effort. The virtue of an early election was that it could precede the campaigning season in Europe. As usual, King's timing was dead on—the election took place on March 26, the Liberals repeating their promise of no conscription for overseas service, and Canadians returned a huge Liberal majority. The Nazis attacked Denmark and Norway in April and the Low Countries and France in May, but the Grits were in power for the duration.

• • •

Based around Aldershot, England, the units began more intensive training at the beginning of 1940 than they had been able to carry out at home. The soldiers started with the basics, carrying out individual training in January and February, unit collective training in March, and brigade and division exercises on a small scale or without troops the next month. These all were rudimentary, neither the division's senior officers nor battalion Commanding Officers having much idea of how to train. General McNaughton himself had little interest in training his command to fight—if the division had modern equipment and reasonably intelligent staff officers and commanders, historian Douglas Delaney wrote, "it could overcome any challenges it might encounter." There was little such equipment, unfortunately, and most of the commanders were older men, unversed in the kind of blitzkrieg war the Germans had unleashed on Poland. In the circumstances, much of the training focused on Great War tactics; indeed, units trained in trenches at Pirbright. People of his age, said D.C. Spry, then a twenty-six-year-old captain in the Royal Canadian Regiment, "considered this was completely retrograde; we were going backwards in tactical doctrine." The plan was to send the division to France to take its place in the British line in May 1940.

The German schedule was different. The Wehrmacht invaded Denmark and Norway in April. Copenhagen capitulated quickly, but the

Norwegians resisted, and the Imperial General Staff looked to McNaughton's men to participate in an attack against Trondheim fjord, occupied by the Germans in the first days of the assault. The 1,300 troops from the 2nd Brigade got as far as Dunfermline, Scotland, but the operation collapsed, the planners fortunately having second thoughts.

Attention quickly changed focus. On May 10, Hitler sent his panzers and paratroops against the Low Countries and France, and the situation turned disastrous with great speed. Towns that had fallen to the Germans in months in 1914 were now taken in days, and the French and British armies were outmatched and outfought. The British Expeditionary Force fell back toward the English Channel, most of its men (but little of its equipment) being miraculously rescued. After Dunkirk, there was a scramble to create a new defence line in France, and the Canadians, considered battleworthy by their commander, readied themselves. On May 23, McNaughton held a conference and told his officers that the Germans had cut the British Expeditionary Force's lines of communication through Arras. A mixed force of Canadian and British troops, under McNaughton, was to establish a protected line of communication from either Calais or Dunkirk—so wrote Harry Foster, a major in the 1st Division. His brigade was to form the advance party. "This is our opportunity to show the stuff we are made of," the General Officer Commanding (GOC) said, according to Foster's diary. "It's going to be a sticky business, you must be absolutely ruthless, and in dealing with refugees remember the fifth column—tell the men we are not particularly interested in prisoners." In scenes of chaos at the docks, the Canadians' orders for France were cancelled.

But then, on June 8, the Canadians received instructions to proceed to France. The 1st Canadian Infantry Brigade's three battalions of infantry and supporting units, some 5,000 men in all, left Aldershot that day, soon arrived at Brest, and proceeded inland by rail, passing refugees in their thousands. At 4:30 a.m. on June 15, with French resistance collapsing everywhere, the Canadians received new orders to retreat to Saint-Malo and Brest, which they did in a hurry. They had faced no action. All but a handful of men who had somehow wandered away from their units and fallen into enemy hands made it back to England; much of their equipment did not. The chaos on the docks was colossal as men scrambled desperately to return to Britain. Foster wrote on June 19 that "the whole of our precious new transport was wrecked at Brest and all our kits burned." The Royal Canadian Horse Artillery's new 25-pounder guns did make it back, however, when the Commanding Officer, Lieutenant-Colonel Hamilton Roberts, forced, at gunpoint, the British officers controlling the loading of ships to take them aboard. Another officer, Lieutenant Robert Moncel of the Royal Canadian Regiment, saved his unit's Bren gun carriers only by ordering his sergeant to shoot the British officer who wanted to destroy them. These guns and carriers would be very rare in England after the fall of France, and the 1st Canadian Division would be just about the best-equipped formation available to meet the Nazi invasion everyone expected soon.

• • •

For the next three years, the Canadians' primary task was to defend the British Isles. McNaughton received a promotion to lieutenant-general and the command of a corps. With a British division, he formed the mobile reserve south of the Thames River. The 2nd Canadian Infantry Division, commanded by Victor Odlum, a politically connected Great War brigadier who had seen some postwar service in the militia in the 1920s, arrived in Britain in the summer of 1940 and, by the end of the year, had joined the 1st Division in the new Canadian Corps.

Mobilization at home quickly picked up speed as well. The "limited war" desired by Mackenzie King and the Finance Department had disappeared, and money was now no object. While there was as yet no shortage of volunteers—so many men were coming forward that there was no need for the government to launch a major recruiting campaign—the National Resources Mobilization Act (NRMA) authorized home defence conscription, initially for thirty days, soon for ninety, and in 1941 for the war's duration. This was unpopular in French Canada, but the defence of Canada—what the NRMA intended—seemed a necessity in the summer of 1940, and the Québécois by and large grudgingly accepted this.

The prime minister of Canada and the president of the United States, fearful that Britain might fall and the Royal Navy be seized by Hitler, created the Permanent Joint Board on Defence at Ogdensburg, NY, in August 1940, effectively guaranteeing Canada's security through joint planning and a pledge of U.S. help in case of attack. The United States military was hardly ready for war, but American rearmament proceeded apace, and the Ogdensburg Agreement let National Defence Headquarters, now much less concerned with home defence, dispatch every available man, gun, aircraft, and ship to assist Britain's struggle to survive.

The decision to raise a third division and an armoured brigade came in the summer of 1940. The 4th Canadian Division and the 5th Canadian

Division came into being in 1941 and 1942, along with a second armoured brigade. This was too big a force to be commanded by a corps headquarters, and the rudiments of First Canadian Army, not created until the early spring of 1942, existed—three infantry divisions, two armoured divisions, and two tank brigades. This large force, the largest ever put in the field by Canada, was the creation of Major-General Harry Crerar, who had become Chief of the General Staff in 1940. He had presided over the home defence conscripts' enlistment and the extension of their service, he had argued for the big army, and he had assured Mackenzie King and his ministers that First Canadian Army could be sustained without conscription for overseas service. Crerar apparently believed this at the time he gave his word, but wartime pledges from generals and politicians are always subject to revision by events.

The first action for the Army in the second World War came not in Britain but in the Crown colony of Hong Kong. Hong Kong was indefensible, a tiny British outpost on the edge of Japanese-occupied China. When Japan moved against Britain and America on December 7, 1941, the two Canadian infantry battalions, one from Quebec City and one from Winnipeg, and a brigade headquarters that had arrived from Canada to help garrison the colony in November were thrown into a hopeless struggle. Their transport had not arrived, thanks to errors in administrative arrangements in Canada. For many of the soldiers, training was less than complete. The British commanders directing the defence were hopelessly incompetent, and, after a costly struggle in which the Canadians showed much courage, the British, Indian, Canadian, and Chinese defenders of Hong Kong surrendered on Christmas Day. Much of the Far East would follow as Japan's army and navy seemed irresistible. For the survivors of the battle who had arrived in November, there were four years to come of appalling treatment in prisoner-of-war cages there and, later, in Japan. Only 1,418 members of the almost 2,000 in the Hong Kong force returned to Canada after V-J Day in August 1945.

• • •

After Hong Kong, Canadians became fully aware that Canada now faced a war on both European and Asian fronts. The Nazis had invaded the Soviet Union on June 22, 1941, and huge battles were being waged on the Russian plains, with the Wehrmacht besieging Leningrad, remaining near Moscow, and pressing east toward Stalingrad. In Egypt, the Afrika Korps always seemed on the verge of taking Cairo and cutting off the Suez Canal, Britain's lifeline to Asia. The Japanese had struck at Pearl Harbor and sunk much of the United States Navy's Pacific Fleet. They had advanced through much of Southeast Asia, taken the Dutch East Indies, and now threatened Australia. Everywhere Britain and the United States were on the defensive, struggling to overcome the Axis militaries.

Could Canada fight this global war without compulsory service, without conscription for the war overseas? Into 1942, men continued to volunteer, but those trained under the NRMA's provisions since 1940 were available for home defence alone, and some ministers in the Liberal government, notably Colonel J. Layton Ralston, the minister of national defence, thought this flatly wrong. So did the Conservative Party's new leader, Arthur Meighen, the architect of the conscription legislation of 1917. The political and military situations encouraged Ralston, and he and other ministers pressured Mackenzie King to change the policy. In

January 1942, King decided to call a plebiscite—not a referendum, which would have been binding—to ask Canadians to release the government from the pledges it had made about military service. As historian Robert Bothwell has written, "Canada was a divided country. There was nothing that could be done about that, certainly not in [King's] lifetime. There were more English-speakers than French-speakers, and there was nothing that could be done about that, either. Yet living with these facts meant that a prudent Canadian leader must avoid, as far as possible, a situation where the English majority would be tempted to impose its will on the French minority. It also meant avoiding any circumstance in which the French minority thwarted the majority over something it deeply desired."

The question of compulsory military service was just that polarizing. English-speaking Canadians voted massively "yes" in the plebiscite on April 27; French-speaking Canadians voted "*non*" in equally strong numbers. The split in public opinion was clear, and Quebec obviously had not forgotten the pain of the conscription crisis of 1917. Nonetheless, King introduced Bill 80 into the House of Commons to remove the restrictions on the NRMA men's employment, but in a famous phrase he declared his policy "not necessarily conscription, but conscription if necessary." The Army had not yet seen enough action to be short of men, but the legislative framework for action was now in place if and when overseas conscription became needed.

• • •

A foretaste of the dreadful casualties that the Second World War would produce promptly occurred. The army's second action was both bigger in scale and an even greater disaster than Hong Kong. With Western Europe under Nazi control, British planners looked for ways to test both enemy defences and their own theories on how best to mount an eventual large-scale invasion. By the early summer of 1942, plans were under way for a big attack on the French port of Dieppe: Could a small defended port be seized? General Harry Crerar had left Canada for England and was acting in command of the I Canadian Corps while General McNaughton was in Canada. Crerar fretted about the corps' "continued lack of participation" in operations and the difficulty of maintaining the "desired keenness and morale." Lieutenant Syd Thompson, later a successful battalion CO, said after the war that his unit was demoralized after "too long with nothing to do." The Canadian generals all knew their restless soldiers needed action, and the troops themselves, tired of being asked by their English girlfriends if they would ever fight, largely shared that opinion. "Like every other soldier," Corporal Robert Prouse recalled, "I was bored to tears with the long inaction and was itching for battle." Lieutenant Hal MacDonald of the North Shore (New Brunswick) Regiment, not on the raid, wrote home regretfully, "We were all tensed, hoping our outfit would go, but no. We had to stand by and watch the other outfits go on board." Everyone wanted—needed—a big raid on the Continent. In the end, the Chief of the Imperial General Staff and Combined Operations Headquarters (COHQ), responsible for the raid, agreed that the 2nd Canadian Division and 1st Canadian Tank Brigade could provide almost 5,000 men for the Dieppe operation. Major-General Hamilton Roberts, two years earlier the CO who had saved his guns at Brest, was the (GOC) of the 2nd Division, and in command of the operation.

The plan, derived at COHQ, was complex and subject to the vaga-ries of weather. In July the operation had to be cancelled because of inclement conditions and the units dispersed. Thinking that the enemy, though it might have heard of the raid, would never suspect the planners of mounting it again, COHQ decided to attack Dieppe in August in an operation dubbed "Jubilee." There were no heavy bomb-ings and no big naval guns in the plan the second time, but the raid nonetheless was to go in on August 19. General Crerar's comment on the revived plan, offered on August 11, was that "given an even break in luck and good navigation," the raid "should" prove successful. Luck should never be a requisite for a successful military operation, but for this operation, luck was the key. Unfortunately, there was to be none in Operation Jubilee.

The plan called for 4,963 officers and men drawn from the infantry battalions of the 2nd Division, an armoured regiment, and a thousand British Commandos to assault Dieppe and surrounding areas from the sea. Covered by seventy-four squadrons of fighters and fighter bombers overhead and ten small ships offshore, infantry from the Essex Scot-tish from southwestern Ontario and the Royal Hamilton Light Infantry, accompanied by tanks of the Calgary Regiment, were to land on the beach in front of Dieppe.

To the east at Puys, Toronto's Royal Regiment of Canada was to go ashore on a tiny beach under a cliff. At Pourville to the west, the South Saskatchewan Regiment and the Queen's Own Cameron Highlanders were to disembark, with the Camerons intending to go almost five miles inland to attack an airfield and a German headquarters and destroy a coastal battery. The floating reserve was the Fusiliers Mont-Royal. The

Commandos' task was to eliminate German batteries east and west of the three main landing areas.

The intention of the raid was to take the town of Dieppe, establish a defensive perimeter, and hold it just long enough to permit the destruction of harbour facilities—and, as we now know, to carry out the heist of a German Enigma code machine and code books from German naval intelligence headquarters in the town. The raiders were then to depart by sea. There were no heavy bombers to soften up the defences, and the Royal Navy declined to assign battleships to support the assault—the English Channel was too risky for that with the Luftwaffe nearby. The German defences at Dieppe were in the hands of the 302nd Infantry Division, and ample reserves were close by. The enemy soldiers were not first-class troops, but their defensive positions were such that they held the high ground that completely dominated the Dieppe area.

The troops boarded their landing craft on August 18 and set sail that night. Very quickly, everything unravelled, starting with the flotilla's bumping into a German coastal convoy. The firing alerted the enemy defences, removing the element of surprise on which the entire plan depended. The Royal Navy landed the Canadians on Puys' Blue Beach thirty-five minutes late, at a time when they could be easily seen by two platoons of Germans on the beach and in a pillbox on the cliff overlooking it. The attackers from the Royal Regiment of Canada were cut to pieces by German machine guns and mortars; only a few made it to the top of the cliff. Those still alive on the beach surrendered at about 8:30 a.m.; those atop the cliff held out until the late afternoon. Only 65 Royals out of almost 600 made it back to England.

At Pourville's Green Beach, the situation was only marginally better.

The South Saskatchewan Regiment landed on time in darkness and achieved an element of surprise, but the Royal Navy landed part of the unit in the wrong place. One company, properly landed, took its objective. The rest, trying to cross the river Scie on a bridge, faced withering fire from the Germans perched on the cliffs on both sides of the landing beach. The South Sasks commander, Lieutenant-Colonel Cecil Merritt, then led his men across by sheer force of will: "Come on over, there's nothing to it," he said, standing up and swinging his helmet. Merritt headed attacks up the hill with his troops, joined by men of the Queen's Own Cameron Highlanders (who had landed with their pipers playing).

The remainder of the Camerons moved inland some 2,000 yards until they encountered very heavy opposition and withdrew to the beach. The landing craft were there as planned to pick them up, but very few of the survivors could reach them through the hail of machine-gun fire the Germans laid down. Merritt stayed to organize the defences that let those who made it get away. He was taken prisoner and soon received the Victoria Cross.

The real disaster was in front of Dieppe, on Red and White beaches. The enemy heard the firing from Puys and Pourville and was at the alert, so there was no surprise, and without surprise there was no chance of good luck. The only advantages the Canadians had were an air attack on the cliffs to the east of the beaches and the strafing of the beach defences by Hurricanes. The infantry came ashore while the Germans tried to collect themselves after the air attack, but the Royal Navy landed the Calgary Regiment's new Churchill tanks late. The big armoured vehicles—not the most effective or reliable of tanks—managed to lay down fire but could scarcely move, most failing to get over the seawall, others unable to use their tracks on the baseball-sized stones that made up the beach.

Brigadier Sherwood Lett remained at sea directly in front of the landing beaches as he continued trying to direct the battle on shore. He wrote that he and his men "were under a regular hail of fire of all kinds from in front and from the headlands on either side. They shot away the ramp in front so that we could not land any more vehicles or get ashore, and they disabled the engines and finally the steering gear of our craft so we could not move in or out, and twice they shot away the aerials from my wireless set." The skipper ordered everyone to abandon ship, but Lett managed to get the engine started and rigged steering gear, "and after what seemed a couple of weeks we got offshore a bit and out of the worst of the fire." Most of his officers aboard were killed or wounded; Lett himself was seriously wounded but made it back to England.

Without immediate fire support, the infantry took heavy casualties from the defenders perched on the cliffs that overlooked the beach, and from the fortified casino at the west end of the beach. Some of the Royal Hamilton Light Infantry (RHLI) broke through the Germans' wire and made it into the town. Like most of the RHLI, the Essex Scottish, raked by fire from the east and west headlands, died or fell wounded where they had landed on the beach. The carnage now was compounded: garbled messages that suggested success led General Roberts to send in his reserve battalion. Montreal's Fusiliers Mont-Royal landed at 7:00 a.m. and met only slaughter. Few made it off the beach. The Enigma machine, like the town of Dieppe, remained in German hands.

What had gone wrong? "Everything" is the only answer. The plan was sadly flawed, and it was as if Dieppe were 2,000 miles from England and not, for decades, a day trip for thousands of English tourists who had lazed on the shingle beach and stood atop the cliffs where the Germans sensibly put their machine guns and artillery. The Germans' 81st Corps' after-action report commented that "the Canadians on the whole fought badly and surrendered afterwards in swarms." But the Wehrmacht's Fifteenth Army disagreed: "The enemy, almost entirely Canadian soldiers, fought—so far as he was able to fight at all—well and bravely." So far as he was able to fight at all—that summed it up.

The luck on which the Dieppe raid depended had disappeared; 907 Canadian soldiers died on the beach in a few hours of slaughter, 586 suffered wounds, and 1,946 fell into German hands. Many of the Canadians captured had been wounded; some of the mortally wounded were killed by German officers as "an act of mercy," or so said the Royal Regiment's Jack Poolton, who witnessed the executions. The British Commandos and Royal Marines had 45 killed and 197 wounded or captured. The Royal Navy lost 28 percent of the vessels it used in the raid and 550 officers and sailors, and the Royal and Royal Canadian Air Forces had 106 aircraft shot down, the heaviest single-day loss since the beginning of the war. In all, 2,200 Canadians returned safely, 600 of them wounded; most of those who got back had not landed. The 2nd Canadian Division, which had provided the infantry for the assault, took a very long time to recover.

So did the towns and cities where regiments in Canada's Army were geographically based. The town of Winona, Ontario, provided a company in the Rileys, as the RHLI were dubbed, and most of the men had been workers at the E.D. Smith Co., which produced jam. The Rileys' C Company was hit hard in the assault; most of its men were killed, wounded, or captured. It was, said one former resident, "quite devastating for the little village of Winona." That shock was replicated in Toronto, Calgary, Montreal, Windsor, and elsewhere.

As historian Timothy Balzer has conclusively demonstrated, COHQ's expert public relations team turned out to be better at preparing media lines for failure than its planners were at drawing up the strategy for operational success. Combined Operations Headquarters instantly claimed that the raid had been a great achievement and learning experience, and they held to that line even after the lengthy casualty lists became public. Two years later, they still maintained that without Jubilee's invaluable invasion tutorial, D-Day could not have succeeded. General Crerar said much the same and, understandably perhaps, so have most Dieppe survivors, not wanting their comrades to have been thrown away for nothing. The British and Canadians still had much to learn about fighting the Germans. There had been more than enough courage on the beaches of Dieppe, but nowhere near enough sensible generalship and clear thinking.

• • •

The Canadians had already set about the task of learning how to soldier. The three divisions of the Canadian Corps in England had come under the command of a tough little British general, Bernard Montgomery, one of the few commanders who had emerged from the debacle of May and June 1940 with any credit. The Canadians were an independent force, but they were for all practical purposes under British control in the United Kingdom. That made military sense because the Canadian Corps needed all the help it could get to become an effective force.

Now, beginning in late 1941, Monty was going to teach the Canadians how to fight. In a succession of inspections and exercises, he set out to get rid of the weak and promote the capable. He told commanders what he thought, and his comments were unmerciful. "I hope to be sending you [Generals] Pearkes, Potts, and Ganong back to Canada shortly," he wrote in a private letter to his former Canadian ADC. "You will find them useful your side [of the Atlantic], I hope, you need some really good officers back in Canada." Pearkes had succeeded McNaughton in command of the 1st Division, Potts and Ganong were brigade commanders, and all three were decorated Great War veterans.

Pearkes, as Montgomery wrote bluntly in April 1942, "is unable to appreciate the essentials of a military problem and to formulate a sound plan. His mind works in a groove and he gets the bit between his teeth, puts on blinkers, and drives ahead blindly. He is a gallant soldier without doubt, but he has no brains." Major-General Basil Price, a militiaman and dairy owner, sacked as GOC of the 3rd Division, was another to suffer from Monty's acerbic pen: "He will be of great value in Canada where his knowledge of the milk industry will help on the national war effort." Monty reached down into battalions and staffs. He didn't always get it right, but his eye for talent was ordinarily excellent. The same month, Montgomery, who had a keen sense of soldiering and was able to recognize good fighting men, said that "the soldiery in the Canadian Corps are probably the best material in any army in the Empire … But they are going to be killed in large numbers unless commanders can learn to put them properly into battle." The Canadians had grown bored with their training, tired of acting as a garrison army, preoccupied with getting leave and with their relations with the locals.

Montgomery was unpleasant—"an efficient little shit," as his British contemporaries called him. But he was right, dead right. In May 1940, McNaughton had believed that the 1st Division was ready to fight in France; it wasn't. By late 1941, he had believed his corps was "thoroughly prepared for battle." It wasn't. Some of the senior officers had neglected training; some were lax. The Commanding Officers—few of them, all the way up to McNaughton, understanding how to train an army—searched for ceremonies, guard duties, and educational classes to occupy the troops.

Good officers understood that they were unready to fight. Major Bert Hoffmeister, a company commander in the Seaforth Highlanders from Vancouver, was one such. In 1941 all this wore on him to such an extent that he had a nervous breakdown over the agony of coping with the poor training that his regiment had received and his sense that he himself had still not learned enough to lead his men effectively into battle. Hoffmeister recalled stepping into a hot bath in a billet he shared with another officer. He felt nothing, but when his other foot went in he was scalded, and he realized that he was almost paralyzed on his left side. He went into hospital, and there, from a Royal Canadian Army Medical Corps psychiatrist, he received a new philosophy that guided him thereafter: "If you are given a job, it is because your superiors think you are capable of it and they expect your best. Do your best then and don't let worries accumulate." Hoffmeister did exactly that and excelled thereafter. So did his soldiers once Montgomery was finished training them.

Montgomery insisted that physical fitness become a priority, that every soldier be able cover ten miles in two hours with full battle order on his back. Starting in late 1941, every Canadian division ran its men through Battle Drill, a rigorous training course to harden the men and to teach them the fire and movement tactics that had to become instinctive. The intent was to develop a simple word-of-mouth tactical manoeuvre plan for use at platoon level. The school in Yorkshire was tough: it used sewers and abattoir offal, and made men crawl through this to accustom them to blood and filth. One second lieutenant wrote home that "the course was great for physical condition[ing]— everywhere we went we ran, with web equipment, small packs, respirator, steel helmet, and rifles." The instructors taught platoon officers and NCOs, and they also worked with carrier platoons. Battle Drill, however, "particularly its parade square facets," historian Jack English wrote tartly, "inculcated a rigidity of thought and action." But it was certainly better than anything that had preceded it in the Canadians' training.

General McNaughton stressed night fighting, so Major Roger Rowley, commanding the Canadian Battle Drill school in 1943, instituted a day/night reversal and sought advice from specialists about using carotene to improve vision; the results, he said, were dramatic as people learned to use their senses. Similarly, big exercises like Beaver III, Beaver IV, and Tiger, which tested commanders and soldiers, increased in tempo. By the time Montgomery went off to find glory in North Africa in the summer of 1942, the Canadians were in much better shape physically and militarily.

The training problems were real and continued, but they were almost inevitable. The tiny Permanent Force of 1939—just over 4,000 officers and men—had expanded once, twice, many times in size, so much so that virtually every junior officer was recently a civilian and every man had been in the Army for only months or a few years. Inevitably, learning to be a soldier, learning how to fight the Germans, was a long process. What must be said is that McNaughton and his senior officers had raised an army but had failed to manage the processes of training successfully. Montgomery had begun to change things; others had to take on the task.

In McNaughton's defence, he had very little to work with in England. The PF had produced no bright young officers who could immediately assume brigade or division command, and all McNaughton was able to do was to use the available older PF officers and militia stalwarts, such as Generals Pearkes, Price, Potts, and Ganong. He knew this. In January 1944, the American business magazine *Fortune* interviewed McNaughton and published a piece on the Canadian Army: "At first McNaughton had to lean on the older militia officers, veterans of the last war, who were middle-aged businessmen rather than soldiers. In one of his homely metaphors, they served as 'a cover crop, to help the younger men through the wilting strain of the first responsibilities, in the same way that older trees are used to shelter saplings through the heat of the day.'" The difficulties here were twofold. Firstly, some of the cover-crop officers had little to pass on to the young comers. Secondly, General McNaughton somehow did not realize that he too was part of the cover crop. Guy Simonds had worked closely with McNaughton, and he was unsparing in his criticism: "General McNaughton tended to be so absorbed in the technical and equipment and organizational problems that to my mind he definitely neglected the operational aspects." There is no more serious complaint that can be levelled at a commander.

The problem now was how to get rid of the General Officer Commanding-in-Chief (GOC-in-C) of First Canadian Army. Hugely popular with the troops and the Canadian public in 1939 and 1940, Andy

McNaughton had by 1942 become unknown to his own men and had begun to wear out his welcome with the British. He had remarkable ability and a fine mind, one of his staff, W.A.B. Anderson, then a major, recalled, but "he would have an absolute conviction about something and get firmly committed to it and then become almost obsessed with it." McNaughton's difficulty was that he was "not very good at noticing that things were changing." His army had remained in England in substantial part because its commander insisted that when it went into action, it fight only together and under Canadian command—*his* command. But it was difficult to expect First Canadian Army, untried and with a commander that few trusted any longer to do well in action, to be thrust into battle and be able to prevail. General Sir Alan Brooke, the Chief of the Imperial General Staff, wrote that McNaughton was "devoid of any form of strategic outlook, and would sooner have risked losing the war than agreed to splitting the Canadian forces." That was harsh but true, and it took a major struggle to get the 1st Division and the 1st Canadian Tank Brigade (soon to be renamed 1st Canadian Armoured Brigade) included in the invasion of Sicily in July 1943. Aware that people at home wanted their army to fight, aware that Canadians wanted Dieppe to be avenged, Ottawa had insisted on this over the general's objections.

This fight had weakened McNaughton's position. What all but finished it was the huge war game called Exercise Spartan in March 1943, when McNaughton—according to British observers—created an "awful muddle" as Army commander. "I felt that I could not accept the responsibility," Brooke wrote, "of allowing the Canadian Army to go into action under his orders." The Army's II Canadian Corps was new; its commander, McNaughton's selection, Lieutenant-General Ernest

Sansom, was less than stellar. And that helped create the muddle. But it was McNaughton's army, his commanders, his men, and his responsibility. Getting rid of the GOC-in-C was a major problem that involved the defence minister, Colonel J.L. Ralston; the Chief of the General Staff, General Ken Stuart; General Harry Crerar; General Sir Alan Brooke; Vincent Massey, the High Commissioner in London; and eventually Prime Minister Mackenzie King. Canadian propaganda had built Andy McNaughton into a modern Napoleon, and it was difficult to sack a giant. But sacked he was, sent back to Canada in retirement because he was "ill." After a brief period in command of I Canadian Corps in Italy, Harry Crerar, a long-time friend and protégé of McNaughton's and one of those who had helped push out the GOC-in-C, would be his successor in command of First Canadian Army.

The 1st Canadian Infantry Division landed in Sicily on July 10, 1943. The attack on Sicily brought the Canadians into Montgomery's Eighth Army, fresh from its victories in North Africa, and alongside American forces. The object was to drive the Italians out of the war and force the Germans to deploy more troops into Italy. That would help the Russians and weaken enemy defences in Northwest Europe. The Canadian aim was to get soldiers "blooded" and experienced.

This last aim was achieved in Sicily. Montgomery had worked with Guy Simonds in England when he was Chief of Staff in I Canadian Corps, and he had decided that the young brigadier was "the real brains," in historian Doug Delaney's words, at the Canadian HQ. Now the 1st Canadian Infantry Division, commanded by Major-General Simonds as part of Monty's Eighth Army, marched up the island's mountainous winding roads, bumping into light German rearguards that forced the infantry into time-consuming deployments. Near Valguarnera on July 17 and 18, a German panzer grenadier regiment and armour stood and fought, and the Canadians learned that the enemy had more and better machine guns and mortars and all the advantages the terrain could provide their defence. The town was taken, but at the cost of 145 casualties. The next seventeen days had more of the same, with major actions at Assoro, Leonforte, Agira, Regalbuto, Catenanuovo, and the river Simeto that helped greatly to break the centre of the German defences. The Canadians had 2,310 casualties, the Allies 19,000 in all in their dozen divisions, and the Germans an estimated 25,000 in their four divisions; Italian losses were estimated at 144,000, including 137,000 prisoners.

The lessons learned fighting the Germans in Sicily had been hard ones, but the infantry and armour had done well and some Canadian commanders had proven themselves. Simonds had led his division with skill, in Montgomery's view, and Brigadier Chris Vokes had fought his brigade with tenacity. So too had Lieutenant-Colonel Bert Hoffmeister, the CO of the Seaforth Highlanders, soon to be given a brigade command.

Then it was the Italian mainland. McNaughton had intended that the Canadians return to England after Sicily, but this made no sense in a war where shipping was always scarce. So the infantry division and the armoured brigade stayed, and in late 1943 they would be joined by the 5th Canadian Armoured Division and I Canadian Corps headquarters. Simonds would take over the 5th and Vokes the 1st Division, while Harry Crerar prepared himself to take command of I Canadian Corps in preparation for his getting the First Canadian Army post in England. But First Canadian Army had been split in two, and Canada's overseas soldiers now had two long supply lines, two reinforcement streams to manage—a very difficult task for a small country of 11 million with a growing Army. This would have major implications down the road.

The Canadians landed on the toe of the Italian boot on September 3, and Italy surrendered on September 7. Mussolini was tossed out of power after two decades of bombast and repression. But the Germans merely took over the country and continued to fight. Initially, the Canadians moved northward as fast as they could go—until the enemy decided to stand on the defensive, inflict casualties, and pull back. This happened repeatedly, the terrain again favouring the defenders, who were constructing a fortified line south of Rome, extending across Italy to the Adriatic town of Ortona.

Getting into Ortona would almost destroy the 1st Canadian Division, now commanded by Major-General Chris Vokes, and to a lesser extent, the 1st Canadian Armoured Brigade. The Canadians had to contest every inch of ground against first-rate German panzer grenadiers and paratroopers. Crossing the Sangro River was especially costly, the Moro River even more so in cold December weather. "We were appalled by the ferocity of the German reaction," Farley Mowat, a lieutenant in the Hastings and Prince Edward Regiment, later wrote, and "realized we had never before seen war in its full and dreadful magnitude." Matthew Halton, now of the CBC, called the slugging match on the Moro "little Passchendaeles of mud and blood." The fighting went on in a deadly cycle of attack and counterattack, with heavy casualties on both sides. Then there was a gully—the Gully, it came to be called—a deep fold in the ground that cost scores of Canadian lives as battalion after battalion in eight attacks battered against the enemy atop the high bank. Crossing the Gully took from December 11 to 19 and a thousand Canadian casualties.

As Christmas 1943 neared, the 1st Division entered Ortona, defended by the Germans' 1st Parachute Division. The paras had created defensive positions in houses and blown up other residences to create interlocking fields of fire. Even tanks had been placed hull down in bombed-out houses. The only way to move was through the walls of connecting row houses, clearing one then mouseholing into the next and tossing grenades to the floors above and below. Tanks blasted strongpoints at point-blank range but came under attack by German anti-tank guns. The enemy cleverly booby-trapped some houses and attractive objects to entice looters, and one explosion caught an entire platoon from the Loyal Edmonton Regiment. On December 25, men who were able to do so left the line for a roast pork dinner, including a bottle of beer, in a ruined church, then returned to their position to fight again. Not every man was able to break free. Major Jim Stone of the Loyal Eddies remembered that "I was on the main street of Ortona, directing a local attack ordered by my C.O. Three of my men were killed on the street before 0900 hrs. My Christmas dinner was a cold pork chop brought forward on a 'Bren' Carrier. A most unhappy day."

The CBC's Halton described the inferno: "If it wasn't hell, it was the courtyard of hell. It was a maelstrom of noise and hot spitting steel. Perhaps thirty or forty Canadian machine guns were brrppping at once. It sounded like hundreds … And the enemy's anti-tank shells and mortars were crashing into the buildings everywhere."

At last, on December 27, the enemy, two of its divisions as battered as the Canadians, pulled out silently. Halton said on air that "the Germans were superb … and when that is said, our Canadians were better. The Boche had all the cards—the prepared positions, the hundreds of booby traps and mines. We had to seek him out and kill him man by man … The attacking Canadians beat two of the finest German divisions that ever marched." They had, but the Canadians had 176 officers and 2,163 men killed, wounded, or captured, along with more than 1,600 evacuated because of illness or battle exhaustion. Half the division's infantry fighting strength had been gutted, and General Vokes's men had shot their bolt. "I am compelled to bring to your attention," Vokes told his corps commander, "that in my opinion the infantry units of this division will not be in a fit condition to undertake further offensive operations until they have had a period of rest." As Vokes said later, "Everything before Ortona was a nursery tale."

Gunner Donald Delaney served in Italy in a Medium Regiment of artillery—guns that fired a 100-pound shell. He wrote his father in Digby, Nova Scotia, in late March 1944 to recount his experiences in a "dirty rotten country like this": near misses, souvenirs, pay problems, the sometimes casual lack of discipline, and especially the food. "We are eating fairly good," he said of a spell out of action. "We are very fortunate at the present to be getting bread three times a day … We also get lots of mutton which we can eat with a mighty effort, if we are hungry enough … Frankly it's awful. For breakfast we get porridge, bacon or egg powder, sausage meat, bread, jam and coffee. For dinner we usually get canned stew … potatoes, carrots. For dessert we have usually, rice or prunes. We have no other means of getting food like in England." Not that the food in England, curtailed by stringent rationing, was very good.

It took time to recover from the carnage at Ortona, and the now established I Canadian Corps did not fight a full-scale action until

May 1944, in the Liri Valley, south of Rome. The corps, commanded by Lieutenant-General E.L.M. "Smiler" Burns (so dubbed because he never smiled) in place of Harry Crerar, who had returned to the United Kingdom to command First Canadian Army, had the still largely untried 5th Canadian Armoured and the now rebuilt 1st Division under command. The 5th's GOC was Major-General Bert Hoffmeister. He had replaced Simonds, who had returned to England to get ready for the D-Day invasion as the commander of II Canadian Corps. A mid-level Vancouver lumber manager in civilian life, Hoffmeister had been a success as an infantry battalion commander, and his brigade had taken Ortona. Now this officer who led from the front had a division.

The big British-led push up the Liri Valley aimed to breach the Gustav and Hitler lines. The difficulty, aside from the great strength of the enemy's superbly fortified defences, was that the Liri was a constricted valley with far too many units in it trying to use too few roads. The Canadians entered the battle on May 16 and advanced slowly; on May 23, the corps launched a set-piece assault near Pontecorvo, running into very intense enemy fire, "worse by far than the fire in front of Ortona," one Seaforths' officer wrote. But the Hitler Line was breached—though again the casualties were terrible: 3,300 killed, wounded, or taken captive, and another 4,000 injured or ill. This was a success, but the Eighth Army commander, the British General Oliver Leese, complained bitterly about Canadian transports jamming the roads and slowing the advance, something perhaps more attributable to his own staff than the Canadians'. Leese tried to sack Burns, but the top Canadian brass refused to agree, and Smiler stayed in place.

The advance went on, rolling toward Rome, which was seized by

American troops on June 4, 1944. It was the first Axis capital to fall and ought to have made headlines everywhere. But the Normandy invasion on June 6 grabbed the top spot, and the forgotten warriors in Italy—"the D-Day Dodgers in sunny Italy," as the rueful song had it—soldiered on.

The next major Canadian battle took place north of Florence in the Apennines. The Germans had constructed yet another defensive position, the Gothic Line, and I Canadian Corps had the job of breaking the eastern edge of this line and opening the road north to Rimini and the Po River Valley. The Canadians reached the Gothic defences on August 27, and General Hoffmeister went forward to do his own reconnaissance before the scheduled attack on September 1–2. Hoffmeister was startled to observe the enemy positions still largely unmanned, the Germans having been convinced by an Allied disinformation campaign that the main attack would come farther west. He persuaded Burns to advance the date of the attack. There were, again, very heavy casualties as the Germans quickly manned their positions when the Canadian assault began, but Hoffmeister's coup and his and Chris Vokes's soldiers' cracking of the Gothic Line forced a German withdrawal on September 1. It was, most Canadian military historians now agree, the finest feat of the war by Canadian soldiers. The "Mighty Maroon Machine"—the soldiers' name for the 5th Armoured Division because of the colour of their divisional shoulder patch—was now "Hoffy's Mighty Maroon Machine." Burns received the Distinguished Service Order for his role, but he was soon sacked. Vokes and Hoffmeister had found they could not work well with him, and the Eighth Army's commander similarly found him difficult. He was replaced by the equally dour Lieutenant-General Charles Foulkes, who had led the 2nd Division in France.

The Canadians remained in Italy until after New Year's 1945, fighting almost continuously and taking casualties every day, until they were ordered to Northwest Europe to rejoin First Canadian Army. I Canadian Corps and its soldiers had formed one of the very best fighting formations in Italy, and they would add their strength and experience to that of their comrades in Holland and Germany. The Italian Campaign had lasted more than a year and a half and had involved 92,750 Canadians; 5,339 officers and men remained behind in Commonwealth War Graves Commission cemeteries, while almost 20,000 Canadians had been wounded and 1,000 captured. In all, there were 26,254 casualties, or well above one in four of those who served.

The Italian Campaign had been intended to tie down German forces, and it did. But in order to do this, the Allies had had to devote their own resources—substantially more of them than the enemy did—to a brutal slogging match. For the Canadians, the long supply lines from Canada and Britain stretched very thinly, and reinforcements had become scarce through the summer and autumn of 1944. It was a long, hard war, and it was far from over. It would be won only by more men and more machines.

• • •

In the course of the Second World War, Canada's factories, mines, and fields produced billions of dollars' worth of goods and food to support the war effort. The nation created and produced more than Canada's one million men and women in uniform needed to fight and win, so arms, equipment, food, minerals, and metals were sold or, if our Allies did not have the money to pay, given away in Mutual Aid for the cause of victory. This was an astonishing feat of production and organization, a massive effort by every sector of the Canadian economy and by Canadian workers and business leaders. Canadians won the economic war.

Canada had been a small and weak country in 1939. The gross national product, the sum total of all the goods and services created by the population of 11.2 million Canadians, was $5.6 billion. The federal government's expenditures in 1939 were only $680 million. Unemployment remained very high, though down from the worst years of the Great Depression. There were still hundreds of thousands on relief, and men continued to "ride the rods" across the country, seeking work anywhere at a time when jobs were few. There were almost no munitions plants in that last year of peace—only one small federally owned arsenal in Quebec City (which primarily made limited quantities of small arms ammunition) and a subsidiary plant in Lindsay, Ontario, which had reopened in 1937. The British government just before the war had placed a small contract with Marine Industries Limited of Sorel, Quebec, to make one hundred 25-pounder artillery field guns. A few tiny aircraft manufacturers produced airplanes on an almost piecework basis (in 1933, no aircraft were produced in Canada; in 1938, 282 were produced, worth $4 million). In Toronto in March 1938, the John Inglis Company had won a contract to build 7,000 Bren light machine guns for the Canadian military and 5,000 for Britain—through a contracting process that produced cries of scandal, patronage, and profiteering and resulted in a Royal Commission investigation. Perhaps the Bren gun fiasco had something to do with the cancellation of the order that had been placed by the United Kingdom in Canada for 100 Bren gun tracked carriers, an order extraordinarily ended by London just after the outbreak of war.

Nor was there much of a legacy from the industrial war effort of the Great War of 1914–18. The British government of the time had arranged its own procurement in Canada through the Imperial Munitions Board, and the Dominion had produced mainly artillery shells—an effort that had proved difficult enough and had generated a succession of scandals and many production failures, all eventually resolved. In all, the industrial effort had generated a billion dollars' worth of munitions, a figure then seen as huge. The country's shipyards had built some small ships, and a few aircraft factories had produced tiny numbers of "flying machines." But the main effort had come in the form of shells, trucks, and automobiles, produce from fields, raw materials and mines.

Few in the dark years of the Depression believed that, should there be another war, Canada could do much more. There had been a "Survey of Industry" in 1936, the first full-scale attempt to catalogue what resources Canada might have for war production. But the difficulty was that few Canadians in government or industry could foresee the creation of war plants in Canada if they were only for equipping the Canadian forces. British orders were needed to make the creation or retooling of factories economical and, the British order for Bren guns aside, orders for Britain's armed forces almost always went to British firms. Nor were there prospects of orders from the United States—America was neutral in word and deed, and its small armed forces used different patterns of military equipment.

Partly as a result of the Bren gun affair, the Liberal government had, in June 1939, passed the Defence Purchases, Profits Control, and Financing Act, which aimed to limit profits from and costs of defence contracts. Profits could not exceed 5 percent, a stipulation that meant that soon after the war began, C.D. Howe, the minister of transport, told the House of Commons that Canada had not managed to place a single contract, there apparently being limits to the patriotism of manufacturers. The act had also created the Defence Purchasing Board to coordinate purchases; in its short life (July 14 to October 31, 1939), the board managed to buy only $43.7 million worth of goods, with three-quarters of the orders placed after Nazi Germany had invaded Poland. One of the first casualties of the Second World War was this system of profit controls, quickly repealed so that war orders could be placed. A second casualty was the Defence Purchasing Board itself, replaced on November 1, 1939, by the War Supply Board. Initially, the new board fell under the control of the finance minister, but in mid-November, in a fortunate move, it came under the ambit of the minister of transport, the newly named, double-hatted Minister of Munitions and Supply, Clarence Decatur Howe. Howe had no department as yet, only a title. But when the War Supply Board was swallowed by the new department on April 9, 1940, just days after the King Liberals' election victory, war production had found its Canadian czar.

Howe was American-born, a graduate of the Massachusetts Institute of Technology, a former Dalhousie University engineering professor, and a man who had made himself rich by constructing grain elevators throughout the west. In 1935, he had won election to Parliament from Port Arthur, Ontario, as a Liberal, and he instantly went into Mackenzie King's Cabinet. Tough, blunt, familiar with business and the men who ran it, Howe proved to be the right minister to lead the nation's wartime industrial mobilization.

But even Howe could do little until the urgency of war began to drive matters. The Nazi invasion of Denmark and Norway in April 1940 was quickly followed by the stunning victory of the Wehrmacht in the Low Countries and France. The Dunkirk evacuation at the end of May was the only grace note in the requiem for the European democracies. But now, at least, the financial concerns that had crimped British armaments orders in Canada and restrained Ottawa's own purchases were gone. Both London and Ottawa wanted everything now—right now. The dollar no longer reigned; the idea that Canada would fight a "limited" war had disappeared, a casualty of the Hitlerian blitzkrieg.

Howe set out to seize the initiative. He began to look to Canadian business for executives who could step in to organize and galvanize war production and to allocate scarce commodities. He expected their employers to pay their salaries; he offered nothing beyond a dollar a year, other than expenses; many of those he brought to Ottawa declined to take their expenses at all. The "dollar-a-year men," as they quickly became known, were the cream of Canadian business—a parliamentary return in February 1941 noted that 107 dollar-a-year men were employed across the government; Howe's department, with its array of executives, accountants, and lawyers, had by far the most. There would be many more as the war went on.

The Department of Munitions and Supply had control over all orders placed by Britain in Canada, soon had similar sway over orders from a rearming United States, and, of course, controlled all Canadian orders. The act that had created the department was amended in August 1940 to give Howe the power to "mobilize, control, restrict or regulate to such extent as the Minister may, in his absolute discretion, deem necessary, any branch or trade or industry in Canada or any munitions of war or supplies."

Moreover, the amended act gave Howe exclusive power to buy, manufacture, or produce munitions and supplies required by the Department of National Defence. Howe was in charge, the one man directing the Canadian industrial war effort. And Canada was the only Allied nation that had one agency handling all war procurement. There was no competition for scarce supplies between the various armed forces. The Cabinet and Howe decided, and Howe's voice was the clearest in the decisions.

Howe and his men did everything in a hurry. Munitions and Supply offered loans and grants, it purchased licences to permit Canadian production of foreign-owned weapons and equipment, and it helped secure the British and American experts needed to help Canadian firms get up and running. This was usually sufficient to get detailed planning under way; getting the actual armaments produced was more difficult.

Canadian industry was small and slow, plants were often obsolete, machine tools were scarce, and skilled workers were always in short supply. Howe's production chief, Harry Carmichael, who had come to Ottawa from General Motors, had the answer—subcontracting. The lead firm could likely produce a few artillery pieces a month, for example, if it worked on its own. But if it could get carefully machined parts from other, smaller plants across the country, parts that could be screwed into place at the main shops, production could be stepped up. That was how the big automobile plants worked, Carmichael said, so why couldn't the same methods be employed in building artillery or ships or aircraft? It required planning and control, a careful allocation of scarce materials, and a high level of inspection to ensure that the requisite quality was maintained, but it could be done. It was a "bits and pieces" program, Howe said. But it worked, and, moreover, it spread wartime jobs across the country and not just through central Canada. That was a political necessity if complaints from the Maritimes and the West that Ontario and Quebec received all the jobs were to be dealt with.

There were inevitable bottlenecks and failures, of course, but one way around them was to create Crown corporations. There was a shortage of rubber? Set up a Crown company to produce synthetic rubber. Need to develop high-tech equipment, including optical lenses and radar? Set up Research Enterprises Limited, with 7,000 employees in Leaside, a suburb of Toronto. Wood veneers for aircraft were in scarce supply? A Crown corporation could do the job. Machine tools? Howe's Citadel Merchandising could get them and make sure they went where they were most needed. In all, twenty-eight Crown corporations came into being during the war, some manufacturing, some purchasing and distributing, others supervising and controlling. The establishment of Crown companies, operating with great flexibility outside the usual bureaucratic restraints, allowed for efficiencies.

Even so, Howe and his advisers believed that private enterprise was inherently more efficient than any government-run operation. The Second World War made the government—or at least C.D. Howe's part of it—operate much like a corporation. The state helped with plant expansion and retooling, and corporate Canada put its own money into wartime growth. It had to—more than half of Canadian war production came from plants that had not existed in 1939. In 1939, some $3.65 billion had been invested in the country's factories. Four years later, capital invested amounted to $6.3 billion, a huge jump. Much of that was government money, but because Howe and his controllers ran what the press called "a graftless war," one almost wholly without patronage and preferment, there were relatively few complaints.

Certainly, Canadian business was paying its full share of the war's costs. Businesses contributed billions of dollars to Victory Loans, helping the government finance the war—for interest rates that ranged from 1.5 to 3 percent. Corporation taxes had increased from 18 to 40 percent. Excess profits taxes produced even more revenue. Profit on government contracts was limited to 10 percent, and by 1942, excess profits were taxed at 100 percent. Corporations, however, could claim double depreciation against taxes for plant renovations, machinery acquisition, and other expenses, and they were to receive a 20 percent rebate on their excess profits taxes after the war, a conscious attempt to help in the eventual reconversion to peacetime production. "No great fortunes," Finance Minister J.L. Ilsley said in 1941, "can be accumulated out of wartime profits."

For most Canadians working in war industry, there were big gains. Average wages increased dramatically, from $956 per year in 1938 to $1,525 in 1943. There was as much overtime as people wanted; many worked fifty or even sixty hours a week. Families that had struggled to keep one breadwinner employed in the Depression years now had a son in the army and two, three, or more family members bringing home good paycheques each week from factory work. The government's National Selective Service system controlled where people could work in an economy struggling to find enough workers for factories and men for the army, navy, and air force. The flood of people from small-town and rural Canada into the urban factories was enormous, not least the huge numbers of women who took jobs outside the home and went into factory work for the first time. By 1943, 261,000 women were employed in war plants and earning wages almost equivalent to those of male workers. Hundreds of thousands more women replaced men in service industries and on farms, and in 1944, women's participation in the paid workforce reached 33.5 percent.

There were also some 50,000 women in the armed services, including nurses, Wrens (in the Women's Royal Canadian Naval Service), WDs (in the Women's Division of the RCAF), and CWACs (in the Army). The Canadian Women's Army Corps provided much of the clerical and kitchen labour for Army bases, and CWACs first went overseas in November 1942. By the spring of 1944, there were 853 other ranks serving in Britain—390 were general duty personnel, with many employed in laundries; 378 were clerks; and others worked as drivers, cooks, switchboard operators, cipher clerks, and dental assistants, and in a host of other occupations. Every CWAC relieved a soldier for other duties, including combat, but CWAC pay was only two-thirds that of a man of equal rank (90 cents a day for a private, compared to $1.30). The pay scale for CWACs increased to 80 percent of the soldiers' in July 1943. Still, for many CWACs, their pay was the first money they had ever earned.

Generally, for both males and females, the growth in wages across the country outstripped inflation, thanks to the federal government's wage and price control system. And wartime Canadians ate better and spent more, despite the rationing of food, gas, and tires, than they had in the 1930s. Housing, however, was in short supply in cities with armament and uniform factories and in small towns near military bases, and many landlords gouged their tenants shamelessly.

Canada's overall war production ranked fourth among the Allies, behind only the United States, the United Kingdom, and the Soviet Union. For a nation of just 11 million people, this was little short of amazing. Orders, for example, went out for $58.4 million in Anson aircraft in December 1940 so that training under the British Commonwealth Air Training Plan could speed up. Canadian firms could build the airframes but none could manufacture the engines, which therefore had to be imported. In 1941, only 88 Ansons came off the lines; in 1942, total production had risen to 1,432; and by the end of 1943, it was up to 2,269. The story was much the same for other aircraft types. More than 16,400 aircraft in all were produced in Canada by 116,000 workers, including 30,000 women. It was a massive, hugely successful effort even if the engines had to be brought into the country or installed in aircraft once the airframes reached Britain or the United States—all the more impressive for beginning from a standing start.

But there were errors. The blitzkrieg of May 1940 had demonstrated the superiority of the enemy panzers, and the Allies scrambled to match them. In Canada, this meant an effort to develop a tank—the Ram—that could be used by Canada's planned two armoured divisions and two armoured brigades. The Ram began with the American Grant tank and grafted on a revolving turret, giving a 360-degree sweep. Two thousand Rams were built in Montreal, but the tank turned out to be expensive and not very effective; it was soon superseded by the American-produced Sherman. The Rams ended the war converted into armoured personnel carriers, the so-called Kangaroos. There were evidently limits to what Canada's small industrial base could produce.

Still, the Canadian and Allied armies were huge beneficiaries of the production of the nation's factories. The major contribution—indeed, arguably Canada's biggest industrial contribution to victory—was in the form of trucks, most particularly Canadian Military Pattern (CMP) vehicles. These vehicles, produced in huge numbers by Ford and General Motors (along with some 180,000 military versions of Chrysler's D60 truck model), came in a bewildering variety. There were 90 types of army vehicles on 12 different chassis. In all, Canada's General Motors, Ford, and Chrysler auto plants produced 815,729 military vehicles that equipped the Canadian and British Commonwealth armies. Britain's Eighth Army, fighting in North Africa and Italy, used huge numbers of CMP vehicles.

Does it overstate matters to suggest that the British Army ran on Canadian vehicles? Yes and no. Large as it was, Canadian war production made up to only 10 percent of total British Commonwealth production. On the other hand, only 34 percent of Canadian war production was used by the Canadian services, while 53 percent went to the British and Commonwealth nations, 12 percent to the United States, and 1 percent to other Allied states. In all, Canadian wartime industrial production was valued at more than $9.5 billion in 1940s dollars (the equivalent in today's dollars would be well above $150 billion). Another $1.5 billion was spent on defence construction and the expansion of war plants, almost all paid by the government. For a nation that had begun the war with a gross national product of $5.6 billion, this was incredible. That Canada's GNP in 1945 was $11.8 billion, more than double the total six years before, is accounted for in large part by the extraordinary production of the nation's workers and factories.

CHAPTER 2

From D-Day to the Closing of the Falaise Gap

I n 1944, the war began to move toward its climax. The battle in Italy continued, with Mussolini being toppled, Rome and Florence being captured, and the Allies pushing north toward and through the Gothic Line. In the Soviet Union, the war's decisive battleground, the vast Russian armies continued to pound the Wehrmacht and press the Nazis back to the west. In the Far East, the Japanese advances ended, and relentless air and sea pressure helped the island-hopping of the American fleet, Marines, and armies. The Second World War was far from over, but the next act—the invasion of France—was set to begin. In this operation and for the remainder of the war in Europe, Canada's soldiers would play their greatest role.

• • •

The average Canadian in khaki in 1944 was a Depression kid. Some two-thirds of soldiers were between the ages of eighteen and twenty-five, and most of the rest, including officers up to lieutenant-colonel, only a few years older. They were largely of British origin, but in the Second World War the Canadian-born were in the majority, as had not been the case until the very end of the First World War. Ethnic minorities were well represented in the Army; French Canadian enlistment too was much better than in the Great War, though significantly less than the percentage of francophones in the population. The soldiers, every one of those overseas a volunteer until the last two or three months of the war, understood, according to surveys and interviews, that Hitler's Germany threatened them and their nation. Most identified strongly with Britain and the Empire, a product of the schooling they had received and the media they read. The songs they sang in Britain and heard on the radio—Vera Lynn singing that "there'll be blue birds over the white cliffs of Dover"—enhanced their pro-British beliefs. Even at home in Canada, the soldiers had listened to the Happy Gang sing "There'll Always Be an England" on each episode of their CBC radio show.

The men had volunteered for a wide range of reasons. Many believed in the democracies' cause and wanted to help beat Hitler and the Nazis. Others thought in terms of proving themselves, or sought adventure, or disliked their job or being out of work. Still more were in unhappy relationships and wanted to escape. Others, happy and in love, believed that they had to serve their country in a time of great trial. Some enlisted out of a fear of being conscripted or being subjected to social pressure. The reasons always varied, but until early 1945 the Canadian Army overseas was the only all-volunteer army on the Allied side. In all, one million Canadians volunteered in the Second World War for the three services, an utterly remarkable record, and some 700,000 joined the Army willingly.

Most likely, the soldiers also knew that the war would be a long, desperate struggle and realized that they might face what their fathers had suffered during the 1914–18 war. "I was born in 1920," war artist Alex Colville, who enlisted in the infantry in 1942, remembered. "This was the year [in] which most of the [Canadians] killed in the Second World War were born. They were in their early twenties. A great many of the people I went to school and university with were killed." The truth was that on-the-job training in battle was terribly costly.

The soldiers, the majority of whom left jobs to join up, first went through their basic training in Canada. They were harassed by sergeants, lectured at church parades by padres, and drilled unmercifully. Journalist and historian Pierre Berton remembered that his recruit training platoon "began to grow a little cocky" and somehow decided that it would win the competition for the best-drilled platoon on the parade square: "Perfection in close order drill became an obsession. It is hard to believe, looking back on it now, that we actually gave up our precious evenings and practised at night in our own time. Of course we won." The next day, Berton said, the platoon broke up and went its separate ways, promising to write, pledging to have a grand reunion at war's end. "In just ten weeks the army had taken seventy-five strangers from all walks of life," he later wrote, "and turned them, for a little while at least, into the closest of comrades." The Army broke men down and built them up; the loyalties forged in units became vitally important. Men would die rather than let down their comrades, and once they joined their regiments, their unit pride grew strong.

As might be expected, officers had more formal education, at least a high school graduation certificate, while under 5 percent held a university degree. Only one in eight enlisted men had completed high school, and an astonishing two-thirds had not progressed past grade 7. In the Régiment de Maisonneuve, the median education level of the 197 fatalities whose records are available for examination was 6.3 years; in the Calgary Highlanders, the 394 soldiers killed in combat had a median of 8 years of education. The average soldier was 5 feet 7 inches in height and weighed under 160 pounds. Most put on weight in the Army, some eating well for the first time in their lives, and after extensive physical training, most were in their best physical shape. Nonetheless, it was evident that the Royal Canadian Air Force and to a lesser extent the Royal Canadian Navy had skimmed off the cream of the nation's youth.

If this was not the best-educated army in the world, its soldiers were adaptable, easy to train, and tough. For one thing, almost all could drive, an advantage they shared with American soldiers. They had adapted well to Battle Drill and hard training, and, while they enjoyed England—and the English girls, who also liked the Canadians, who were better paid than their own British soldiers (though not as well paid as the Yanks)—they wanted to get into action and, like all soldiers, to prove themselves. "When grown men cry 'cause they're not with their unit today carrying out their jobs," wrote Lieutenant Hal MacDonald of the North Shore (New Brunswick) Regiment, who had charge of his battalion's reinforcements still in England on June 6, D-Day, "well that's an indication of the fighting spirit of the 3rd Cdn. Div." Someone else might be killed in battle, but it would not be them. They would get their opportunity to experience war now.

• • •

The necessity of invading Europe had dominated the thinking of Allied political and military leaders for almost three years, indeed almost since the blitzkrieg had driven Britain off the Continent in June 1940. The Americans had argued strongly in 1942 before the Combined Chiefs of Staff that the Allies should invade France, while the British, having faced the German army in France, Greece, and North Africa by this time, were very wary. The American military chiefs were flatly wrong, and the British were correct to advocate clearing North Africa and striking at Sicily and Italy first. Not until May 1943, at the first Quebec Conference, did Prime Minister Winston Churchill and President Franklin Roosevelt and their military chiefs (Mackenzie King and his military staff were present at Quebec but had no role in the high-level discussions) agree definitively to land in France. Even then, Churchill continued to have his doubts. Nonetheless, for the next thirteen months, the invasion planners did their preparatory work, gathering the landing craft and supporting naval ships, assembling the troops and training them, and assigning the bombing targets. It was war, and nothing went precisely according to plan, but the preparations were thoroughly and ingeniously made.

The planning team, made up of British and American officers, operated under the direction of a British officer, Lieutenant-General Frederick E. Morgan, the COSSAC, as the Chief of Staff to the Supreme Allied Commander was called. The Supreme Allied Commander had yet to be named, and the Chief of the Imperial General Staff, General Sir Alan Brooke, and the U.S. Army's Chief of Staff, General George C. Marshall, both wanted—and deserved—the job. Neither could be spared, however, and as the Americans now had much the greatest power in the Anglo-American alliance, the SAC had to be American.

The post fell to General Dwight Eisenhower, a career soldier who had worked for Marshall in Washington and then been tapped to direct the invasions of North Africa, Sicily, and Italy. Eisenhower had the knack of getting on with even the most difficult of men, and he succeeded in being scrupulously fair in leading the British and Americans, not always kissing cousins. His most difficult subordinate was General Bernard Montgomery, and the Eighth Army's feisty, opinionated, and victorious commander was designated to be in charge of the Allied armies once the lodgment in France had been made. The overall naval and air commanders were also British.

COSSAC's draft plan called for a three-division assault supported by parachute drops. Because of a global shortage of tank landing craft, Morgan, the COSSAC, estimated the Allies could land only three divisions in the first assault—"the destinies of two great empires," Prime Minister Winston Churchill moaned, "seem to be tied up in some God-damned things called LSTs," or "Landing Ships, Tank," as the military called them in its usual backward nomenclature. But once they'd arrived in England to take up their roles, once they had reviewed COSSAC's plan, both Eisenhower and Montgomery considered this too weak an assault force. They directed that the plan be altered to put five divisions on the beaches, with three divisions of paratroops landed on the flanks. Somehow the additional LSTs would be built or redirected to England. COSSAC's chosen landing site, the beaches of Normandy, remained the objective, and the operation, dependent on the tides, was scheduled to proceed in May or June 1944.

The Germans knew an invasion was coming, but they did not know where or when, and learning this was complicated for them by the Allies' elaborate and effective security and disinformation measures. Led by Field Marshal Erwin Rommel, Montgomery's foe in North Africa, the Nazis had greatly strengthened the French portion of their Atlantic Wall, a 3,000-mile system of fixed obstacles and bunkers along the European coast. There were tens of thousands of mines everywhere—in the water and on the beaches—plus vast numbers of tank and troop obstacles planted in the water or the sand, stakes driven into the ground in likely landing places for gliders, and hundreds of huge concrete bunkers dotted along the beaches to provide interlocked fields of fire covering possible landing spots. (Many of these bunkers remain intact today on the Normandy beaches.)

Manning these defences were divisions of varying quality. Most of the Wehrmacht deployed in the east against the Russians or in Italy against the Allies; the troops defending the Normandy beaches, including Juno Beach, where the Canadians were to land, came from the 716th Division. This formation was made up of the young and the old, the ill and those recovering from wounds, and men from Osttruppen—Red Army prisoners conscripted into the Wehrmacht and ordered to defend the Atlantic Wall. The 716th had little transport, (much of it horse-drawn), employed mostly heavy weapons captured from the Czechs or French, and had generally low-grade officers. But in mid-March 1944, Hitler's intuition told him something might be up in Normandy, and he posted a high-quality division, the 352nd, into the coastal region. This reduced the frontage assigned to the 716th Division and thickened up the defences. Even bad troops fighting in well-sited concrete bunkers could take a heavy toll, and they did. But there were good troops in France too, elite panzer divisions and the best of Hitler's well-armed and highly skilled Waffen-SS panzer formations, generally located inland but within an easy march to the coast. All would fight well, even the "volunteers," so long as they were in their bunkers and their officers enforced discipline. The Germans' intent was to drive the Allies back into the sea, to force another Dieppe on any American-British-Canadian invasion attempt.

One great advantage the Allies had was that the Germans, aware of the enormous difficulties in landing a huge force across the English Channel, reckoned that an assault would come at Pas-de-Calais, the French landfall closest to Britain. Hitler's headquarters believed this was the most likely place, and the Führer was the one to ultimately decide if an invasion was a feint or the real assault, and to determine when to release the panzers to try to drive the Allies into the sea. Getting ashore was to be no easy task for the Allies; staying ashore might be even more difficult if the Germans promptly sent their full force against the Normandy landing. Another advantage for the Allies was that the Nazis, unlike the forces of the democracies, still depended on horsepower. The mobility of the German armies defending the Channel coast depended on horses, 67,000 of them, hauling artillery and supply wagons in infantry divisions.

The Allies knew the locations of most of the German units. They had the benefit of extensive air reconnaissance, the results of investigations of the beaches by navy frogmen, and reports from the French Maquis, the underground fighters who tried to keep the spirit of resistance in France alive. They had established air superiority over most of France; their fighters and bombers, with a ten-to-one advantage over the Luftwaffe, were able to roam almost at will. The German navy also had been subdued, its forces now limited to a few destroyers, small craft, and fast, torpedo-carrying E-boats. The U-boat fleet, checked in the North Atlantic by the combined efforts of the British, American, and Canadian navies in the course of 1943, still posed a threat, but not an immediate one to any landing.

Much thought and planning had been put into supporting the troops once they had effected a lodgement. No port on the Normandy coast had been selected as the invasion site—one of the few true lessons from the Dieppe raid was that an attempt to seize a fortified port would likely be fruitless—but ships carrying backup troops and supplies were needed. How could they be unloaded? The answer: two artificial ports, dubbed Mulberries, each the size of the harbour in Dover, England, were to be created out of scuttled ships and huge concrete caissons towed into place. (Much of the historical information on the planning for the two Mulberries is located in the McMaster University archives in Hamilton, Ontario.) An underwater pipeline, PLUTO, was to be built to carry gasoline. British, American, and Canadian troops required tons of supplies of all kinds to fight, and everything had been taken into account (except the weather, as it turned out). Airfields needed to be seized or constructed to provide close air support, and these required heavy equipment. One advantage the Allies had, with their almost total control of the sea and the skies, was that destroyers, cruisers, and even battleships could stand offshore and direct heavy gunfire to support the landings and subsequent operations. Such support would continue to be extremely critical into July.

The sites for the landings on the Normandy coast had been carefully surveyed: there were five beaches—Omaha and Utah to the west, where the Americans were to land; Gold and Sword for the British; and Juno, between the two British beaches, for the Canadians. The date for the invasion was finally fixed for June 5, 1944.

• • •

The designated Canadian landing force was the 3rd Canadian Infantry Division, supported by the 2nd Canadian Armoured Brigade. The 2nd Canadian Infantry and 4th Canadian Armoured divisions were designated as follow-on forces, as were the headquarters of II Canadian Corps, commanded by Lieutenant-General Guy Simonds, and First Canadian Army, commanded by Lieutenant-General Harry Crerar. In all, the frontline Canadian forces numbered some 60,000 men, with additional thousands in supporting and specialist units. The follow-on forces were to arrive in France when there was room in the bridgehead. Once ashore, they would form a part of General Montgomery's 21st Army Group. First Canadian Army—with the II Corps and its three Canadian divisions—could have British or other Allied forces serving under it, at least until I Canadian Corps' two divisions and an armoured brigade, fighting in Italy, were reunited with it, whenever that might be.

The 3rd Canadian Division GOC was Major-General Rod Keller, who had been in command since September 1942. A Permanent Force infantryman from the Princess Patricia's Canadian Light Infantry, Keller was short and stocky, tough-talking, and popular with the troops. As an instructor at the Royal Military College before the war, he had been dubbed "Captain Blood," after a swashbuckling movie character played by Errol Flynn. But Keller drank too much and caroused too much, and because he had a mistress in England whom he was determined to visit, he was sometimes less than assiduous in following the restrictive rules of the pre-invasion period. He had a good staff, however. His key staff planner, the General Staff Officer, Grade 1 (GSO1), was Lieutenant-Colonel J.D. Mingay, whom many thought Keller allowed to run the division. His Assistant Adjutant and Quartermaster General (AA&QMG) was the capable Lieutenant-Colonel Ernest Côté, and his Commander, Royal Artillery (CRA), Brigadier Stanley Todd, was a Great War veteran and so aged—forty-six!—that he was known as "Uncle Stanley" by the relative striplings at division headquarters. (Todd was also a superb artilleryman.) The division staff had been working for months with its counterparts at Britain's I Corps, under which they would initially serve in Normandy.

The 7th, 8th, and 9th Infantry Brigades, which formed the 3rd Division, were led by Brigadiers Harry Foster, from the PF, and K.G. Blackader and D.G. Cunningham, both militia officers. The 7th Brigade consisted of the Royal Winnipeg Rifles, the Regina Rifles, and the Canadian Scottish. The 8th Brigade had the Queen's Own Rifles, the Régiment de la Chaudière, and the North Shore (New Brunswick) Regiment. The 9th Brigade was formed by the Highland Light Infantry, the Stormont, Dundas and Glengarry Highlanders, and the North Nova Scotia Highlanders. The division had four, instead of the usual three, Royal Canadian Artillery regiments—plus two British field regiments and a Medium Regiment with sixteen 4.5-inch guns. In addition, the British 62nd Anti-Tank Regiment, with forty-eight 17-pounder guns, was added to the 3rd Division's resources. All the usual supporting elements—engineers, signallers (supply and transport included)—were also present.

The infantrymen had trained extensively for the invasion since November 1943, practising getting ashore from landing craft, clearing obstacles, and, using fire and movement, moving inland. They had worked on company, battalion, and brigade exercises, practised their cooperation with tanks, become accustomed to receiving air and naval support, and psyched themselves up for their task. The artillery, using self-propelled "Priests"—105mm guns mounted on tank chassis—practised firing from their landing craft. The armoured regiments trained on the tanks they would "swim" to shore. The task of preparation was all-encompassing.

The 3rd Division's difficulty was that it had not seen action, its service having been confined to Canada and England. Some of the officers and NCOs had been brought back from Italy to provide a leavening of battle experience; a few had been sent to serve for a time with British units in North Africa. But the 3rd Division—like the 2nd Canadian Infantry Division and the 4th Canadian Armoured Division, which were to follow on into Normandy in the days ahead—was green. "I don't think there would be more than four or five people in the brigade who had ever seen a shot fired in anger before landing in Normandy," said the 9th Brigade commander, Brigadier Cunningham.

It was the same in the 2nd Canadian Armoured Brigade, led by Brigadier R.A. Wyman, who had assumed command on April 15, 1944, after serving in Sicily and Italy. His regiments were the 1st Hussars, the Fort Garry Horse, and the Sherbrooke Fusiliers. All were good units, well trained and ready. Each of the assault regiments acquired two squadrons of new Duplex Drive Sherman tanks, which could use a propeller to swim ashore, shed the canvas flotation gear that kept them from sinking, and then operate on land. The troopers had to learn to employ their new weapons, but many had never fired the main gun on their tanks. The real difficulty, as they would discover to their cost, was that the Sherman, running on flammable high-octane gasoline, was markedly inferior in its armour and its main gun to the enemy's panzers, especially the Panther and Tiger tanks. U.S. tank crews were said to consider five Shermans to be the equal of one Panther, and eight Shermans equal to a single Tiger. It may have been so. One officer who served with the British Columbia Regiment (BCR) in the 4th Armoured Division, James Tedlie, later a major-general, recalled that his regiment lost 105 Shermans, 44 Stuart light tanks, and one Crusader cruiser tank in action. The tank strength of the BCRs was 44. The two Allied advantages were, firstly, that there were in reserve many more mass-produced Shermans, thanks to the United States' vast industrial plant, than the Germans had in comparatively handcrafted Tigers. Secondly, the Sherman was much more reliable—it kept running without breaking down, unlike the Tiger—and it could sustain a speed of 25 miles per hour for long periods. That was scant comfort, however, to the soldiers of a troop of Shermans facing the enemy panzers. Why the Allies, with their great industrial resources, did not develop a tank better able to counter the Wehrmacht's armour remains one of the great mysteries of the Second World War.

The soldiers gathered in their pre-invasion concentration areas. The staff planners made the final calculations on the loading tables, trying to ensure that what the attackers needed first, other than what they carried on their backs, could be put ashore quickest. The last applications of waterproofing sealant went onto the tanks and trucks, and the gunners on the Priests made sure their ammunition was close at hand. The LSTs—the Landing Ship, Tanks—were loaded, carrying huge cargoes;

LST-543, for example, headed for Juno Beach with 66 vehicles, artillery, and Bren gun carriers, plus 354 soldiers.

Offshore, minesweepers—many from the Royal Canadian Navy and manned by some 10,000 Canadian seamen—worked to clear the designated landing areas, while heavier gunned vessels prepared to steam into the English Channel to escort the landing craft and to shell beach targets. The Royal, Royal Canadian, and United States Army Air Forces loaded their bombers to plaster the beaches and likely targets just inland. Phantom formations based in England increased their wireless activity, hoping (successfully) to keep the enemy's codebreakers focused on the Pas-de-Calais, awaiting the "real" invasion there. And the French Resistance fighters listened for the coded signal that would set them afoot to interfere with German troop movements. Everything was ready for the invasion to go ahead on June 5. The tides were right, but the weather, unfortunately, would not cooperate; a strong storm blew through the Channel. The next day—the last day for a month that the tides would be favourable—looked almost as bad, but the meteorologists noticed a break in the storm and informed Eisenhower, and he gave the order to proceed. June 6, 1944, was D-Day.

• • •

RCAF pilot Murray Peden's D-Day task was to drop "window" aluminum strips to shield the invasion from enemy radar. He wrote in his memoirs that on his aircraft's way back to England, "a tremendous awesome aerial armada was passing us in extended formation a mile or two on our left side … I thought of the men squatting nervously inside and felt like a slacker. After five or six hours in the air, we were on our way home, heading back to a good breakfast and a clean bed. They were only a quarter of an hour away from going in by parachute or glider—to face what? We flew in silence for some time."

Another RCAF pilot, Tony Selfe, flying a Halifax bomber with a load of 11,000 pounds of 500- and 1,000-pound bombs, cruised at 2,000 feet over the Channel and was astonished at how crowded the water was with shipping, the air full of aircraft returning after dropping the para-troops on the flanks of the invasion. Selfe's mission turned hair-raising when a bomber flying above him dropped a 500-pound bomb that went through the wing of his aircraft. Selfe managed to get the aircraft turned around, and the crew bailed out safely over England.

One of the first Canadians to land near Varaville in Normandy was Private Mark Lockyer of the 1st Canadian Parachute Battalion, part of the 6th British Airborne Division. The paras had the task of blowing bridges over the river Dives in an attempt to cut off enemy forces attack-ing the Allied beaches from the east. Lockyer's Dakota took off at 9:00 p.m., and he could soon see the huge invasion fleet filling the English Channel. "It looked like you could almost jump from ship-to-ship to get back to England," he wrote. "What a wonderful sight. It made you feel good that you were part of a tremendous effort." Lockyer's "stick" jumped at about 12:45 a.m., and he and many others landed in water— the Germans had flooded low-lying areas to slow any invaders trying to attack the bridges. The paras were scattered by the winds, but enough of the Canadians collected together near the bridge at Robehomme to blow it up at 3:00 a.m. Then the roughly fifty Canadians dug in and pre-pared to hold off the enemy for as long as it took.

While the paratroops were digging in, the first of the assault troops were closing in on the beach. Two battalions from each of the 3rd Division's 7th and 8th brigades were in the first wave to hit Juno Beach. Fortified small towns like Courseulles-sur-Mer, Saint-Aubin, Bény-sur-Mer, and Bernières-sur-Mer provided the hard core of the German defences. Once the beach defences were cleared, the advance would press inland. The plan called for the British to seize the city of Caen on the Anglo-Canadian front the first day.

Rifleman Jim Wilkins of the Queen's Own Rifles, a Toronto regiment, much later told his story of the 3rd Canadian Division's assault on Juno, first providing information on "how the army works": "The generals always like to have reserves so they hold back one full brigade of three regiments totaling 2400 men who would come in about three-quarters to one hour later. So now we are down to two brigades of 6 regiments or 3200 going in. Now the Brigadiers of the two brigades want to hold back one regiment each for [their] reserve or 1,600 men, so we are down to only 4 regiments … going in. Next the Regimental colonel decides to hold back 'C' and 'D' company for twenty minutes as his reserve or 480 men. So who the hell is going to make the first assault?" he asked. "Two companies [each] out of 4 regiments—'A' and 'B' companies of the North Shore Regiment, 'A' and 'B' of the Queen's Own Rifles, 'A' and 'B' from the Winnipeg Rifles and 'A' and 'B' from the Regina Rifles and one company from the Highland Light Infantry. Nine companies in all, plus assorted extras like engineers, medics, signalers, etc. Each company has 5 boats so the total was 45 boats consisting of about 30 men each or a total of 1350 men who are to be in the first wave assault on Juno beach. We started out with 15,000—where the hell was the other 13,650??"

The Queen's Own Rifles (QOR) had been trained to hit the sand hard and fast. After a very rough night on the stormy Channel—"Everybody got sick," Rifleman Jack Hadley remembered—with reveille at 3:15 a.m. and breakfast at 5:00, the first wave landed. Every man had been briefed on what he was to do when he went ashore at Bernières-sur-Mer, Company Sergeant Major Charlie Martin wrote, and yet, as Martin's boat came closer to the shore, he thought, much like Wilkins, that he and his soldiers had never been so alone in their lives. "Ten boats stretched out over fifteen hundred yards is not really a whole lot of assault force," he recalled of the first wave to get ashore. A football field's worth of space separated each of the assault craft. The tanks supporting the Queen's Own, frustrated by the high seas, could not swim ashore and had to be put directly on the beach—late. Worse, the soldiers could see the shore from their assault boat, and the houses looked undamaged, the enemy's pillboxes and obstacles manned and untouched by bombs or shellfire. The heavy bombing and naval guns had not accomplished much. And once the boats grounded just after 8:00 a.m., machine-gun and mortar fire began to fall heavily on the beach. "Move! Fast! Don't stop for anything! Go! Go! Go!" he shouted at his mates. And they did. Ten of the first eleven of the riflemen who got ashore in one QOR landing craft fell dead or wounded to machine-gun fire.

Gilbert Coutts of the Royal Winnipeg Rifles remembered that as his landing craft approached the beaches, "shells were hitting the side of the boat. You could hear them ricocheting off the sides … When the ramp went down I was in waist-deep water, and we ran like little rabbits across that beach. There was a hole in the wire and we went tearing through there, and across this field. We got to the other side and found out it was a mine field." Somehow, most of the men found their way through. The riflemen of the Royal Winnipeg Rifles and the Queen's Own, much like those of the North Shore Regiment and the Regina Rifles, made the difference between victory and defeat.

The experiences of the Queen's Own Rifles in the first hours after landing were not untypical. The men faced withering enemy fire and belts of land mines. One platoon of A Company ran into an 88mm gun, not spotted by pre-invasion reconnaissance; ten minutes later all that was left of the platoon were five or so unwounded survivors. D Company unluckily landed directly in front of a bunker, and half its strength was lost in a 200-yard dash to the protection of the sea-wall. Not until three riflemen took out the bunker with hand grenades pitched through the firing slits could the advance proceed. The rifle-men soon cleared Bernières, and the owner of an *estaminet*, a little wine shop, quickly popped up from his cellar and, with bullets still flying, started to sell wine.

Some bunkers faced by the Regina Rifles on their beach in front of Courseulles-sur-Mer were huge—thirty-five feet wide, the concrete four feet thick—and had underground chambers, again protected by concrete and steel, for the defenders. Fortuitously avoiding the enemy's mines, the landing craft of A Company grounded on the sandy beach and the company commander immediately fell wounded. Pinned down and taking more casualties from heavy machine-gun fire and an 88mm gun inside a concrete emplacement that had survived the naval bom-bardment unscathed, the men huddled on the beach. The fate of the "Farmer John" company's assault hung in the balance. Then initiative and courage came into play.

Lieutenant Bill Grayson, a platoon commander, had jumped from his landing craft and run across the bare expanse of sand to the first row of houses facing the sea. There, he took cover behind a house near the 88mm gun emplacement, where he was invisible to the crew inside. There was a German machine gun between him and the 88mm gun, and Grayson noticed that the machine gun's fire came in timed bursts along a fixed arc. He checked the timing and estimated that he could get past the machine gun and run to the side of the emplacement, where he could toss a grenade through the gun slit. Immediately after the next burst, he dashed for the emplacement and threw in his grenade. He heard the explosion, dived in after it, and leapt up in time to see the 88's crew fleeing. The last German turned and threw a grenade at him. Grayson caught it and threw it back.

He then followed the Germans through a zigzag trench to a covered shelter. He looked in, made out a few figures, and heard shouts of "*Kamerad.*" He motioned with his pistol for them to come out and was astonished when thirty-five men emerged with their hands up. With the 88mm gun out of action—thanks to Grayson's courage, which won him the Military Cross—A Company was able to get off the beach. But the landing craft carrying D Company of the battalion, minutes behind the first wave, ran into mines offshore; only forty-nine men made it onto the beach.

The Royal Winnipeg Rifles, tasked with clearing part of Courseulles, faced enemy units that had completely escaped bombing. "The bombardment having failed to kill a single German," the unit's war diarist noted, the Little Black Devils "had to storm their positions 'cold'—and did so without hesitation." B Company had its 120 men reduced to

27 after the morning's action. A medical officer, Major Charles Baker, saw enemy shellfire destroy a self-propelled Priest carrying a 105mm gun. The ammunition and fuel exploded and set the grass on fire. "The men who had been unlucky enough to stay … under and around the S.P. art[iller]y were burned alive," he wrote. "As they burned up, they screamed blood-curdling screams that I can hear yet." Baker himself suffered multiple wounds.

In most cases, the tanks of the 2nd Canadian Armoured Brigade, intended to precede the infantry ashore, arrived late or not at all. The armoured regiments' Duplex Drive Sherman tanks, able to swim over calm seas and support the attacking infantry, were slowed by the heavy waves. Some landing craft decided to put their tanks on the beach; others sent them afloat and many of these sank, their crews lost. In all, only twenty-one tanks made it to shore on Juno in the first hours of the invasion. Confusion inevitably resulted, compounded by losses from mines and from anti-tank gunfire. Almost everywhere, the tanks got into action after, not before, the infantry, but the guns of the 1st Hussars' Shermans, for example, turned on the enemy strongpoints, greatly helped the Regina Rifles get into Courseulles. As the regimental history noted of the squadron supporting the Royal Winnipeg Rifles, "as soon as the anti-tank guns on the beach had been liquidated, the seven DD tanks began to cruise up and down the beach engaging the machine gun nests. At first the fire was so intense that the crew commanders had difficulty in locating the targets, but gradually these were found and neutralized, permitting the infantry to sweep on over the dunes to begin their push inland." Also on the beach in the first waves were small British subunits of "funnies" from the 79th Division. These specially designed tanks included flails that cleared mines and the Armoured Vehicle Royal Engineers (AVREs), vehicles that threw a 40-pound shell at bunkers; both were critical in the success of the landing.

The North Shore (New Brunswick) Regiment landed to the west of the formidable resistance nest at Saint-Aubin-sur-Mer. Minefields, pillboxes, 50mm anti-tank guns, two 75mm field guns, bunkers, and tunnels awaited the assault companies after they fought their way across the beach to the coastal road. Before the assault, the resistance nest was struck by USAAF bombers, then shelled by a destroyer, followed by 120 rounds per gun from a field regiment's 24 guns fired from landing craft, and a thousand 27-kilogram rockets from a Landing Craft, Tank (Rocket). Bad weather upset things, and most of the supporting tanks were lost or failed to arrive, but the North Shores got ashore and cleared the town. They suffered heavily in the process, losing 124 killed or wounded by the end of the first day.

Private William Smith of the North Shores wrote in his (illegal) diary that when his landing craft approached the beach, he had felt reassured by General Eisenhower's message to the troops: "The free men of the world are marching to victory!" Smith added that his reassurance did not last very long: "I could not hear myself think because everything was exploding around me. I knew that I would fight with all my heart for my country ... But now, words are jumping out at me. I still can't describe the horror I saw yesterday ... [We] got in the water, some guys were really scared, I could see it in their eyes. Hell," he admitted, "we were all scared. The water was freezing. As I approached the beach, I saw my own friends a few feet away from me, have their arms shot off or even worse die instantly in front of me ... Right now a third of my company … are hiding out in a pit until darkness sets in so we can start looking for the others. I don't even know where the hell we are!"

The Régiment de la Chaudière, the reserve battalion in the 8th Brigade, landed just behind the Queen's Own Rifles at Bernières-sur-Mer. The Toronto unit was still fighting to clear the beach defences. Mines destroyed some of landing craft, but the surviving Chauds soon moved inland, where the infantrymen found themselves held up by a battery of three deadly 88mm guns. A radio message quickly whistled up fire support from the destroyer HMCS *Algonquin* offshore, one of some 110 Royal Canadian Navy ships involved in D-Day. The ship fired fifteen shells from its 4.7-inch guns at the enemy. A remarkable thirteen landed on target, and the infantry moved ahead unmolested. Some supporting units carried bicycles. "That," Brigadier Cunningham recalled, "was Monty's idea—they were the most useless, bloody things. Our troops couldn't carry bicycles … They were never used."

The soldiers of the 3rd Division and the armoured brigade had fought exceptionally well on D-Day. They had cracked the Atlantic Wall and gone ashore in the face of heavy fire and high casualties. None of the Canadian units (and no other Allied units)—except for a single troop of four tanks from the 1st Hussars—reached their D-Day objectives. The British certainly had not captured Caen; it would not be liberated for another month. But every Canadian unit had moved well inland, and the 3rd Division was close to joining up with the British troops on Gold and Sword beaches, adjoining Juno. In all on D-Day, the Canadians had lost 340 killed in action, 574 wounded, and 47 taken prisoner. It was a terrible toll, the highest on the three easternmost landing beaches; that it was much less than had been predicted by the planners was little consolation.

Only on Omaha Beach, well to the west of Juno, had the Allied casualties (almost 9 percent of those landed) exceeded estimates, and the U.S. troops there had had to fight exceedingly well to secure any lodgement at all. But the Allies at last were back on French soil. Their task for the coming days was to build up their strength, expand the bridgehead, and hold off the inevitable enemy panzer counterattacks that would aim to drive them into the sea.

· · ·

As mandated by German tactical doctrine, counterattacks there would be. The enemy response had been delayed by the strong belief in Paris at Wehrmacht headquarters and at the Führer's headquarters that the Normandy invasion was a feint, the Pas-de-Calais still the real objective. It took time to get the counterattacks authorized, and the relentless strafing of German vehicles on the roads delayed matters further. Field Marshal Rommel stated on June 12 that "our own operations are rendered extraordinarily difficult and in part impossible to carry out [because of] the exceptionally strong and, in some cases, overwhelming superiority of the enemy air force." But as the Allied forces moved inland—150,000 men and innumerable tanks, trucks, and guns had been put ashore in the first twenty-four hours—they soon bumped into the enemy.

The first Canadians to meet the Germans inland were men from the North Nova Scotia Highlanders and the Régiment de la Chaudière. On the night of June 6–7, they faced scattered opposition and took prisoners, mainly Russians and Poles forced to serve in the Wehrmacht. The next morning they began an advance that aimed at the airfield at

Carpiquet. At Buron, a squadron of Shermans from the Sherbrooke Fusiliers and a company of North Novas knocked out two 88mm guns. But at nearby Authie, the North Novas came under a fierce attack from the 12th SS Panzer Division Hitlerjugend.

The 12th SS was a vicious formation that would bedevil the Canadians for the next two months. The division had been formed by almost 21,000 fanatical Hitler Youth teenagers equipped with 164 Mark IV and Panther panzers and more than 300 armoured vehicles of different types. It had been well trained and was led by battle-tested officers and NCOs, many originally from the 1st SS Panzer Division Leibstandarte SS Adolf Hitler, a famously effective formation that had served in the brutal fighting on the Eastern Front. The attacking regiment, about four times the size of the Canadian forces being attacked, was led by Standartenführer Kurt Meyer, an experienced soldier at thirty-four, a committed Nazi, and a ruthless fighter.

The best recent account is by historian Marc Milner. Meyer's seventeen- and eighteen-year-old teenagers drove back the Canadians, who could not get into contact with the artillery or the ships offshore, from Authie and Buron, overrunning whole platoons; his Panther and Tiger panzers raised havoc with the Sherbrooke's Shermans. But the green Canadians gave as good as they got, and the 12th SS did not have an easy time of it. The 12th SS lost 17 panzers and more than 300 men, thanks to six hours of fierce resistance from the 9th Brigade; other German units from the 21st Panzer and 716th Infantry divisions lost more men and tanks as well. The Canadian regiments had 302 men killed, wounded, and captured and 28 tanks destroyed. The Shermans—the enemy dubbed them "Ronsons" (after the popular cigarette lighter) or, more graphically, "Tommy cookers"—easily burst into flame when their gas tank or ammunition exploded. The Canadians had been pushed back, but in its first counterattacks the enemy had completely failed to reach the Channel or disrupt the landing.

A later analysis of destroyed Shermans calculated that 89 percent had been penetrated by German shot and 82 percent had "brewed up," or burned. The Sherman gun, moreover, was none too successful against enemy armour plate; only the Sherman Firefly, equipped with a high-velocity 17-pounder main gun, could readily knock out the panzers. The difficulty was that the gun made the Firefly distinctive, and there was only one in each troop of four tanks.

The next night, the 12th SS launched additional hasty forays at the Regina Rifles and Royal Winnipeg Rifles near Bretteville and Norrey-en-Bessin. The Winnipegs, having lost the equivalent of a company on D-Day, lost another and more when they were driven out of most of Putot-en-Bessin and had 150 men taken prisoner, but once again the Canadians inflicted heavy losses on the 12th SS. The Canadian Scottish recaptured the hamlet the next day. The Farmer Johns had an equally difficult day and night. At least a dozen panzers roamed between two companies of the Reginas. The panzers, said Gordon Brown, commanding D Company, "overran one platoon ... crushing anti-tank guns, carriers and soldiers." A German dispatch rider rode his motorcycle down the main street of Bretteville; the Reginas' CO, Lieutenant-Colonel Matheson, killed him with his Sten gun. Then a confused German officer apparently drove his Kübelwagen very near to the Reginas' HQ, got out and gazed around for a few seconds, and disintegrated when he was hit by a 3-pound Projector, Infantry, Anti Tank

(PIAT) round. At daybreak, fearing air attack, the panzers retreated, already having had six Panthers destroyed, most by anti-tank guns; but "large numbers of Panzer Grenadiers" attacked in full daylight. "Down to 45 men and two officers," D Company fought back until Brown called in a 105mm barrage from the Canadian artillery. "The accuracy of the shelling was unbelievable," Brown said. "It was the best shoot I ever saw in my nine months of action. The Germans were caught in open ground and had to withdraw." Lieutenant-Colonel Fred Clifford, the Commanding Officer of the 13th Field Regiment, which had fired that shoot, said later that "the Germans thought we were fucking Russians! They did stupid things and we killed those bastards in large numbers." The Canadian and British guns supporting the 3rd Division this time, as on many other occasions, made the difference.

A second attack by 12th SS Panthers failed disastrously when a squadron of Shermans caught them with their less well-armoured flanks exposed and, at a range of a thousand or so yards, knocked out seven of the panzers in four minutes. One Firefly Sherman from the 1st Hussars, commanded by Lieutenant Gord Henry, claimed to have destroyed five Panthers. British historian Michael Reynolds called the Johns' defence "one of the finest small unit actions of WWII." The Canadians had fought the 12th SS to a standstill, and they had stopped the panzers.

The Hitlerjugend had nonetheless taken many prisoners on June 7 and 8. Most were marched back to Meyer's headquarters at the Abbaye d'Ardenne and interrogated. Seven of the captured Canadians refused to answer questions. Told that they were to be killed, "the young Canadians shook hands with one another, some with tears streaming down their faces, and said their goodbyes. One by one," wrote a historian, "they were led to a small garden and shot in the back of the head, their bodies left in a bloody heap. Witnesses would later describe the soldiers walking to their deaths with their heads held high, in one last act of resolute courage." Other Canadian POWs were murdered then placed on a road heavily travelled by panzers and trucks; their remains were pulverized and French civilians were not allowed to remove the bodies for six days. There seems little doubt that Meyer either ordered or acquiesced in these murders—prisoners only consumed German rations, he was said to have remarked. In the next few days, Meyer (who took over command of the division on June 13) and other officers of the 12th SS directed or condoned the murder of 156 Canadian prisoners in all, an extraordinary one in seven of the Canadians killed by enemy action between June 6 and 11. Even German troops called the 12th SS the "Murder Division."

Surrendering in battle was always a risky proposition. A machine gunner who put up his hands after mowing down an infantry section was not likely to be greeted affectionately by his captors. Soldiers pressing forward sometimes had no way to accept prisoners, and many captives likely were killed because of the inconvenience (and danger) they caused shorthanded soldiers moving forward under fire. But there is a vast difference between a battlefield killing, which, while not excusable, takes place in the heat of the action, and a calculated execution occurring after interrogation at a headquarters. The 12th SS soon became the enemy unit most loathed and most feared by Canadians—"They were bastards," Brigadier Cunningham said—and few of its teenagers survived capture. One soldier recollected that "we had a saying in Normandy" about 12th SS POWs: "Take these guys to the beach and be back in ten minutes." In other words, shoot them. Indeed, many 12th SS troopers killed themselves to avoid capture, or so their commander, Kurt Meyer, said.

There were further German counterattacks in the next few days, and the Canadian advance failed. But German efforts that aimed to drive the attackers back into the sea also gained nothing, and the beachhead, soon forming a continuous line across all five landing beaches, remained intact. The Germans fought fiercely and well, but their attacks had tended to be small in size, strictly local, uncoordinated, and aimed at strongpoints rather than at the weakest sections of the line. If the 12th SS had attacked in division strength instead of with single regiments, it might have prevailed, though the effectiveness of Canadian anti-tank guns and artillery and the weight of the naval guns off the beachhead made this more than a slightly dubious proposition. Moreover, Meyer's men could and did make tactical mistakes—"The German attacks," said Brigadier Harry Foster of the 7th Brigade, "were launched without any semblance of tactical sense … straight against the strongest points." Historian Marc Milner stated bluntly that the 12th SS "was not a very effective military formation: brainwashed Hitler Youth led by thugs from the Nazi Party were a recipe for ferocity, not efficiency." Adding enormously to the German difficulties, Allied tactical aircraft, acting on intelligence intercepts, located and destroyed the headquarters of Panzer Group West on June 11, killing thirty-two officers and men, including the entire operations staff, decapitating the enemy's most formidable weapon. Command and control was lost, and the Nazi attacks on the beachhead effectively ceased.

But the 3rd Division could err too. A hastily prepared armoured and infantry attack at Rots and Le Mesnil-Patry on June 11 ran into heavy SS tank and gun fire. The 1st Hussars lost 37 tanks, and the Queen's Own Rifles, going into battle riding atop the Shermans, lost 55 killed, wounded, and captured. Canadian POWs again were executed. This costly debacle was the last major Canadian engagement until July, as newly arrived British units took over most of the action.

The six days of fighting in Normandy cost the Canadian division and armoured brigade 1,017 men killed and more than 1,700 wounded. The 3rd Division now had a few weeks' time to rethink its tactics, lick its wounds, and absorb its replacements, all the while holding the line. And while it did, the headquarters of Guy Simonds's II Canadian Corps and Harry Crerar's First Canadian Army crossed to France. So too did the 2nd Canadian Infantry Division.

· · ·

General Bernard Montgomery commanded the Allied land forces in Normandy for the first three months. His plan was to attract the bulk of the German armour to the eastern end of the bridgehead, making it easier for the Americans to break out. But the Yanks were stuck in the hedgerows of the Norman *bocage* and making slow headway. This put the enemy's main forces in front of the British and Canadians, with Caen as the critical point. Holding them there and taking Caen and the ground south of the city became the objective.

Montgomery was very clever and highly opinionated, convinced that everything he did was always right and that his critics were complete fools. He had beaten Rommel in North Africa, and he believed he could beat him again in France. He had no high opinion of General Eisenhower, his superior, and he had little praise for the American army's fighting skills. Monty was no kinder to the Canadian commanders. He had little time for Harry Crerar—"He is very prosy and stodgy, and he is very definitely not a commander," Montgomery said, "a very poor soldier, and has much to learn." As British historian Antony Beevor observed, "Senior Canadian officers detected a supercilious attitude toward them." Indeed they did.

Only Guy Simonds among the Canadian senior officers merited Monty's praise. Monty believed that the Canadian soldiers were very good material if properly led, but he would have much preferred to have had British commanders rather than Canadians if this had been possible. Canadian national interests and pride said that this wasn't, so Monty had to make do with the situation and with the commanders as he found them.

A British attack on June 26 failed to budge the enemy, and the Canadians, rejoining the fighting on July 4 in Operation Windsor, struck at the village of Carpiquet and its airport, the airport that had been almost in their grasp on June 7. The infantry battalions of the 8th Brigade plus the Royal Winnipeg Rifles and the Shermans of the Fort Garry Horse faced only 150 men from the 12th SS Panzer and had supporting gunfire from the Royal Navy battleship HMS *Rodney* off the coast. But the SS troops were located in fortified positions in the village and in concrete bunkers at the airfield, and they were heavily supported by artillery, mortars, machine guns, and panzers. The casualties were terrible, the Canadian soldiers cut down by heavy fire as they advanced through a wheat field "like automat[on]s. Not running," Matthew

Halton reported. "Walking, steady as robots … Not one man wavering unless he was wounded or killed." Too many of them were, the casualties marked for stretcher-bearers by rifles stuck bayonet-first into the soil.

The village fell to the North Shore Regiment and the Chaudières, who resisted repeated counterattacks by 1st SS Panzer troops and killed scores of the enemy. The airfield proved much more difficult, the SS resisting even when naval gunfire, fighter-bomber aircraft, and flame-throwers were used against the bunkers. The Royal Winnipeg Rifles' assault on the southern hangars failed with heavy losses; the northern hangars did fall, but in all the attackers had sustained 377 casualties with only a partial success as compensation.

For Captain Hal MacDonald of the North Shores, after Carpiquet the enemy were "all bastards, rotten, sneaking, back-shooting, double-crossing devils. Only one good thing for them." A corporal said the SS youth "look like babies" but "they die like mad bastards." Private Smith of the North Shores ended his diary on July 7: "I'm going back home. I lost my right foot on those new German [Schu] mines. We were under fire and I was running to hide in the fields and next thing I knew I was laying in my pool of blood in great pain. But it's over, the nightmare is over." Carpiquet was not completely in Canadian hands until July 9.

Private Smith's nightmare would last as long as he lived; the 12th SS's trauma had only a few more weeks to run. By July 9, the division had lost its reconnaissance battalion, one artillery battery, one complete regiment, and 140 tanks. Its effectiveness had been greatly reduced, and Meyer had to reorganize his formation into three battle groups. His SS teenagers would, nonetheless, continue to fight.

One soldier in the Canadian Scottish near Carpiquet wrote later that in the early morning he had spotted a flash from a church steeple. Private Wayne Arnold continued to watch the flashes, decided that it was a signalling mirror, and realized that mortar fire kept hitting his position, likely because of the flashing signals. "Finally," Arnold recalled, "I drew a sight with my rifle and fired." Later, he was told that "I had got him square between the eyes . . . it was more than a thousand yards away."

General Miles Dempsey, the commander of I British Corps, under which the 3rd Canadian Division continued to serve, had been unhappy with the events at Carpiquet and with the GOC, General Keller. Keller's own staff were unhappy too, seeing their boss as very jumpy, so much so that the serious joke among the 3rd Division's senior officers was that "Keller was yeller." Major Peter Bennett of the 7th Brigade recalled Keller at a D-Day or D Plus 1 Orders Group staying in a slit trench to give his orders while everyone else stood up top around him. Montgomery had watched the 3rd Division's performance and leadership, and he soon wrote, "I am not too happy about the Canadians. Keller has proven himself to be quite unfit to command a division; he is unable to get the best out of his soldiers—who are grand chaps." But it was up to the Canadian high command to act. When II Canadian Corps became operational, Guy Simonds met with the 3rd Division GOC and spoke to Keller about the adverse reports. Keller actually indicated that he thought he might be medically unfit. But the division had taken heavy casualties, and Simonds, worried about its morale if Keller, who remained popular with his soldiers, was sacked, oddly only told him to think about matters, and allowed Keller to remain in command.

Such mercy was unusual for Simonds. He was forty-one years old, one of the youngest corps commanders in the Allied armies, and he had risen fast because of his great ability and intelligence, but also "largely because he had ascended in a vacuum," or so the acerbic historian Jack English wrote. Simonds knew he was abrupt and had a hot temper. As he said, "I am impatient of stupidity, dullness and indifference—or gaucheness, and I know I sometimes lose my temper when I shouldn't." He "could never forgive or forget," said Colonel Clement Dick, who served with Simonds in Italy. "There were guys who were majors at the beginning of the war who finished there because they had crossed him." He had fired officers in Sicily because they failed to live up to his standards or his expectations—"You either did it his way," Dick said, "or you had it." It was exactly the same before D-Day. Brigadier (later Lieutenant-General and Chief of the General Staff) S.F. Clark said that when Simonds had come to II Canadian Corps at the end of January 1944, he met his staff officers by saying, "Good morning, gentlemen. There are some of you in whom I have not much confidence. I will see you all individually the next day and tell you why." The Chief Engineer and Chief Medical Officer were sacked. The Chief of Staff, Brigadier Elliot Rodger, stayed, and only one or two more were kept. Clark remembered Brigadier Darrell Laing, the corps' senior administrative officer as DA&QMG, saying, "I've been through and not sacked. What about you?" Simonds wanted people who could make good, quick decisions and stick to them. This was very Monty-like. Clark stayed as Chief Signals Officer. He remembered Simonds asking him what he was doing one day. Trying to get a line communications system that worked better, Clark replied. "Well, you'd better." As Brigadier Rodger noted, "Never have I worked for anyone with such a precise and clear and farseeing mind—he was always working to a plan with a clear cut objective which he took care to let all of us know in simple and direct terms." For an officer who had had only a few months' command of a single division in battle in Sicily and Italy, his grasp of the task of fighting a war was extraordinary.

Simonds was ruthless and very demanding. He expected high performance from his staff and his subordinate commanders. His own issued orders were clear, his plans thought through with care. Simonds was the commander, and he projected toughness and confidence. His staff's task, his subordinate commanders' task, was to implement his orders fully. Gruff he may have been, but you liked working for him, said Lieutenant-Colonel C.B. Ware, who commanded the Princess Patricia's Canadian Light Infantry in Italy in Simonds's 1st Canadian Division. "You knew what he wanted and you didn't screw it up. His briefings were good," Ware said, "even if he wasn't a great success—unlike Montgomery—at calling troops around his jeep for pep talks." The problem, however, was that Simonds, never having commanded an infantry battalion, did not seem to understand the effect casualties could have on a battalion's ability to fight. His friend George Kitching noted that Simonds took a long time to comprehend that a battalion with only a hundred men could not do what one of five hundred could.

Another difficulty Simonds faced was that his divisions and their GOCs in Normandy were sometimes simply not up to the task. Keller was demonstrably weak, and Simonds believed that General Charles Foulkes, the GOC of 2nd Canadian Division, was also "NBG"—no bloody good, as he told Kitching. The 3rd Division had been battered badly in the June fighting and at Carpiquet, and the 2nd Infantry and 4th Armoured divisions, when they got into action, would be as green as grass. A more cautious commander might have factored these considerations more fully into his planning.

As it was, Simonds believed that centralized control of the battle—by him—was essential, the enemy to be defeated by carefully organized attacks, heavily supported by artillery. Artillery was the key for Simonds, a gunner, and the infantry's job was to bite and hold ground then to beat off the counterattacks the Germans always threw at the Allies. That tight control was the way to harness his weak commanders and get the most from his green troops. Simonds was the boss, far above his subordinates, who were unconsulted employees, not shareholders in a common enterprise. He was driven, a striver, and hugely competent tactically. But, as Harry Crerar told Colonel J. L. Ralston, the defence minister, "he must be ridden like a temperamental race horse with soft but firm hands."

Next for the Canadians was Caen. A huge bomber attack devastated the city, killing civilians but scarcely harming the enemy, who had moved into the suburbs. At Buron, the Highland Light Infantry fought a day-long battle that cost the regiment 262 casualties, including its CO. But the HLI took the village and, with the invaluable help of British self-propelled anti-tank guns, stopped cold an enemy counterattack with tanks, the Germans losing thirteen panzers. After a stiff fight and 200 casualties, the Regina Rifles captured Kurt Meyer's Abbaye d'Ardenne headquarters—the bodies of the murdered POWs buried there would be discovered some time later—but the skilful Meyer led the defence and extracted most of his soldiers to fight again. Captain Gordon Brown of the Reginas found a large stash of champagne and liquor and a basket of cherries in Meyer's bedroom in the Abbaye. "We drank some champagne and ate the cherries," Brown said. Authie also fell, and by July 9, the Canadians held the ruins of Caen. The price was another 1,200 killed and wounded.

Simonds's II Canadian Corps fought its first battle as a corps on the left flank of Operation Goodwood, a major British attack that promptly ran into trouble from the enemy's 88s and Nebelwerfers, the rocket-firing "Moaning Minnies." Two armoured divisions, the Guards and the 11th British, suffered terrible losses, with some 186 of their tanks destroyed or damaged. In Operation Atlantic, the Canadian part of the attack, the 3rd Canadian Division got across the river Orne and into the Caen suburbs of Cormelles and Vaucelles with substantial difficulty, the Germans fighting hard from the ruins of a heavily bombed steel mill at Colombelles. Even the senior officers came under fire. Robert Moncel, then a lieutenant-colonel on Simonds's staff, and Brigadier Harry Foster, commanding the 3rd Division's 7th Brigade, had taken shelter from enemy shelling in a doorway when two privates jumped in with them. "You're a general?" "Yes." "You can do what you want?" "Yes." "Well, if I was a general I'd get the hell out of here."

As part of Atlantic, on July 18 and 19, the 2nd Canadian Division staged its first attack since the Dieppe raid, with the 5th Brigade's Régiment de Maisonneuve seizing Fleury-sur-Orne and Montreal's Black Watch taking Ifs. The 6th Brigade moved over the Orne against Verrières Ridge with heavy artillery support on July 20, took some of its objectives in a drenching rain, and then faced a strong German counterattack led by tanks that overran the South Saskatchewan Regiment, the Essex Scottish (who had been added to the 6th Brigade for the attack), and many men from the Fusiliers Mont-Royal. The enemy tactics centred on holding forward positions lightly but with interlocking zones of fire; their panzers and self-propelled guns, from the 12th SS, were held in reserve at the main defence line under cover for counterattacks. The German mortars, able to fire 15 to 25 shells a minute at ranges from 100 to 1,500 yards, and always skilfully employed, invariably caused heavy casualties, as much as 70 percent of the Canadians killed and wounded in Normandy and after. Enemy mortars were dug in, their ammunition safely below ground. The Canadians understood the German tactics and had been trained to meet them, but they were very difficult tactics to counter, especially when the enemy mortars, artillery, and panzers knocked out the anti-tank guns. Some men in 6th Brigade apparently broke and ran to the rear, and the CO of the Essex Scottish was fired for "nervousness."

The casualties were heavy in 2nd Division—1,149 in all, with 249 killed in action. A young replacement officer in the South Saskatchewan Regiment, Lieutenant Harvey Burnard, initially wrote home that the action had gone well "because of our superior artillery and tank support." But a day later, after he had talked to some of his regiment's officers and men, he amended that to say the battalion ran into "some German tanks ... and things went bad. The Infantry," he added, probably with a bit of exaggeration, "were dead scared of Canadians and could hardly wait to surrender but the tanks were a different story." The casualties were heavy and the South Sasks "had to come back [to the rear] and get re-organized." Burnard would be killed in action a few days later.

Another account, by John S. Edmondson, a company commander in the South Sasks, suggests a complete breakdown in command and control; a lack of artillery, armour, and support from the brigade commander, Brigadier H.A. Young; and weak divisional HQ planning. To Edmondson's disgust (and that of the fired CO of the Essex Scottish), the failure of a bad plan made by division and corps commanders was quickly blamed on infantry battalions that lacked the resources and support to fight a well-trained, well-equipped enemy holding the key ground. The soldiers weren't at fault, in other words; the higher-ups had messed matters up. Messed them up again, some said bitterly. Captain Britton Smith, an artillery Forward Observation Officer with the Fusiliers Mont-Royal, noted that at one point, the FMR "could have used some mutual support" from the Stormont, Dundas and Glengarry Highlanders a quarter mile away, "but we did not know their radio frequencies and evidently they did not know ours, they being 3rd Division and we 2nd Division." According to Kurt Meyer, the Germans probably knew the radio frequencies being used, and, if they didn't, the lack of wireless security in units and the orders in clear given by senior officers let the Germans react quickly to Canadian moves. The first action of 2nd Division inevitably failed because of inexperienced commanders leading game but equally inexperienced troops. Historian Jack English, himself a lieutenant-colonel, called the failure of Operation Atlantic "by any measure a complete disaster and humiliation of Canadian arms."

Many men suffered from battle exhaustion after Atlantic, crying without cease, shaking, shattered. "They were in shock," one medical officer noted, "but with no visible wounds. The doctor in charge of them would give them sedatives and get them to sleep." Captain Hal MacDonald of the North Shores wrote his wife that after his unit had been hit hard by mortar fire, "three men went windy and nuts entirely. Got two pacified and two evacuated, using strenuous methods." Private Wayne Arnold remembered that after he had driven dead and wounded comrades to the rear, "I started crying and shaking ... I was not wounded but I was shook up. I was put on a lorry for Chateau Beauregard, north of Caen, an army rest camp." But after two nights, "I requested the Camp Commander send me back to my unit because the Germans dive bombed us all through the night. I told the Camp Commander I felt safer in the front lines."

MacDonald's and Arnold's stories were not untypical, but General Crerar worried about the large number of cases and fretted over "the natural, but in the circumstances of war, reprehensible objection of a small proportion of other ranks ... to risk death, or serious injury for their country." Discipline had to be tightened, Crerar said, and all ranks had to be educated that "escapism" was "a shameful thing." Most battle exhaustion cases were genuine, the GOC-in-C believed, but many were "unstable mental characters." If it was not considered disgraceful to become an exhaustion case, he feared that lead-swingers and slackers would "seek this way out." Discipline was tightened, and the worst cases among the battle exhausted went to England; others went back to their units after a few days' rest. The enemy remained formidable.

General Simonds's ambitious plan for his first action as a corps commander had been for the attackers to "be prepared to exploit to capture" the high ground north of Saint-André-sur-Orne and the village of Verrières, on the ridge overlooking the Route Nationale to Falaise. This high ground, none of which fell to II Canadian Corps in Operation Atlantic, would test the Canadians and their commanders for the next three weeks.

The GOC of 2nd Division in its first actions was Major-General Charles Foulkes, a "cold fish" whose rise had apparently occurred because of his abundant skills as an Army politician rather than any magic gift of leadership. "He had none of the innate intelligence of ... Simonds,"

Douglas Delaney wrote unsparingly, "and the rapidly expanding Canadian Army of 1939–43 had too many training handicaps to ensure that raw material such as Foulkes developed into capable senior commanders. Foulkes was a survivor, however." Dour, pudgy, and intelligent, Foulkes had begun the war as a major, and he got on well with Harry Crerar, but much less well with Simonds, his other superior officer in Normandy. Crerar clearly saw Foulkes as a kindred spirit; Simonds, the corps commander, viewed him only as a weak leader with powerful friends higher up. On one occasion, Robert Moncel recalled, Foulkes's division was to stage an attack, and Simonds was just behind the division HQ waiting for the scheduled attack to go in at 6:00 a.m. The barrage was twenty minutes late and Simonds said, "I'm going over to relieve the Division com[mander]." Moncel urged delay, saying it wouldn't help the battle. Simonds looked at him with his hawklike glare and grumpily agreed: "You owe me one." The battle was a disaster, Moncel said, like everything Foulkes touched.

Foulkes's new GSO1, appointed a few days after the division's baptism of fire, was Lieutenant-Colonel C.M. "Bud" Drury, a very capable gunner who ended the war as a brigadier and commander in the 4th Canadian Armoured Division and later became a Liberal Cabinet minister. His three brigade commanders were the highly competent Sherwood Lett, who, after recovering from wounds suffered at Dieppe, was wounded again on July 18 and replaced at the 4th Brigade by J.E. Ganong; W.J. Megill, a PF officer, commanding the 5th Brigade; and H.A. Young, leading the 6th Brigade. Neither Ganong nor Young would last long, both eventually taking the fall for the weaknesses of their division commander in the August fighting to come.

THE BEST LITTLE ARMY IN THE WORLD

The 2nd Division brought together some of Canada's most famous regiments. The 4th Brigade consisted of the Royal Regiment from Toronto, the Royal Hamilton Light Infantry, and the Essex Scottish from Windsor and southwestern Ontario. The 5th's regiments were the Black Watch from Montreal, the Régiment de Maisonneuve, and the Calgary Highlanders. The Fusiliers Mont-Royal, the Queen's Own Cameron Highlanders from Winnipeg, and the South Saskatchewan Regiment formed the 6th Brigade.

Until the 4th Armoured Division got into the fighting, the 2nd and 3rd divisions made up Simonds's II Canadian Corps, with support from the 2nd Armoured Brigade. The 3rd Division was badly bruised, the 2nd still new to battle but shaken, and the troopers of the 2nd Armoured Brigade now knew all too well the weaknesses of their Shermans. The Germans were short of men and rapidly running out of panzers, but they had the benefit of battle experience. In Normandy, said Brian Reid, the historian of Operation Totalize, "the German army knew how to fight and the Allies were learning as they went along."

The Canadians had two great strengths, however. First, their field and medium artillery were very good, the gunners capable of concentrating massive gunfire on any given position on short notice. Second, Allied tactical air power, most of it now based on airfields in Normandy, could—and did—strike enemy positions and road movements with deadly rockets and strafing attacks ... whenever weather permitted (as it had not during Operation Atlantic). The Typhoons—called JaBos, short for Jäger-Bombers, by the enemy—were greatly feared by ordinary German soldiers, with good reason. The North Shores' Hal MacDonald wrote that "if I ever run into Typhoon pilots I shall go down on my knees before them. They've given us an awful lot of support and saved us from some bad attacks." One example, he said: "quite a while ago I observed 6 Tigers, carefully camouflaged on a crest opposite our position, obviously planning a breakthrough. Phoned in a report and within 12 minutes 12 Typhoons came over and rocketed hell out of them—a beautiful sight." The Typhoons probably destroyed fewer tanks than their pilots claimed as kills, but they shook German morale, and many panzers were abandoned intact, their crews fleeing. From Britain, the heavy bombers, once again concentrating on targets in Germany, could also be used against the enemy forces in Normandy if a sufficient case could be made for this by the ground commanders.

• • •

The battle of the bridgehead remained in stasis through late July. The Germans had suffered heavy casualties, not least Field Marshal Rommel, grievously wounded when his staff car was strafed, but their tactical proficiency held the Allies in check. Allied forces had also sustained substantial losses, but Montgomery's campaign had succeeded in forcing the enemy to keep most of its strength—14 divisions and 600 panzers— on the British and Canadian front. The Americans, however, facing only nine enemy divisions, had not yet been able to break out. At this point, on July 23, First Canadian Army Headquarters, led by Harry Crerar, became operational. A few days earlier, a group of Wehrmacht officers tried and failed to assassinate Hitler. This should have weakened the morale of German troops in Normandy—but did not; indeed, ordinary soldiers were infuriated at the attempt on the Führer's life and seem to have redoubled their efforts. Rommel would be swept up in the investigation and eventually forced to commit suicide in October 1944.

But by July 25, the Americans believed they were ready to roll. A clever sergeant had designed a blade to be put on tanks to cut through the thick hedgerows of the *bocage* and reduce the German ability to fight under cover, field by field. Another attack south of Caen was necessary in order to keep the German attention focused on the east side of the bridgehead and away from the Americans. This big attack, Operation Spring, was to strike at the 1st SS Panzer Division Leibstandarte SS Adolf Hitler and the 272nd Infantry Division, bolstered by panzer grenadiers from the 2nd Panzer Division and the 10th SS Panzer Division. The 1st SS was likely the best panzer division the Germans had. In the German rear areas, close at hand, were the main bodies of three more panzer divisions. This defensive system in depth was the strongest enemy position in Normandy.

The Canadian plan, drafted by Simonds, was to launch in full darkness in the middle of the night on July 25. The objective for the 2nd and 3rd Canadian and British 7th Armoured divisions was to take the ground immediately south of Verrières Ridge, followed by the seizure of Point 122, the dominant feature in the area. Then would follow further unspecified exploitation. Simonds later claimed that he knew the strength of the enemy dispositions and expected no such gains as his orders specified. To him, after the fact, Spring was a holding attack, nothing more. As he wrote later, "Of all the operations of the war the 'holding attack' is that least understood by the layman for casualties seem to be out of all proportion to apparent gains." The units involved did not, could not, know this.

The 3rd Division's task was to drive the 1st SS out of Tilly-la-Campagne, a tiny village held by a battalion of panzer grenadiers and a company of tanks, so that the British armour could move through to take the high ground. On the right, the 2nd Division was to seize the villages of Verrières, May-sur-Orne, and Rocquancourt. The enemy, commanded by SS General Sepp Dietrich, had its deadly mortars and artillery and a full supply of 88mm anti-tank guns to shoot up the Shermans. The Germans also had the equivalent of nineteen infantry and six panzer battalions facing or very near to the Canadians, more force than the attackers could muster.

The attack jumped off on schedule, the soldiers helped—for a time—by artificial moonlight, created by bouncing searchlight beams off the clouds. Unfortunately, the dull light silhouetted the advancing troops, and German fire stalled the 3rd Division's assault with heavy losses of men and tanks. Ordered to resume the attacks in daylight, two battalion commanders in the 9th Brigade refused, a position supported by their brigade commander. A battalion at full strength had four rifle companies of some 150 men each, as well as a support company with heavy weapons; but after the initial phase of Operation Spring, the infantry companies that did the fighting numbered under a hundred, and platoons could be down to fifteen to eighteen tired, shocked men. In such circumstances, attacks could not and did not go ahead with much chance of success.

But staff officer Robert Moncel, a month later a successful armoured brigade commander, talked about how a senior commander could not believe a CO who refused to attack because he said the men were tired. Too often it was the commander who was tired. Moncel recalled Simonds once being told troops were "pinned to the ground" and, on going forward, finding the men lying in the sun. He fired all the commanders. They ought to have been going forward to see things themselves. A brigadier, Moncel continued, should go down to company level to see what is up. Moreover, good brigadiers had gone to Staff College and had a sense of all-arms cooperation and of the resources available. He recalled sitting in on a brigadier's Orders Group when, on being offered extra artillery and armour support, the brigadier refused. The attack was a disaster and two hundred soldiers died. Officers got tired and stopped caring, he said. They ought to have been relieved—with honour.

Matters went little better on the 2nd Division front. The Calgary Highlanders took heavy casualties in their assault, as did the Royal Regiment; only the Royal Hamilton Light Infantry, the Rileys, led by Lieutenant-Colonel John Rockingham, took their objective, Verrières, and held it against a determined counterattack by elements of the 1st SS. A troop of 17-pounder anti-tank guns and British tanks helped the RHLI hold its position. The Australian-born Rockingham, one of the ablest Canadian field commanders of the war, galvanized the defence, sending out patrols to hunt down machine gunners, and, though he lost three of his four anti-tank guns, he managed to survive an attack by eight panzers that rolled over and through his position. RAF Typhoons helped blunt repeated counterattacks by the enemy against the Canadian foothold on the ridge.

The real disaster fell on the Royal Highland Regiment (the Black Watch), from Montreal. In the fighting between July 19 and 24, the regiment had lost two of four rifle company commanders and eight platoon commanders. Now it was to go into its most severe test thus far. Ordered to move past May-sur-Orne, held by the enemy, and to get to the summit of the ridge and take Fontenay-le-Marmion on the reverse slope, the Black Watch lost its CO in the opening stage of the advance. The acting Commanding Officer, twenty-four-year-old Major F.P. Griffin, consulted his brigade commander and Major Walter Harris, the officer commanding the 1st Hussars squadron in support, and then led his brave men up the ridge in full daylight without tank support, which had been hammered by the enemy at May-sur-Orne. Deadly fire, coming from men of the 272nd Division and a battle group of tanks from the 2nd Panzer Division, hit the regiment hard. Of the 339 Black Watch officers and men who started up the ridge, perhaps 60 made it to the top, only to be surrounded there by panzers. Griffin ordered the survivors to get away and 15 made it. He was killed along with 120 others; 211 were wounded or captured. In all, another 14 officers became casualties, making the loss in two weeks of battle 63 percent of the Black Watch's officer establishment. Major Harris of the 1st Hussars was wounded but survived to become finance minister in the government of Louis St. Laurent in the 1950s. The Black Watch casualties were the most suffered in the war by a single Canadian unit, the Dieppe raid excepted.

Spring had been a debacle, only the RHLI taking and holding its objective. The Rileys' stubborn battle, great though it was, could not relieve the gloom of defeat. The 1st SS Panzer Corps reported proudly that "the enemy took high bloody casualties," and July 25 had been the worst day of the campaign for the Canadians, with at least 450 men killed and 1,100 wounded. Callously, furiously, Simonds concluded that his plan had failed because of "a deterioration of ... fighting efficiency" and "a series of mistakes and errors of judgement in minor tactics." The fault, Simonds believed, lay elsewhere, not with his plan. To a substantial extent, he was correct. The 2nd Division's GOC and two of his three brigade commanders had not performed well. They remained untouched for the moment, but the corps commander duly sacked brigade and battalion commanders in the 3rd Division's 9th Brigade, and the RHLI's Rockingham became the new brigade commander.

Perhaps the old adage that "the fewer you use, the more you lose" had been proven. Operation Spring was a large attack, but it threw single battalions at heavily fortified defensive positions. If there had been fewer objectives and more brigade-scale assaults, II Canadian Corps might have done better and might even have reduced the casualty toll. Perhaps.

A few days later the CBC reporter Matt Halton wrote privately that the Spring operation had been a "folly" and a "massacre," and he quoted a dispatch rider shouting to a group of officers, "When are you going to give us a rest instead of fucking us around?" However, the benefit of Spring—to mask the seriousness of the American breakout to the west—was real. After five days of fighting, the U.S. forces reached the Atlantic coast at Avranches, and General George Patton's Third U.S. Army turned east. The German front was broken, but Hitler compounded the coming disaster by ordering a counterstroke at the Americans at Mortain. The opportunity to catch the German armies in Normandy in a great pocket had suddenly opened up—when the Germans sent their forces west against the Yanks, they could be trapped by the British and Canadians, driving south from Caen along the twenty-mile highway to Falaise, and the Americans, moving east and north. The Normandy campaign had reached its decisive moment, and the II Canadian Corps, now including the 4th Armoured Division, was to play its full part.

By this time, news of the murders of prisoners in Normandy had reached the troops. At General Crerar's request, an Anglo-Canadian court of inquiry was set up to investigate, and leaflets promising to bring the perpetrators to justice were dropped behind German lines. Crerar warned his men not to take revenge by retaliating in kind, urging instead that anger be converted to a hard determination to destroy the enemy in battle. But he also warned that to surrender to the Waffen-SS was to invite death.

· · ·

Guy Simonds was fertile in invention. He realized that Operation Spring had failed because the German main positions, from which their counterattacks sprang, had been left untouched. Their forward defence lines might be hit hard when the enemy possession of Verrières Ridge was neutralized by darkness, but unless the Germans' main positions to the rear were hammered equally hard, their control of the high ground and their superior tanks, 88s, and fighting skill could prevail. Now his plan, called Operation Totalize, was to achieve tactical surprise by attacking at night and to hit the forward and main positions at the same time, using a combination of artillery, bombers, and fighter aircraft to neutralize the enemy.

The Germans had well-prepared defensive positions to protect the route to Falaise, and they had dug in sixty panzers. They had in addition some ninety 88mm guns to use as anti-tank weapons, and their lines were manned by the 12th SS, the newly arrived 89th Infantry Division, and the 272nd Infantry Division. Farther to the rear was the 85th Infantry

Division. These units were of varying quality, and the 12th SS had been greatly reduced in strength, if not in ferocity, by two months in action. The Nazi soldiers, however, were confident. One panzer grenadier in the 12th SS Hitlerjugend wrote that "it was made known to us that we would have to fight as we had not fought before. We felt that we had the measure of the Canadians and that their armoured effort would be as slow and ponderous as usual. We knew that we could hold."

Simonds's Operation Totalize called for the three divisions of his corps, plus the British 51st Division, a British tank brigade, and the newly arrived 1st Polish Armoured Division to smash the enemy positions. But how? The plan was for 1,100 bombers to strike at night to support an attack in darkness by his divisions and—a new innovation—the use of seventy-six Priests converted from self-propelled artillery into "Kangaroos," armoured personnel carriers that could move infantry in relative security onto their objectives.

The Kangaroos, a way to get infantry safely through the storm of fire, appear to have been Simonds's own idea. Indeed, after the war he sought a monetary reward from the War Office in London for his idea but was refused. The Priests were the 105mm self-propelled gun that Canadian artillery regiments had used on the Norman beaches. Now these had been replaced by regular 25-pounder guns or Sexton self-propelled 25-pounders. Simonds realized that if the Priest's gun was removed and the gap in front of the tracked vehicle was replaced with armour plate, the result would be a vehicle that could carry twelve infantry safe from airbursts, deliver them onto the objective, and, moreover, keep up with the tanks.

The orders to "defrock" the Priests went out on July 31, and over the next week the Royal Canadian Electrical and Mechanical Engineers (RCEME) worked frenetically to convert seventy-two Priests to Kangaroos. (Kangaroo, the code name given to the workshop near Bayeux where the conversions were under way, soon became the name of the new armoured personnel carriers.) Simonds inspected the first prototype on August 3, and all the Kangaroos had been completed and armed with a .50 calibre heavy machine gun by August 6. They were ready to receive their baptism of fire in Totalize on the night of August 7–8. The Kangaroos did in fact reduce infantry casualties; the infantry using them sustained fewer casualties than those that marched. Simonds later pressed for the creation of the 1st Armoured Carrier Squadron to support his corps, and in late October a carrier regiment was established with Lieutenant-Colonel Gordon Churchill, later a member of John Diefenbaker's Cabinet, in command. The defrocked Priests were replaced in October 1944 by Kangaroos created from the Canadian-produced and -designed Ram tank, which had been used by Canadian armoured units in England before the invasion of France.

Simonds ordered that Totalize be led by the 2nd Canadian and 51st British divisions preceded by two armoured brigades, engineers, and anti-tank guns, all to move forward in three huge columns, each consisting of four vehicles abreast on a 17.5-yard frontage, that being the width that could be cleared of mines by four tanks equipped with flails. Every ten feet, there would follow four more vehicles. Each column was to be headed by two tank troops, followed by two flail troops and an engineer troop. One armoured officer wrote, "I left my tank and walked back to the end of my regimental column, we were closed so tight that my feet never touched the ground. I just stepped from tank to tank."

Then came infantry in Kangaroos or half-tracks. Farther back were the rest of a tank squadron, two anti-tank troops, a machine-gun platoon, and a section of engineers. The rear of the column was covered by an armoured regiment. The columns were to break through the enemy line in the dark and consolidate on their positions in the morning, able to repel any counterattacks, and then the 3rd and 4th Armoured divisions would push through the gap behind another heavy bombing run. Way-finding was to be assisted by tracer fire, radio beams, and artificial moonlight. Finally, the 4th and 1st Polish Armoured divisions would roll on to Falaise, catching the enemy in a huge pocket.

Once it got under way, but not before, the attack was to be supported by a massive artillery concentration that required the drivers and trucks of the Royal Canadian Army Service Corps to run their biggest ammunition-dumping program thus far in the war. Two hundred thousand rounds of ammunition had to be brought up to the guns, up to 650 shells for each of the 700 guns supporting the operation, with more being required each day of Totalize. Then gasoline, some 150,000 gallons, had to be trucked forward to the tanks, armoured carriers, and self-propelled guns. Gunner James Brady of the 4th Medium Regiment later recorded that the guns backing Totalize had fired "184,000—25-pdr., 87,000—5.5 Mediums—6,500 Heavies 9.2 Long Toms."

Simonds's plan was complex, especially so as it was to be staged at night. The senior officers briefed on the plan cautioned that a night attack like this had never been done. "That's why I'm doing it," Simonds answered. The Royal Air Force doubted that its aircrew could bomb accurately enough in the dark. That was a problem. There were also genuine difficulties with supplies, and the battlefield was chaotic, as

Brigadier Bruce Matthews, the corps' artillery commander, recalled. Red smoke shells arrived only at the last minute, for example. But the real difficulty was that everything had to be done at once, and that there was never enough time. For example, the old idea of registering artillery targets—that is, determining their positions in advance so that their exact coordinates were known—was scrapped; the gunners shot by the map, and the maps were not very accurate. The pressure, the magnitude of the operations, Matthews said, was unbelievable.

Simonds was genuinely innovative, but he likely overestimated the capabilities of his soldiers at this stage of the war. The fact was that the Canadian divisions that had been in Spring were bloodied and bruised. The Polish division was untried. The 4th Canadian Armoured Division, led by Simonds's close friend Major-General George Kitching, was similarly green; it had acquired new tanks just before embarking for Normandy, and its training in England—where it had never conducted a divisional exercise or operated off the roads—had been spotty. The division's engineers, Simonds's Chief Engineer, Brigadier Geoffrey Walsh, said, were not yet very capable, and crucially neither were the signallers (nor their wireless sets). Moreover, the armoured columns in Totalize could be stalled any time a vehicle was disabled or collided. Still, the operational plan was brilliant, a new way of breaking through the enemy lines, and only Guy Simonds among Canadian senior officers could have devised it.

Predictably, unfortunately, everything went wrong when the attack jumped off on August 8, 1944, twenty-six years to the day after the great Canadian attack at Amiens began the Hundred Days that brought the Kaiser's Germany to surrender in the Great War. More than a thousand

Royal Air Force and Royal Canadian Air Force bombers arrived on schedule at 11:15 p.m., but only 660 dropped their payloads, the rest being called off by the master bomber because the target was obscured by dust and smoke. The bombs nonetheless plastered the enemy lines. The columns moved off at 11:30 p.m. and almost at once ran into difficulty from dust and the dark; drivers were unable to see the vehicles ahead of them until those vehicles turned on tail lights. Elements in two of the three columns soon got lost. The Germans had been initially stunned by the bombing, and many men of the 89th Division fled toward Falaise until Kurt Meyer appeared to stop them. Meyer stood in the middle of the road and asked if the men were going to leave him alone to deal with the Allied attack. Some returned to their positions.

Nonetheless, by noon, most of the attackers were intact and near their objectives—"Fuck me," one British infantry CO said when his unit took its objective on the east side of Totalize, "we've arrived"—while the 6th Brigade worked to clear out bypassed villages. The penetration of the German lines was five miles wide and four deep, and casualties had been light. Field Marshal Günther von Kluge, commanding the German armies in Normandy, was stunned: "A breakthrough has occurred south of Caen such as we have never seen." Unfortunately for the attackers, bypassed German-occupied villages and farms did not surrender but continued to resist strongly.

Now, after some delay, Phase 2 began, and the 4th and 1st Polish Armoured divisions found themselves stuck in a gigantic traffic jam waiting on the bombers to level little Norman villages with their defenders. At 1:00 p.m., 492 aircraft from the United States Eighth Air Force attacked the enemy positions, but 24 aircraft dumped part of their bomb load on the Canadians and Poles below, killing and wounding hundreds. The North Shore (New Brunswick) Regiment lost 37 killed and 78 wounded, and Hal MacDonald wrote that he'd been in the middle of it: "I've seen blood and death on battlefields but not as concentrated … When we got up you could reach out anywhere and pick up limbs. It was frightful … very demoralizing." One of those wounded was General Keller of the 3rd Division, whose headquarters was bombed. He was said to have yelled at his batman, "Roberts, give me my revolver. I'm going to shoot the first goddam American I see."

Gunner James Brady wrote that the aircraft passed overhead. "Then the front waves suddenly loosed an avalanche of heavy block-busters and anti-personnel fragmentation bombs. In a moment huge orange-coloured flame blossomed upward … Blinding smoke and fumes enveloped us … When the smoke cleared away and the bombers passed, the first person I saw was … my immediate superior, almost cut in two by a bomb fragment … [The Medium Regiment] suffered 19 men killed, 47 wounded, whilst 11 guns and 27 vehicles were destroyed." Munitions dumps exploded and continued to do so for forty minutes, further disrupting the advance. One staff officer, Captain Brian Dickson, was gravely wounded in the friendly-fire debacle and woke up at a field hospital, where he groggily realized that the triage process had placed him in the row of wounded who were deemed to be beyond help. An Army surgeon from Winnipeg, Dickson's hometown, passed by, recognized him—"Brian, what are you doing here?"—and took him into the operating theatre, where, although he lost a leg, his life was saved. Dickson later became Chief Justice of the Supreme Court of Canada because of his chance encounter with a friend.

Beyond the Canadian and Polish casualties, very little damage was done to the Germans by the 1,500 tons of bombs dropped by the USAAF, but with Keller injured and Brigadier Booth, the commander of the 2nd Canadian Armoured Brigade, also grievously wounded when the HQ of the 4th Armoured Brigade was almost wiped out by German 88s, the command structure of the attackers was in difficulty.

At this critical moment, Brigadeführer Kurt Meyer, commanding the much-reduced 12th SS Panzer Division, took advantage of the delay in beginning Phase 2 of Totalize and personally took charge of organizing the defence. Meyer sited his deadly 88s along the Caen–Falaise road, and these guns—some of the most effective weapons of the war, capable of knocking out Shermans at a range of more than 2,000 yards and setting the gasoline-powered "Tommy cookers" alight—brought the hesitant drive of the two armoured divisions to a crawl. As night fell, the two divisions stopped and began to move into harbour, exactly as they had been trained to do. Simonds raged in frustration, and the 4th Armoured Brigade cobbled together a battle group out of the Lake Superior Regiment and the Canadian Grenadier Guards, sending it off in the dark toward Bretteville-le-Rabet. The British Columbia Regiment and infantry from the Algonquin Regiment, dubbed "Worthington Force" after the BCR's commander, set off at 2:30 a.m. on August 9 to take the high ground, Point 195, southwest of Quesnay Wood and astride the Falaise road. They made good progress, breaking through the German defences. Then, in the dark, the BCR tanks stopped on what they thought was the objective.

But at the dawn, the little force discovered to its shock that it was in an open field, Point 111, three miles north of the objective and under the guns of a nearby 12th SS battle group with twenty panzers, including five Tigers. The hopeless battle lasted all day, and, as no one at II Corps or the 4th Armoured Division HQ could find the BCRs, no help came. Curiously, Typhoons regularly attacked the enemy during the day but failed to report the location of Worthington Force. The Poles used different codes than the Canadians, but nonetheless were two miles away and at one point came to within a few hundred yards of Point 111 before being driven back. They also appear not to have reported the BCR's position to Simonds's headquarters. The artillery Forward Observation Officer with the BCRs had contact with his guns to the rear, but inexplicably no information appears to have been passed to 4th Armoured Brigade HQ. The armoured regiment and infantry battalion lost 240 men, including both COs, and 47 tanks. Another attack on heavily defended Quesnay Wood by the 8th Brigade had no better luck, and Simonds called Totalize to a halt. The operation had gained eight miles, something unprecedented for British and Canadian troops and, indeed, the only decisive corps-level penetration of a German defence line in Normandy. Totalize was demonstrably a success, despite its failings, but it had also not advanced quite as far as its creator had hoped. Still, Meyer knew the end was near: "Further Canadian attacks will inevitably lead to a catastrophe," he wrote. "We are at the end of our tether."

(Soviet Red Army officers who toured the Normandy battlefields forty years later studied Simonds's Operation Totalize and said to their conducting officers that the Red Army's method of getting the job done would have been to threaten commanders with execution if they failed to reach Falaise by the end of August 8. If he had not been included in the list of those to be shot, Simonds might have agreed.)

By now the German attack at Mortain had failed dismally, smashed by the Americans and Allied airpower, and the enemy's only aim was to flee eastward as quickly as possible. The Allied task was to put them in the bag, and with the Americans moving east fast and turning north, Montgomery ordered II Canadian Corps to get south to Falaise and Trun to seal the trap.

Simonds was unhappy. On August 13, he met with as many of his senior officers as he could bring together and gave "a very tough and unpleasant" briefing in which he "blasted armoured regiments for their lack of support for infantry ... He demanded much greater initiative from arm[oure]d regiments," Major-General George Kitching recorded. "Drive on—get amongst the enemy etc. Forget about harbouring at night—keep driving on ... Don't rely on the infantry to do everything for you." Simonds's next plan, called Operation Tractable, was to jump off on August 14.

Tractable was as innovative as Totalize. A daylight attack screened by smoke to hamper the enemy's visibility, it consisted of two 150-tank squares, one based on the 4th Armoured, the other on the 2nd Armoured Brigade and the 3rd Division. The squares were to go straight at the enemy defences, their flanks covered by large smokescreens and heavy bombing by more than 800 aircraft from Bomber Command. Massive artillery resources were allocated, and every effort was taken to guarantee surprise. That last effort misfired when an officer of the 2nd Canadian Division's 8th Reconnaissance Regiment wandered into enemy lines in his scout car, was killed, and was found to be carrying the plan for the attack.

Tractable began on schedule just before noon, but again bombing fell among the Canadians and Poles, this time from 77 RAF and RCAF bombers, killing or wounding almost 400 men, of whom 204 were Poles. An officer of the 12th Field Regiment, Captain T.J. Bell, wrote that "the giant planes came over at less than a thousand feet and as they approached we could see the bomb doors open and the bombs come tumbling out … They not only bombed us but they machine-gunned us as well. No Germans ever presented a finer target than we did … with all our guns pointing unmistakably south and all our vehicles with their clearly visible white stars."

Once the vehicles began to roll, the dust rose—"dust like I've never seen before!" wrote a unit commander—blinding drivers. Then the Germans began firing into the closely packed squares and killed scores, guaranteeing confusion. The tanks nonetheless reached the Laison River, a supposed trickle of a stream that instead had wooded banks and a muddy bottom that was difficult to cross. Under fire, the attack stalled there then got under way again when the tanks found a ford, and Germans, fresh from soft occupation duties in Norway, began surrendering—until the tanks of the 1st SS Panzer Corps arrived on the scene, hit the 1st Hussars hard, and once more slowed the advance on Falaise.

The Shermans "brewed up" when hit, burning so quickly that the troopers had only a few seconds to bail out through the turret hatch. Only a few made it. One officer recalled that "when a Sherman was hit by anti-tank fire, particularly from the 88, there seemed to be an immediate explosion and flames roared 20 or 30 feet out of the top of the turret. This was followed by two or three explosions of high octane gas and the high explosive shells and the ammunition racks exploding." Tanks were supposed to fight "buttoned up," their hatches closed, but most crew commanders chose to drive with them open, preferring the threat of being sniped to that of being burned to death. In wooded country, as on the Laison, the odds against the armour were heavy, and the Germans' 88s were deadly. A 1st Hussars squadron lost eleven of nineteen tanks trying to find a way across the stream. Infantrymen worried that tanks attracted fire, and they were right to do so. But they frequently needed the firepower the tanks could bring, and they always complained when the tanks pulled back to refuel and rearm. As far as the foot soldiers were concerned, armour was almost never there when needed.

The carnage everywhere after Totalize and the first day of Tractable was awesome. Matthew Halton reported over the CBC on August 15 that he had walked along the Falaise road, where, he said, "you can see everything that is meant by the word 'War' ... The destruction of life, the destruction of smiling fields, the destruction of culture and the treasures of the past. The monstrous bomb craters, the shambles at every crossroads, the million shell-holes. The crosses of the dead and the dead still being collected ... The twisted and burnt-out vehicles and tanks and guns. The road to Falaise." A staff officer at Simonds's corps headquarters, Major Gerald Levenston, wrote home to Toronto, "one of my jobs is to provide working parties to bury the dead ... Some day I will be able to tell you ... of the unbelievable horror of it all."

That same day, Hitler ordered Field Marshal von Kluge to hold Falaise at all cost, prompting the German commander in Normandy to tell his aides that "he's absolutely out of his mind." The next day, much too late, Hitler ordered the units that had struck westward at Mortain to withdraw through the shrinking pocket. Von Kluge, implicated in the failed plot to assassinate Hitler, killed himself on August 17.

Meanwhile, Simonds had regrouped, issuing new orders that sent the 4th Division and the Poles to bar the German retreat out of the Pocket, now sealed in the south by U.S. troops at Argentan, and the 2nd Division to take Falaise. German general Hans Speidel later recalled that "two army commands, four corps commands, nine infantry divisions, and about five Panzer divisions were being pressed together in a square about six to ten miles in size between Falaise and Argentan, under converging artillery fire of all calibers and exposed day and night to continuous bombing." Some 100,000 Germans scurried east in their efforts to escape the trap, their long lines of vehicles and horse-drawn wagons and carts under constant air attack by rocket-firing Typhoons and every strafing aircraft the Allied tactical air forces could put in the skies. The death on the roads was such that pilots claimed that they could smell the rotting human and horse flesh as they flew above. Soldiers who had to march or drive through the slaughterhouse on the roads tried to wrap kerchiefs around their noses and mouths, so terrible was the smell of death.

The 2nd Division captured most of Falaise on August 17 and cleared the rest of it one day later. So chaotic was the fighting that at one point the Essex Scottish troops were slowed in their advance by trucks on the road ahead of them. The CO, Lieutenant-Colonel Peter Bennett, recalled that he went forward, whipped back the tarpaulin on the last truck, and saw Germans fleeing the Pocket. Still, one major crossroads was now blocked. The Poles moved into position to contain the enemy fleeing the Pocket and to battle a German westward thrust that aimed to keep the escape route open, their tanks taking up positions on Mont Ormel, an 859-foot-high mace-shaped hill three miles north of Chambois that controlled the road over which the Germans had to pass. The Poles' commander dubbed their hill Maczuga, Polish for "mace."

At the same time, the Canadians drove down the Falaise–Trun road, and the 9th and 10th brigades dug in along the river Dives. From the 4th Canadian Armoured Division, a squadron of fifteen Shermans from the South Alberta Regiment, commanded by thirty-two-year-old Major David Currie, and a company each of Hamilton's Argyll and Sutherland Highlanders and the Lincoln and Welland Regiment moved to seal the Gap. The Argylls were led by Lieutenant, A/Captain, A/Major Ivan Martin (the acting ranks denoting his temporary promotions to fill positions vacated by casualties), and Currie's force took position in the town of Saint-Lambert, where the sole bridge over the Dives that could carry tanks still stood.

This was the bloody climax of the battle to close the Falaise Gap. The 1st Polish Armoured Division clung to Maczuga, inflicting vengeance on their traditional oppressors but at heavy cost. The few armoured vehicles and two hundred men at Saint-Lambert fought off the Tigers and the desperate enemy, knocking out 88s, brewing up panzers, and killing hundreds. Currie single-handedly knocked out a Tiger, and Martin moved to destroy a machine gun firing at his men. He went to a slit trench and told an Argylls private, "Help me get that machine gunner." The reply: "You're kidding, of course." Martin went alone, killed the machine gunner with his Sten, and returned with the machine gun over his shoulder. Shortly thereafter he fell, killed by a shell, but Major Currie, the only surviving officer, continued to rally his men as they destroyed seven tanks, a dozen 88mm guns, and forty vehicles, and killed, wounded, or captured an extraordinary 12,000 Germans. Currie won the Victoria Cross; had he died and Martin survived, the latter likely would have had the VC. At Maczuga, the Poles destroyed seventy tanks and five hundred vehicles and took 6,000 POWs. They lost 1,400 of their 2,000 men and two-thirds of their tanks.

A little farther east, on August 21, two machine-gun platoons of the Cameron Highlanders found themselves in position on high ground just north of the highway between Trun and Chambois. Just before six o'clock that morning, enemy panzers and infantry put in a violent local counterattack through the neighbouring village of Magny. One tank approached the machine gunners' position, followed by infantry. The tank was damaged by a PIAT bomb and hastily sheered off, and the Vickers guns took "a dreadful toll" of the men on foot. Caught on rising ground, there was no cover for them. Those who were not hit ran toward the dead ground in the draw to their right. Their attack was completely disrupted, and for two hours, the machine gunners fired at whatever they could see. During this time, hundreds of the enemy crowded in to surrender. Many others were unable to give up, for every move to do so brought bursts of fire from SS troops patrolling the low ground behind them in a half-track to discourage surrendering.

That day, August 21, the tanks of the Canadian Grenadier Guards finally relieved the Poles and sewed the Falaise Pocket completely shut. The picture at Maczuga, the Guards war diarist wrote, "was the grimmest the Regiment had so far come up against. The Poles had had no supplies for three days; they had several hundred wounded who had not been evacuated, about 700 prisoners-of-war lay loosely guarded in a field … Unburied dead and parts of them were strewn about by the score … The Poles cried with joy when we arrived."

The Germans had managed to extract some 50,000 men before the Canadians closed the Gap. They lost between 10,000 and 20,000 dead and 40,000 to 50,000 taken prisoner in the fighting to August 21; their total losses in the Normandy campaign likely approached a half million. It was, some Nazi survivors said, "Stalingrad in Normandy." Kurt Meyer's 12th SS, which had had more than 20,000 troopers and 159 tanks on D-Day, June 6, had, according to some estimates, only 300 men and 10 tanks after the Gap battles. Allied operational researchers counted more than 8,000 damaged, destroyed, or abandoned vehicles, including 456 tanks and self-propelled guns and 367 other armoured fighting vehicles. An estimate of uncounted vehicles suggests that the actual total was 12,000. Tactical air power—Allied fighters, U.S. Thunderbolts, and RAF Typhoons had flown 2,029 attack sorties on August 17 and 3,057 on August 18—and artillery had done the job, but 20,000 vehicles, including tanks and self-propelled guns, escaped across the river Seine.

Meyer himself survived, only to be taken prisoner by Resistance fighters in Belgium the next month. He would stand trial in December 1945 for the executions at the Abbaye d'Ardenne and elsewhere and be found guilty at a Canadian court martial. Brigadier "Budge" Bell-Irving was a member of the court, and he still believed years later that Meyer was "a splendid man and fine soldier … whose original sentence of death by firing squad was intended to be a step up from hanging." The senior officer on Meyer's court-martial panel was Major-General Harry Foster. He told his son and biographer, "What struck me as I sat in my comfortable chair looking down at this hardnosed Nazi was that not one of us sitting on the bench … could claim clean hands in the matter of war crimes or atrocities or whatever you want to call them. It hadn't all been one-sided. Our troops did some pretty dreadful things to the Germans. Didn't that make all of us who were commanding officers just as guilty as Meyer?" Meyer's sentence was commuted to life imprisonment by order of Major-General Christopher Vokes, who later said that Meyer had been convicted on evidence that was "sort of second hand." He wrote that he knew, "and knew very well as a divisional commander in war, that certain things probably [went] on that were not always according to The Rules and Usages. I did absolve my own troops, post facto, of bits of hanky panky now and then, of various degrees of seriousness." In other words, Canadians sometimes shot prisoners too. The SS officer served a prison term at Dorchester Penitentiary in New Brunswick. On his release in 1954, still an unrepentant Nazi, Meyer became a beer salesman servicing the messes of Canadian troops based in Germany on North Atlantic Treaty Organization duties.

The Canadian toll in the final battles of the Normandy campaign was dreadful: from August 8 to 21, II Canadian Corps lost 1,470 dead, 4,023 wounded, and 177 POWs. In the Normandy campaign as a whole, 18,444 Canadians became casualties, more than 5,000 of them killed, their remains now interred in the two large Commonwealth War Graves Commission cemeteries at Bény-sur-Mer and Bretteville-sur-Laize in the Norman countryside. To cite one example, one common among the infantry units of the 3rd Division, the Regina Rifles lost 926 officers and men from June 6 to August 23, substantially more than the battalion's establishment strength of 845 on D-Day. Extraordinarily, Canadian soldiers died at a higher rate for each thousand soldiers in the field than they had in the mud of Passchendaele in the autumn of 1917.

And, as historian Terry Copp has argued, the 2nd and 3rd divisions were in intense combat for more days than any of the British divisions they served beside in Normandy and hence had more casualties. Those killed and wounded always included the bravest and best officers, NCOs, and men who could never really be replaced. Still, reinforcements soon filled the ranks, and experienced lance corporals became sergeants while twenty-one-year-old lieutenants took over as company commanders.

What can we make of the Canadian performance in their first battles in France? General Simonds believed his subordinates' poor leadership, not his battle plan, had led to the slow progress of Operation Tractable, and he sacked George Kitching, perhaps his closest friend, as GOC of the 4th Canadian Armoured Division. "Simply put," Brian Reid wrote in his fine history of Totalize, "Major General George Kitching was just too nice a man to properly command" his division. Command of the 4th fell to Harry Foster, who had commanded a D-Day brigade in the 3rd Division. Newly promoted Major-General D.C. Spry, thirty-one years old, came from Italy to replace the wounded Keller of the 3rd Division. (When he reported to First Canadian Army, he was met by Brigadier Ted Beament, the Brigadier General Staff, and called Beament, a few years older and now junior in rank to Spry, "Sir.") At the same time, Simonds replaced one of the 4th Armoured's brigadiers, E.L. Booth, who had been killed in action, with Robert Moncel, from his corps staff, and sacked two of three brigadiers in the 2nd Division. Inexplicably, it took five days from the time Booth was killed, on August 14, for Moncel to take up his new post. Simonds still wanted to oust Charles Foulkes, the 2nd Division's GOC, but he could not do so because of Harry Crerar's continuing support for Foulkes. In all, in July and August, the II Canadian Corps commander fired a division commander, six of nine brigadiers, and fourteen of twenty-four battalion commanders. This was not wholly surprising, for battlefield leadership is vastly different than directing troops in training. The new commanders were men Simonds correctly believed had proven themselves in battle.

Battle casualties also affected the Canadian regimental leaders. In the 4th Armoured Division's 4th Armoured Brigade, for example, 48 percent of the officers became casualties between the beginning of August and the twenty-sixth. At one point, the Canadian Grenadier Guards' acting CO was a captain. More striking, as noted by Lieutenant-Colonel Angelo Caravaggio, the leading student of the 4th Canadian Armoured Division's history, 56 percent of majors and lieutenant-colonels in the 4th Armoured Brigade were killed or wounded, a figure that includes two regimental commanders among those killed. The losses among other ranks were also very high, and in the late stages of the Falaise Gap battle, the 4th Armoured Brigade had only 46 operable tanks out of the 220 it had originally. That the brigade functioned at all in such circumstances was remarkable.

Simonds himself might have been judged as the innovative tactician he most certainly was, but also as one who failed to factor into his too complicated, too elaborate plans the condition of the divisions he moved around on his maps. All were shaken by casualties, some were brand new to combat, and the German troops were skilfully led and generally ferocious in battle, using their superior weaponry with great proficiency. Caravaggio stated that for Simonds to have depended "on two weakened, inexperienced armoured divisions [the 4th Canadian and the 1st Polish] to plug the escape routes of over 200,000 German soldiers was an unrealistic expectation and militarily unsound." This is surely so. Major-General Harry Foster, the 7th Infantry Brigade commander in Normandy and the most competent brigade commander in the 3rd Division, conceded that Canadians "were no match for the Germans once they were dug in … We held the advantage; in the air, at sea, and on the ground. Yet every time our troops got beyond the range of supporting artillery or sour weather grounded our fighter-bomber cover, the Germans stopped us cold." Charles Foulkes, no great field commander as he demonstrated repeatedly in Normandy, said much the same: "When we went into battle at Falaise and Caen we found that when we bumped into battle-experienced German troops we were no match for them. We would not have been successful had it not been for our air and artillery support." The Wehrmacht and the Waffen-SS were a mighty war machine.

Still, the raw Canadians had eventually prevailed against what was still the best army in the world; they had fought with great courage, and they had learned how best to defeat the enemy. Simonds's high reputation came out of the campaign unsullied—indeed, much enhanced. He was and remains the only Canadian senior officer of whom the British and Americans at the time, and their historians since, thought highly.

The closing of the Falaise Gap was at best a partial success; the blame game started in August 1944 and continues among scholars. Whose fault was it that so many Germans got out? The Americans had stopped moving north in mid-August for fear, they said, of bumping into the Canadians and Poles. Montgomery had failed to give the Canadians enough resources to break through in Totalize and Tractable. And the Canadians were simply slow, too slow-moving and cumbersome, to slam shut the trap.

All of these criticisms are correct. The U.S. Army ought to have moved north in strength, relying on close liaison to avoid interfering with the advance southward of the Canadians and Poles. (In fact, and extraordinarily, the 4th Canadian Armoured could not establish direct contact with the Americans located a few miles away; instead, division HQ had to go through II Canadian Corps, First Canadian Army, and then the U.S. chain of command. This inevitably delayed and complicated matters.) Montgomery should have put more men and resources into II Canadian Corps' drive south from Caen. And, yes, the Canadians were too slow, too uncoordinated, some too poorly trained and too weakly led in a complex, fluid battle, and simply too green to beat a desperate, skilled enemy.

Canadians like to think of themselves as showing initiative, but their army at this stage of the war was still very much a top-down organization, with very few officers, junior or senior, showing any willingness or ability to react on their own to meet a changing situation. For a nation of hockey players, supposedly skilled at seizing an opportunity and an opening to score, it seems odd that in Normandy they should have formed such a slow, ponderous army. But war was different from sport, and perhaps General Simonds was correct in insisting on tight control—or as much control as he could exercise over the sometimes indifferent leadership of his GOCs and brigade commanders. Detailed plans came from Simonds at Corps headquarters; there was centralized staff planning, heavy reliance on artillery support, and cautious exploitation of success. In historian Bill McAndrew's very apt phrase, Canadian attacks followed the "slinky toy method," the offensive moving forward only far enough to keep artillery support in range, then slowing or stopping until the guns moved forward. The artillery was the Canadians' great advantage, to be sure, but it was nonetheless a ponderous way to fight. Historian Stephen Harris summed it up when he noted that "the gunner-dominated Canadian Army [was] unable to develop its own doctrine to foster genuine all-arms cooperation and movement" and "remained overly dependent on the artillery to shoot everyone else forward." Matters improved greatly as the war went on, but in Normandy, First Canadian Army was not yet the best little army in the world. Indeed, it had sometimes been ponderous and poorly coordinated in action.

Oddly for the army of a monstrous dictatorship, the Germans' leadership put more trust in soldiers, giving every man the sense that he was part of a shared enterprise of vital importance to the Führer, to Germany, and to his own comrades and family. (This statement, while true, needs to be read in conjunction with the fact that the enemy executed 13,000 to 15,000 of its own men during the war. Fear—and fear of the SS—ruled the Wehrmacht.) The enemy's battlefield leadership and initiative was better at every level, better in coordinating all-arms operations (although the Waffen-SS and Wehrmacht were often at cross-purposes and unable to coordinate), and far quicker to respond to events. In contrast to the Allies, who believed the commander should be at his headquarters with good communications, the Germans expected commanders to place themselves at the critical point in action. There was simply no Canadian senior officer in Normandy above battalion level who could have stepped up and, by sheer force of will and innate tactical sense, transformed a battle as Kurt Meyer did.

Moreover, and crucially, the terrain south of Caen greatly favoured the defence. Verrières Ridge presented a formidable obstacle, and every reverse slope, little hamlet, and farm had been turned into a fortified machine-gun post and bunker. The ridge was only 250 feet high, but it dominated the landscape south of Caen and north of Falaise and provided fine lines of sight for the enemy's deadly mortars and 88s. Moreover, the Shermans simply could not fight on equal terms against the Tiger and Panther panzers. Only the weight of numbers and the availability of replacement tanks kept the Canadian (and British and American) armoured regiments going.

Still, the Wehrmacht and the Waffen-SS were soundly defeated in Normandy, losing from 300,000 to a half million men and 27 divisions. The seven panzer divisions that had fought in Normandy now could muster only 100 to 120 tanks among them. The Allies had lost 206,700 men, but they had prevailed. Optimism in the Allied high command soared, and the war seemed almost won. The race was on to the east, to liberate Paris, to free the Channel ports and the remainder of occupied France, and to beat Hitler once and for all before Christmas.

On Remembrance Day 1944, the superb reporter, writer, and broadcaster Matthew Halton gave the Canadian Broadcasting Corporation's audience his reflections on the war's course. He noted that he had gone to Vimy Ridge in September, a few short weeks after the closing of the Falaise Gap. His thoughts, he said, "went back to Normandy, to that road from Caen to Falaise, and if there were ghosts around Vimy Ridge as we swept past that day, I wonder if they were saying something like this—'Listen, what are you going to do after this war? Perhaps you're going to build a memorial twice as high as this one on the road from Caen to Falaise—to commemorate our sons, the dead and damned battalions, the Black Watch and the North Nova Scotias and the rest.' Arras,

Ypres and Vimy Ridge. That was the anthem of the damned youth of one generation. Bretteville, Caen, Tilly and Falaise—that's the anthem for the damned youth of another. 'We died. Our sons died. What are you going to do?'"

CHAPTER 3

Clearing the Scheldt

With the closing of the Falaise Gap, the task of First Canadian Army now was to clear the Channel coast, liberating fortified towns like Dieppe, Boulogne, Calais, Le Havre, and Ostend, and the larger inland city of Rouen. The Germans were in full retreat eastward and Paris was liberated on August 25, but the German stay-behind units in northern France were determined to hold out long enough to let their divisions and what remained of their armour escape.

The Canadian troops moving east on the left flank of the rapid Allied advance neared the river Seine in the last week of August and suddenly ran into very stiff resistance in the Forêt de la Londe, the Germans fighting for time to allow the remnants of their armies from Normandy to cross the river. Allied aircraft, whenever the weather permitted, attacked the retreating enemy columns, and concentrations of vehicles at the crossings were easy targets for the Typhoons. British operational researchers studying what they called "the Chase" later tallied 3,648 destroyed vehicles and guns (including 150 tanks and self-propelled guns), noting that the total was incomplete and that the largest mass was on the south bank of the Seine at Rouen, where 20 armoured fighting vehicles, 48 guns, and 660 other vehicles lay abandoned or destroyed. They estimated a grand total south of the river of 12,000 motor vehicles. The 5th Panzer Army, however, recorded that between August 20 and the evening of August twenty-four, some 25,000 vehicles (including horse-drawn transport) crossed the Seine. Most crossings were on ferries, many of which were also destroyed during the fighting. British investigators concluded that twenty-four separate crossing sites had been used, the most heavily trafficked being a pontoon bridge at Poses, four miles east of Pont-de-l'Arche, where a civilian counted 16,000 vehicles crossing during a period of five nights. The Germans apparently dismantled the bridge in daylight to hide it from Allied aircraft; there was no road there and no bridge to attract attention. Even in defeat the Germans were very effective.

The defensive screen covering the retreat, provided by the Wehrmacht's 331st Division, met the Canadians with heavy machine-gun fire on the near side of the Seine. Their resistance was heavy enough that the battalion COs of the understrength Royal Regiment and Royal Hamilton Light Infantry in the 2nd Canadian Division argued "that this task was beyond the powers of a battalion composed largely of reinforcement personnel with little training." The General Officer Commanding the 2nd, General Charles Foulkes, nonetheless ordered the units to attack. They dutifully did so, and the two regiments took heavy losses and withdrew. Lieutenant-Colonel Douglas McIntyre, then commanding a company of the Essex Scottish, wrote later that "we were already aware of the GOC's stubborn haughtiness and apparent disregard for the well-being of an infantry regiment." The 3rd and 4th divisions also faced opposition, but the enemy pulled back on August 29—"on his own bloody time," McIntyre said—and the city of Rouen was liberated on August 30. The Forêt de la Londe had cost the Canadians 577 killed and wounded; the South Saskatchewan Regiment's four companies mustered only 60 men after the fighting. The Germans still had teeth.

The reality was that most infantry battalions in the 2nd and 3rd divisions had taken heavy losses in the Normandy fighting—76 percent of Canadian casualties in Normandy fell on infantrymen, compared to pre-battle "wastage" estimates of 48 percent (*wastage* was the callous British term for losses of all kinds that depleted unit strength)—and much of their leadership had drained away. The French-speaking battalions were worst off, each short from 200 to 331 men, a very serious shortfall that meant that platoons were missing 10 to 15 men each. The reinforcements coming forward to all battalions inevitably were less well trained than the men who had been lost in action—certainly they lacked battle experience—and until they formed bonds with their new mates, moreover, they lacked any support system.

Major Stewart Bull of the Essex Scottish Regiment, in his memoir of his war, talked of his batman in Normandy, who "was busy digging my slit trench. I came upon him and I said, 'Well Bachkofsky, how are you doing?' He said. 'All right sir.' And I said, 'What's new?' And he said, 'This is my second anniversary.' I said, 'Two years in the army, eh?' And he said, 'No, sir. Two months.' Two months before he had been walking down the street in Winnipeg, and he turned into the recruiting office and they had taken his name, and signed him up, and given him a month of basic training. After that he had been sent with others to Halifax for the trip across the ocean." Then, Bull wrote, Bachkofsky "landed in England, found his way to the Essex Scottish headquarters, and was sent across the Channel on the next boat. And he had arrived about two days before in Normandy. He was a very cheerful little guy with red hair," eighteen years old, "being shoved in against a tough and experienced enemy." Reinforcements were supposed to be better trained than Private Bachkofsky, and almost always were, but matters grew worse as infantry casualties mounted and the pressure to find more men grew.

Complaints about the training of reinforcements seem to have been a common theme in every army at this stage of the war, but the criticism in late August, September, and October in First Canadian Army began to reach a crescendo. One brigade commander in the 2nd Division, W.J. Megill, recollected that, while some infantry reinforcements were untrained, the blame lay on the Canadian Reinforcement Units in England. They didn't get good men to run them—"all the duds were there," officers and NCOs found unsuitable by their units and shuffled away. A junior officer wrote later that the Armoured Corps Reinforcement Unit "was overseen by the scum of the Armoured Corps, spat out by regiments, but not returned to Canada for the menial labour to which they were so patently suited." There were hundreds of men in England suitable only for pioneer units—light engineering companies often made up of men with medical problems who weren't otherwise needed. There were also many fit men doing clerical work.

Thus, by the late summer of 1944, the infantry battalions were short of men. The higher infantry casualties meant that headquarters in London and Ottawa had to make ever greater efforts to keep battalions at or near full strength and therefore had to scrape the bottom of the manpower barrel. Wounded men were returned to action quicker than they should have been, and many soldiers, trained to be truck drivers or ordnance specialists or anti-aircraft gunners, found themselves given a crash course and remustered as poor bloody infantry. The Allies had based their reinforcement planning on the Luftwaffe's continuing to inflict casualties on the front and rear, but their air superiority had all but eliminated the enemy's airpower and hence fewer rear-area reinforcements were required; similarly, Allied planners had not counted on German resistance continuing to be so determined for so long, and this meant more infantry casualties, frequently more than 75 percent of all casualties. The result was too many support troops and far too few infantry reinforcements. Too much tail, in other words, and not enough teeth.

In their letters home, soldiers began to grumble about the situation, commanders complained to their superiors, and in late September, Colonel Layton Ralston flew to Europe to see the situation for himself. The minister of national defence told his former deputy minister privately that "towards the end of August he began to feel uneasy as to the reinforcement situation." His conversations in Italy and Northwest Europe had persuaded him that there was already a shortage of reinforcements, and that a major crisis loomed. As he later stated in the House of Commons, "I found that on account of the heavy infantry casualties, the infantry reinforcement pool which had been established in France on D-Day had been completely exhausted." Remustering men to infantry from other corps had been tried, but the pool had not been refilled. This situation, already difficult in late September, would become critical in October and November as the casualties suffered in clearing the Scheldt mounted. The only possible source of infantry, it soon became clear to Ottawa, was from the National Resources Mobilization Act men—the

NRMA home defence conscripts, or Zombies, as the public referred to them after the soulless living dead of Hollywood horror films.

• • •

On September 1, the Canadians took Dieppe without a fight. The honour of entering the town was given to the 2nd Division, which had been bloodied there two years before. The troops marched through the streets to the cheers of the populace, and a ceremony was held, with appropriate speeches. After the parade, some of the survivors of the raid—there were relatively few still with the division—went up the cliffs to look down at the shingle beaches and marvel at the planners' idiocy that had put them there in August 1942.

One additional incident arose from the Dieppe parade, where the General Officer Commanding-in-Chief (GOC-in-C) of First Canadian Army, Lieutenant-General Harry Crerar, had taken the salute. Field Marshal Montgomery, the Commander-in-Chief of 21st Army Group and just promoted to that highest of ranks, had called a meeting at his headquarters and directed Crerar to attend. He replied that the Dieppe ceremony had special Canadian meaning and suggested that the time of Monty's meeting be altered. The Field Marshal was outraged and repeated his order; Crerar, heading to Dieppe, directed that this message go unanswered. When the two commanders finally met, Montgomery asked why Crerar had failed to follow his instructions. Crerar explained that he had to be at Dieppe, and in response, "the C-in-C intimated that he was not interested in my explanation—that the Canadian aspect of the DIEPPE ceremonial was of no importance compared to getting on with the war."

Crerar replied that "I had, as previously explained, a definite responsibility to my Government and country which, at times, might run counter to his own wishes. There was a powerful Canadian reason why I should have been present ... In fact, there were 800 reasons—the Canadian dead buried at Dieppe cemetery." Still furious, Montgomery said "our ways must part," and Crerar, a quiet man but one who was not afraid to fight, replied that he would report this matter to the Canadian government. Monty then backed off, but relations between the two, not good for months, grew extremely cool. Montgomery thereafter could never bring himself to admit Crerar's competence.

Crerar was a nationalist, yes, but he was an Empire man too, convinced that Canada and Britain should and must always work together. Yet he understood the British well. They were influenced by two factors: "the Englishman's traditional belief in the superiority of the Englishman" and the "military inconvenience" of Canadian troops not being immediately interchangeable with the Imperials. As Crerar put it even before the Dieppe dust-up with Montgomery, "no Canadian, or American, or other 'national' Comm[ander], unless possessing quite phenomenal qualities, is ever rated as high as the equivalent Britisher." It wasn't that British troops were so effective; they had been battered by the Germans throughout most of the war, until "Monty Almighty" had defeated them at El Alamein, in Tunisia, and in Sicily. It was simply that in the eyes of men like Montgomery, the British always knew best. The Canadians—and the Americans too—were amateurs who simply could not be trusted to fight the war. Crerar was an amateur, his generals and soldiers were ill equipped for leadership, and the war would certainly go better if British officers controlled First Canadian Army.

Lieutenant-Colonel W.A.B. Anderson, the General Staff Officer, Grade 1 at First Canadian Army HQ and later a lieutenant-general, thought Crerar was the right man for the GOC-in-C job. Crerar spoke for Canada very effectively even if he wasn't the best field commander, and he had a strong sense of the proper relationship to the British Army and Montgomery. One problem, however, was that Crerar had the charisma of a turnip, was completely cold, and almost useless in a discussion. But, recalled Major-General W.J. Megill, he could write a beautifully organized paper on that discussion. He was a natural staff officer but not a natural commander. Still, Crerar's Great War experience told him how important it was for Canadians to stay together and be distinctively Canadian. And he was ordinarily smooth and civilized in achieving this. Every time he had a problem, Anderson stated, one part of Crerar's mind asked, "How will this look in the history books?" Crerar was also very conscious of his role as the Senior Combatant Officer, the one man in the field directly responsible to the government of Canada for the country's troops. Crerar had earlier written that "though in practice I expect to be treated, and behave, as any other Army Commander, in principle I ... am not. I am the Canadian Army Commander and, as such, am in a different category to the British Army Commander." That explained his insistence on being at the Dieppe ceremony.

Harry Crerar was an emotional man, full of strong feelings that he struggled, usually successfully, to control. He was serious, had a sense of responsibility, and drove himself hard. He was a very professional soldier who didn't like dabblers or tolerate sloppiness, and self-control was his personal watchword. Although he was less nationalistic than McNaughton, the officer he had replaced as GOC-in-C, he was a Canadian first and last, conscious of his responsibilities. As Simonds's Chief of Staff, Brigadier Elliott Rodger, said, Crerar wanted to ensure "that Canada is 'done right by' as far as it is humanly possible."

Montgomery, likely seeing Crerar as more of a senior civil servant or a Quartermaster General than a soldier, was certain that the Canadian was no field commander. Long after the war, in 1969, Montgomery wrote to Trumball Warren, a Canadian officer who had served at his side several times as an aide, that Crerar was unfit to command an army in the field. "What I suffered from that man! Canada produced only one general fit to hold high command in war, and that was Guy Simonds." After the Dieppe incident, Monty schemed to put Simonds at the head of First Canadian Army. That would happen temporarily a few weeks later, when Crerar fell ill with dysentery and anemia and flew to England to recuperate for six weeks. Until then, Monty bypassed Crerar as much as possible, greatly preferring to deal with the commander of II Canadian Corps. Still, this little incident at Dieppe had demonstrated that Crerar was the commander of the troops of a nation, fighting in a coalition in its own national interests. It was in some ways his finest hour.

It must be said, however, that Crerar as a leader had no superb moments, as Brigadier G.E. Beament, his Brigadier General Staff at First Canadian Army, recollected years later. He was a fine staff officer, a cautious man who never made a serious mistake. Brigadier Stanley Todd knew Crerar socially before the war and served under him during it. He thought of him as a well-trained, slow, serious man who he doubted ever laughed. Crerar thought through every problem systematically, weighing all the options and possible threats, on everything he had to think about, took his time, and came up with the right answers. In no

THE BEST LITTLE ARMY IN THE WORLD

way was he glamorous. He was an excellent officer, 100 percent sound and very real, Todd stated, but one problem was that it took too long for people to get to know him.

And if Crerar did err, he inevitably managed to skate away skilfully from the mess, avoiding blame. He had done this as Chief of the General Staff in Ottawa when he urged the government to send troops to Hong Kong and they were lost on Christmas Day 1941. He repeated this escape by not taking the rap for the Dieppe raid in August 1942, and he had connived to help get rid of his friend Andy McNaughton in 1943. He was correct in at least two of these actions, just as he was correct in the way he dealt with Montgomery over the Dieppe ceremony. Crerar was a very skilful political animal, to be sure, but the way he always emerged unscathed from his brushes with the disasters that threatened his position was uncanny.

• • •

The key for the Allies was now the need for ports to bring in supplies. Dieppe was the only Channel port taken easily and with its dock facilities intact, but its capacity was limited to a maximum of 7,000 tons a day. The Germans clearly realized that the lack of ports was hampering the Allied efforts to supply their troops. On Hitler's direct orders, all the Channel ports were to be defended as fortresses, a decision that threw away thousands of men when the same objective could have been achieved by levelling the docking and unloading facilities—which the Germans did in any case.

The Canadians had masked Calais, from which huge gun batteries shelled Dover across the Channel, since early September 1944. After a week-long fight to seize the town and its fortifications ended on October 1 with 7,500 prisoners, Major-General Dan Spry, the General Officer Commanding the 3rd Division, spoke to the Wehrmacht commander. One of the Canadian staff officers wrote later that the German "was content enough about the defeat; it was an objective fact, no tears shed over it all. But he was burningly interested in knowing the details of the Canadian tactics: 'Now why did you come in from the precise direction you did, when we were sure that you would come in from over here? What an interesting piece of tactics ... Had you come in just here, where we also expected you, do you suppose you could have succeeded? We had a warm reception prepared for you ...' What he was interested in," the Canadian wrote, angered and more than a little bemused by the German obsession with war, "was the tactical lessons ruling this particular exercise; he wanted to file them away in the Berlin Military College for the meditation of future tacticians. This is not exactly stupidity, I suppose; but then, what is it, if not what the divisional commander called it—'Damned nonsense'?" Spry had been a twenty-six-year-old Permanent Force lieutenant in 1939 and had risen very quickly on the battlefield to the command of a division. While he was a professional soldier who had won this particular battle, he was no war lover, not one to admire what his staff officer called the "pedantic core" of the German general staff.

The port of Le Havre had fallen to I British Corps, under First Canadian Army, on September 12. It had been defended by some 11,300 Germans and had most of its civilians still in residence. Lieutenant-General Sir John Crocker, with Crerar's concurrence, ordered the city bombed by the Royal Air Force. Le Havre had more tonnage fall upon it than had been used to create the firestorm at Hamburg a year earlier, and there were some 2,000 casualties, mainly civilians. An estimated 82 percent of the town was destroyed. The Germans surrendered, but it took a month to bring the port's facilities into operation.

At Boulogne, the 3rd Division had another stiff fight. The North Shores had to attack a massive concrete fortress housing three 12-inch guns, part of the outer works protecting the city, an assault that took three days. It was, Captain Hal MacDonald wrote, "the strongest position we've ever hit—75 yd. long pillboxes or forts housing huge [C]hannel guns & hundreds & hundreds of men. So heavy that our shells bounced off them & a 500 lb. bomb just dug earth away from the side." In a letter to his wife, MacDonald detailed the part he had played then wrote, "The men are marvelous—full of guts. I can't begin to quote the instances of outstanding bravery—hundreds of them. That's what makes us stick there—just the courage of those men hanging on like ants hanging onto a huge barrel." In a second letter, MacDonald wrote that "the Hun had enough, food, ammunition & weapons to hold [us] off for months & it was only sheer guts & tenacity that took these places." The port city, its shipping facilities largely destroyed, was not seized until September 22, once again after a heavy bombing raid affected German morale. The enemy fought until the Canadians neared their pillboxes, then gave up, "in many cases," the Army official historian wrote, "having their kit packed, ready to surrender." The enemy taken prisoner numbered 9,500 men, and the Canadian casualties 634.

Meanwhile, the Royal Hamilton Light Infantry of the 2nd Division had liberated the medieval city of Bruges, Belgium, on September 12.

The regiment was mobbed by "delirious" citizens, so much so that "literally thousands of people swarmed about and prevented the vehicles from moving for close to an hour." One artillery officer, Elmer Bell, wrote home from Belgian territory on September 23 to say that the country did not seem as ravaged as France and, moreover, the local Resistance was much more helpful than the Maquis had been in France: "While the French wait for us to clear roads, these fellows fixed them for us and made our pursuit of the Germans much faster." Bell added that the Belgian welcome had been "tumultuous," but "all Europeans are strictly business of course and in money dealings they figure we are all rich and therefore fair game. So we generally pay through the nose for anything that we buy."

With the exception of Dunkirk, besieged by the 1st Czechoslovak Independent Armoured Brigade, which was serving as part of First Canadian Army, the Canadians had taken all the ports on the English Channel by October 1—too slow, some historians have argued, a position that Canadian scholars have suggested underestimates the difficulties and the Canadians' lack of men and material resources for the task. Moreover, the enemy had done a masterful job of wrecking the facilities, and no ports (except Le Havre) could be restored for use before November. As Major-General A.E. Walford, Crerar's chief administrative officer, noted, a truck was now worth more than a tank, so short had supplies become.

The capture of Antwerp should have solved all of the Allies' supply needs. The great Belgian port could handle a thousand merchant ships at a time, and it had 10 square miles of docks, 20 miles of waterfront, and 600 cranes. Allied planners reckoned that Antwerp could handle 40,000 tons of supplies a day—once it was captured. But Antwerp was about 50 miles from the open sea on the river Scheldt. Between the port and the sea were the islands of Walcheren (a very heavily defended part of the Atlantic Wall), North Beveland, and South Beveland, which was attached to mainland Holland by a small isthmus—all held by the Germans, who could do a great deal to disrupt the flow of shipping into the port. On September 3, Montgomery had ordered General Miles Dempsey of the British Second Army to occupy Antwerp. The British 11th Armoured Division did just that on September 4, but although the Germans were shattered and might have been readily pushed out, Montgomery gave no orders for the Scheldt estuary to be seized. This was the Field Marshal's single worst error of the war.

The reason was that Montgomery's mind had focused on dealing a death blow to the enemy—a bigger objective, to be sure. His Operation Market Garden, launched on September 17, aimed to secure bridges over the Lower Rhine and Maas rivers to permit an early assault on the Ruhr, Germany's industrial heartland. British and American parachute divisions were dropped to take the bridges while armoured divisions pushed through the enemy to link up with them. The plan, clever as it was, failed dismally. The British paratroops were forced to surrender or withdraw by September 25, their casualties very heavy. The German panzers, even if not at full strength after their beating in Normandy, savaged the Allies. Now the enemy planners saw their chance, recognized that Antwerp was the key point, and understood that the port could not be used if the Scheldt River was not cleared. Their army quickly, amazingly, rejuvenated itself, and the enemy now occupied the estuary in force. It fell to First Canadian Army, on the left flank of the Allied advance eastward, to drive the Germans out.

The first orders to the Canadians about clearing the approaches to Antwerp came from 21st Army Group on September 13. Uncharacteristically for Monty, his instructions seemed to vacillate between emphasizing the capture of the Channel ports and clearing the way into Antwerp. It took longer for Montgomery's headquarters to give priority to Antwerp and much longer still before First Canadian Army received sufficient resources to do the job. As it was, small Canadian units had reached the Leopold Canal around this time, crossed it, and been driven back with heavy casualties. The Germans had been ferrying large numbers of troops and equipment across the West Scheldt since early September—amounting in all to nine divisions, with 100,000 men, 6,000 vehicles, and 750 guns, by September 20—and had begun putting their men into position on Beveland and Walcheren. Their determination to fight for the Scheldt approaches now became clear; if Montgomery had sent his lead British units at a completely shaken enemy at the beginning of September, the coming struggle might have been avoided. And, some critics have suggested, the chances of defeating Hitler in 1944 disappeared with Monty's failure.

First Canadian Army staff had already begun making plans for the Scheldt operations when General Crerar fell sick with serious dysentery and anemia, and on September 27, Lieutenant-General Guy Simonds took over as acting GOC-in-C of First Canadian Army. II Canadian Corps came under the acting command of Charles Foulkes, and Brigadier Holley Keefler became acting GOC of 2nd Division. As Army commander, Crerar had essentially dealt with the broad strokes, logistics, and air support, largely leaving the operational details to his two corps commanders. But this hands-off approach was definitely not Guy

Simonds's style: while he was acting in command, First Canadian Army Headquarters would plan, direct, and control events.

The challenge of clearing the Scheldt was horrendous. Virtually the entire area was below sea level, with dikes holding back the North Sea and much of the land being polders—reclaimed land drained over the centuries by hard work and protected by dikes. These dikes, sometimes fifteen feet high, and two broad canals offered the Germans good defensive positions, and the enemy forces were well supplied. Too often, the only way forward for the Canadians was atop the dikes, and it was easy for the Germans to site their weapons to make this very costly.

Crerar's staff planners had already done their appreciations, assessing all the possibilities for Operations Switchback and Infatuate, the plans to clear the Scheldt approaches. Simonds was not happy with them, and he attacked the plans as hypothetical and based on misconceptions about enemy strength. He pointed to the advantages held by the defenders of Walcheren and South Beveland. A water assault on Walcheren might be necessary, Simonds thought, even if it was very difficult. The key to him was bombing the dikes, flooding the islands, and isolating the enemy defenders. Crerar's planners had considered this but ruled it out because of Royal Air Force criticisms and political objections from the Dutch government-in-exile. And the chief engineer at the headquarters, the able Brigadier Geoffrey Walsh, did not believe bombing could breach the dikes. Crerar had accepted this; Simonds would not.

As soon as Simonds took over, as First Canadian Army's Brigadier General Staff Ted Beament recalled, "We gave him the facts, and he went away to his quarters and made his own appreciation of the military situation, called together a meeting of everybody involved and said 'Gentlemen, this is what we are going to do' … Everybody gulped a couple of times," Beament continued, "and we got on with it." His plan was clear: 3rd Canadian Division, assisted by the 4th Canadian Armoured and the British 51st divisions, would clear the south bank of the Scheldt, what had come to be dubbed the Breskens Pocket. The 2nd Canadian Division would then free South Beveland. Finally, Walcheren Island, controlling the entrance to the Scheldt estuary, would be attacked over the narrow causeway joining it to South Beveland and by assault from the sea.

Simonds's plan for Walcheren showed him at his best: over Dutch complaints that this would ruin land that had been reclaimed from the sea only by decades-long efforts, he argued that breaching the dikes with bombs would flood the interior and cut off resupply to isolated German garrisons. Simonds's concern, quite properly, was to clear the estuary, minimize casualties to his soldiers, and make their task as easy as possible. Isolating the Germans could do this. For Simonds, those necessities outweighed the Dutch desire to preserve farmland.

As it was, clearing the Scheldt was an extraordinarily difficult mission. Eighteen months of extensive construction since March 1943 had transformed Walcheren into one of the most formidable defensive positions along the Atlantic Wall. The town of Flushing had been turned into a concrete fortress protected by water-filled anti-tank ditches, wire, and hundreds of thousands of mines. Walcheren's powerful heavy gun batteries also commanded the mouth of the Scheldt. Thus, Simonds pressed his case against Royal Air Force objections that his Walcheren bombing would interfere with Bomber Command's campaign to pulverize Germany and might not even work. The air marshals argued that bombing had not been very effective against bunkers and gun emplace-ments and likely could not burst the dikes—but, Simonds said, if the bombing failed, nothing would be lost. Persisting, Simonds met with senior RAF officers in the caddy shack on the golf course at Ghent, Bel-gium, and there his arguments carried the day. This was "real leader-ship," Beament recalled. The GSO1 at Army, Lieutenant-Colonel Bill Anderson, said, "Simonds was a commander in the classic mould—he made the plan, the staff had to make it work, and his job was to see that what he wanted was done."

This was not how Crerar had operated, but it was Simonds's way, and he and the staff made it work: beginning on October 3, the RAF's bombers flew 2,000 sorties and dropped 10,000 tons of bombs. They created a large gap in the 400-year-old great earth wall near Westkapelle, and in the following days blew three additional breaches. The RAF had done its job and Walcheren began to flood; over the next three weeks, more than 80 percent of the island ended up under water, killing civilians and livestock and destroying livelihoods. Most important for Simonds, interested in opening Antwerp as quickly as possible, the flooding made the Germans' supply problems insurmountable. The general proved correct. The Scheldt campaign, arguably the most gruelling struggle of the war for the Canadians, was set to begin.

. . .

The Canadian infantry battalions that would fight on the Scheldt estu-ary had been reorganized in May 1943 to give them more firepower and a better anti-tank capability. Strength was fixed at 38 officers and

1. Prime Minister Mackenzie King with the High Commissioner in London, Vincent Massey. King directed Canada's great war effort but never understood the military.
LIBRARY AND ARCHIVES CANADA

2. General Andrew McNaughton (*left*) commanded in succession the 1st Division, the Canadian Corps, and First Canadian Army. Highly intelligent and nationalistic, he was nonetheless sacked in late 1943.
LIBRARY AND ARCHIVES CANADA

3. Lieutenant-General Guy Simonds, here with Defence Minister J.L. Ralston, was the only senior Canadian commander of whom Allied leaders thought highly.
LIBRARY AND ARCHIVES CANADA

4. Major-General Chris Vokes (*right*), commanding the 4th Armoured Division, confers with Brigadier Robert Moncel in Sögel, Germany.
LIBRARY AND ARCHIVES CANADA

5. Lieutenant-General Harry Crerar, driving the jeep, arrives with General Bernard Montgomery at Monty's HQ in France.
G.K. BELL/LIBRARY AND ARCHIVES CANADA

6. Charles Foulkes, the GOC of the 2nd Division, drives through Falaise after the closing of the Falaise Gap in August 1944.
M.M. DEAN/LIBRARY AND ARCHIVES CANADA

7. Major-General Rod Keller, the commander of the 3rd Division, arrives with General Crerar for Dominion Day activities on July 1, 1944, in France.

8. The 5th Canadian Armoured Division's Bert Hoffmeister in his command tank.

9. The Canadian army had to be created from nothing—with mock anti-aircraft guns built of wood and Great War–vintage tanks.

10. Recruiting for the artillery in Montreal in the autumn of 1939. The uniforms were Great War vintage, but this militia artillery battery had a truck; most did not.
LIBRARY AND ARCHIVES CANADA

11. Soldiers of the South Saskatchewan Regiment departing Weyburn, Saskatchewan, in 1939.
CANADIAN WAR MUSEUM

12. Training in Britain was initially not very advanced. Here soldiers of the Westminster Regiment look determined for the camera in April 1941.
L.A. AUDRAIN/LIBRARY AND ARCHIVES CANADA

13. An anti-conscription rally in Montreal during the plebiscite in the spring of 1942. "No Conscription," the sign reads. "Youth want peace."
THE GAZETTE/LIBRARY AND ARCHIVES CANADA

14. The Dieppe raid of August 1942 was a disaster, and the Germans circulated photographs worldwide of surrendered Canadians.
CANADIAN WAR MUSEUM

15. This home-front gas station in Toronto did its bit, collecting salvage, preaching conservation, and calling for victory to avenge Hong Kong.
CITY OF TORONTO ARCHIVES

16. A soldier's gift pack with candy, hot chocolate powder, razor blades—and, especially, good socks.

17. The Second World War was a total war—and Canada mobilized all its citizens for the war effort with great success.

EVERY CANADIAN
MUST FIGHT

18. Reinforcements come ashore on D-Day at Bernières-sur-Mer. The bicycles would be quickly scrapped.

19. German POWs under guard on the beach on D-Day, with Canadian wounded behind them.
LIBRARY AND ARCHIVES CANADA

20. The fighting in the Normandy beachhead was immeasurably aided by naval gunfire just offshore. Here HMCS *Algonquin* fires a salvo at an enemy concentration.
HERBERT JESSOP NOTT/LIBRARY AND ARCHIVES CANADA

21. Canadian infantry from the 3rd Division rest at the side of the road near Caen while tanks go forward.
LT. H.G. AIKMAN/LIBRARY AND ARCHIVES CANADA/DND

22. A German soldier, wearing the ribbon of the Iron Cross, surrenders at Carpiquet on July 4, 1944.
M. M. Dean/library and Archives Canada

23. Soldiers from the Fusiliers Mont-Royal carry a wounded comrade to safety during the Falaise Gap battle.
Library and Archives Canada

24. A dead German sniper killed by Canadian troops at Falaise in August 1944.
Library and Archives Canada

812 men. Battalion HQ had 6 officers and 58 men, and a Headquarters Company handling signals, supply, and administration encompassed 5 officers and 94 men. There was a new support company—7 officers and 184 other ranks—with six 3-inch mortars, an anti-tank platoon with Universal Carriers to tow six 6-pounder anti-tank guns (now able to fire the new armour-piercing shells that could knock out a Tiger at up to a thousand yards), and a carrier platoon to provide mobility. Support Company's pioneer platoon was essentially the battalion's engineering subunit, able to build or destroy structures and do mine clearing. Then there were the four fighting companies. Each rifle company had 5 officers and 120 men at full strength, with a headquarters and three platoons. Platoons had a headquarters and three sections, and sections fought with a Bren gun group and a rifle team. The company HQ had its own 2-inch mortars and Projector, Infantry, Anti-Tank (PIAT) weapons, the much less effective British version of the American bazooka or the German *Panzerfaust*. It could destroy a panzer, but the PIAT crew had to get in very close to have a chance.

The soldiers who would do the fighting for the Scheldt estuary each carried a heavy load of at least sixty pounds. Every private soldier had a Lee-Enfield .303 rifle and one or sometimes two bandoliers holding 50 rounds. He usually carried four 30-round magazines for his platoon's three or four Bren light machine guns, at least two No. 36 or No. 69 hand grenades, and likely a two-pound bomb for the 2-inch mortar or a three-pound anti-tank projectile for the company PIAT. A full water bottle hung on his web belt along with his bayonet; many men also carried a knife. On his back was an entrenching tool, the absolutely indispensable spade or pick needed for digging in. Soldiers were to carry a gas mask and gas cape, but few did. Many had been provided with heavy, hot body armour; again, many soldiers found it too uncomfortable to wear. In the soldier's backpack, he carried a rubberized groundsheet, a few tins of food out of ration packs, hard tack for emergencies, cigarettes (everyone smoked) and a lighter, an extra pair of wool socks, a sewing kit (or a "housewife," as it was called), extra eyeglasses, shoe polish, shoelaces, a shaving kit and a toothbrush, a condom or two in case unexpected opportunities arose, aluminum mess tins, a mug, a folding knife, spoon, and fork, and usually mail from home, a deck of playing cards, and a few photographs. Bren gunners had to lug the light machine gun, weighing almost twenty-three pounds, and wireless operators carried the bulky radio with its telltale aerial sticking up high. Most non-commissioned officers carried Sten submachine guns; officers had binoculars, a compass, a Sten, and a pistol. Sometimes Tommy guns were used.

The normal uniform for a soldier in action or out was battledress, a two-piece khaki wool uniform, ordinarily worn done up at the neck, though officers often wore the neck open with a khaki shirt and tie. Senior officers frequently had their tailored battledress made of Barathea cloth. Tank crews, including armoured officers, usually wore coveralls in action. The soldiers' loose pants—with a pocket designed to hold a field dressing—were worn with gaiters and hobnailed boots. Pressed and tailored, with rank and unit badges, medal ribbons, and a blancoed web belt, the uniform could appear quite smart. Although the Canadian battledress was of much better quality than British patterns, it was hot in summer, not warm enough in cold weather, and rough against the skin at all times. In action, the uniforms absorbed dirt and mud, and they quickly became sodden in wet weather. They might be covered with a heavy wool greatcoat or a field parka in winter, occasionally even with white ski pants and jacket.

Soldiers and officers in the field, when out of action, wore a beret—khaki for most units and black for armoured regiments—and, when expecting fire, a steel helmet with a chinstrap and a camouflage net. The helmet provided no protection to the back of the neck, was very uncomfortable, especially while running, and, unlike the American helmet, could not be used as a cooking pot because its rubberized lining was not removable. New battledress and underwear might be issued by a Mobile Bath and Laundry Unit (MBLU) when soldiers were out of the line or if an MBLU managed to get forward far enough to let soldiers, always dirty and often infested with lice, get clean. Major Stewart Bull of the Essex Scottish recalled an MBLU getting to his unit's HQ "and there, oh blessed 'there,' was an overhead shower. We all got undressed and got a good shower and got cleaned off. We had lots of soap and we got a clean feeling. Some of us [got] some clean clothes—clean underwear and socks, and got them on … That was a bonus for the day."

There was no comfort in action, however. Unless they could find a barn or a house to occupy for a night, soldiers learned quickly that they had to dig a slit trench to have a chance of surviving enemy artillery fire. Living below ground was hot in the summer, cool at night, and freezing in winter. Uniforms grew grubby, faces and hands became filthy, and lice and fleas infested everyone. There was no privacy, no place to perform bodily functions away from one's mates. The soldiers lived together, fought together, and, far too often, died together.

So long as they lived, soldiers waited for mail from home or from their girlfriends in England, though sometimes the letters carried bad news. Family members died or were ill; too often wives and girlfriends sent a dreaded "Dear John" letter, bringing a relationship to an end. Some 640 women served in the Canadian Red Cross Corps overseas, and one, Lois MacDonald, worked as a hospital aide in Bruges, Belgium, in March 1945. "We offer advice to the lovelorn," she said of her patients, "sympathize and laugh, too, when their gal at home turns off and marries a Zombie." The wives at home, of course, also wondered what the war could do their husbands—death or wounds, unfaithfulness, personality changes. Rhoda Colville, the spouse of Lieutenant Alex Colville, a war artist, noted that "everything was changed suddenly" by the war and its long separations—"You couldn't count on going ahead and having the kind of life you'd been thinking about. You think what will this do to us, what will we do now." The soldiers overseas fretted anxiously about precisely those questions too, their answers coming only when they returned home, if they returned home.

But while overseas, they waited eagerly for the food parcels that provided a link to Canada and to those they loved. Private Geoff Turpin of the Royal Montreal Regiment, which provided the defence battalion for First Canadian Army's sprawling headquarters, wrote his family on July 25 that "I got a most welcome parcel a few days ago which is the first mail I got here. The mail has been absolutely lousy. I've just got 3 letters from Kay written between the 1st & 4th of July. Your parcel was most appreciated, as you can imagine. It was the composite one from Nan, including chocolate from Cunninghams, chocolate bars from Nan's canteen & life savers from an ex-RMR. McBride (my hole mate) & I melt the chocolate & dip army biscuits in the result. Chocolate biscuits! It also makes good hot chocolate." He added that "our hole now includes a shower, a stove and a wash basin all scrounged or made out of biscuit tins. A certain amount of dexterity with a pocket knife & some biscuit tins, and you can make almost anything." But he still needed some things from home: "Cigarettes are the problem at the moment, because we can only buy 60 English ones a week. Very cheap at 20 francs for 60. But I still love my Winchesters. Also reading material, second hand magazines such as the New Yorker, Cosmopolitan, Red Book, American, Colliers, can all be sent as a parcel, I believe. I don't mean subscriptions, but a monthly round-up of old magazines would always be appreciated by anyone over here. Letters, too, are even more important here than in England, if that's possible."

Jewish soldiers looked eagerly for parcels containing wurst (salami), or so both Eddie Goodman in the Fort Garry Horse and Barney Danson in the Queen's Own Rifles recollected. Another soldier, Sergeant Harry Clark, serving at First Canadian Army Headquarters, thanked his parents for a parcel he had received: "Very glad to receive your most welcome parcel of 3 July containing all those good things which make service life more worthwhile. The socks and towel will come in very handy, as well as all the candy and gum enclosed. The oranges arrived in excellent condition and are very tasty—thanks a million." That oranges, imported to Canada from the United States, could be mailed from London, Ontario, and be received in good condition in France suggested that the Canadian Postal Corps, the army's mailmen, did a good job.

Their parcels from home aside, the men ordinarily received a diet heavy on bread, potatoes, beans, and meat that aimed to provide at least 3,000 calories each day. Whenever it was possible, depending on the situation at the front, unit cooks sent hot meals forward or organized a chow line if they were in reserve. This was never fine dining—nothing slopped into a mess tin with dessert on top of meat could be—but it was hot and filling. Essentially, soldiers "ate when they could." A sergeant in the Cameron Highlanders remembered grabbing a bully beef sandwich from the cook. "If you had an opportunity to have a hot meal, you did … But you didn't stop and say 'This is dinner time' and 'Oh wait it's five o'clock, it's time to eat for supper.' You didn't eat for two days [and] you didn't eat properly … But to sit down … have a leisurely meal, no, you never did," he went on. "You could be having breakfast when all of a sudden hell would break loose and Jerry shells you, so that was the end of your breakfast."

When rations could not get forward, the troops ate whenever they had the chance from composite rations, the dreaded compo pack. This British-produced ration for fourteen men for twenty-four hours came in a wooden crate. It included toilet paper—a paltry six squares per man—seven cigarettes for each soldier (often made in India from what seemed to be factory sweepings), matches, and soap tablets, guaranteed to generate no suds. There was tea—but no coffee— sugar, and milk powder, all mixed together. Very useful was the tin of canned heat that could be used to warm tinned goods. While the menus varied, breakfast might be hardtack biscuits and sausage that could be eaten cold or heated in the tin for an hour or fried with the margarine that was provided. Soldiers considered the margarine to be little more than canned yellow wax, but this was more appealing than the meat and vegetables, called by one soldier "unidentified scraps of fat and gristle mushed up with equally unidentifiable vegetables." There would be cheese, canned and processed; jam that all believed to be made from turnips rather than the strawberries proclaimed on the label; hard candies; and sometimes chocolate. The only truly edible food in the compo ration, soldiers thought, was the dessert (or pudding), especially the treacle variety. "You dine on that for a couple of weeks," Major Bull remembered of compo rations, "and it gets pretty monotonous. But we managed and we kept alive."

George Blackburn, an artillery Forward Observation Officer (FOO), recalled that he and his comrades were desperate for sweets one night and began opening parcels sent from Canada for soldiers already dead. They found candy in one, along with a mother's note urging her boy to keep dry. As they read it, the son's freshly killed body was lying just outside the door in the rain, face up.

Of course, soldiers liberated what food they could from civilian homes and farms. One officer wrote home from German soil that he had seen a dispatch rider with a dozen chickens fastened to the back of his motorcycle and "two soldiers pushing & pulling a pig & another sharpening a knife on a grindstone. Don't blame them a bit either. Have no compunction about men taking anything & am lacking in sympathy for the people. They have asked for everything they are getting."

Officers could eat well out of action, though at the front they tended to eat what their men received. The North Shores' Hal MacDonald wrote on July 22, 1944, that his "batman-gunner is frying meat patties—bully beef, onions, potatoes, and crumbled hard tack. They look and smell very good." A unit's officers' mess, if well back of the front, had better food, paid for by its members' "extra messing" funds, and there might even be officers' mess dinners with, depending on the unit, silver on the table. Harry Crerar's "A" Mess in Normandy and after—the mess where the GOC-in-C and his key staff ate—always had silver and tablecloths, and officers could get a drink or two before and after meals. Toward the end of the war, Crerar's mess frequently had a string quartet playing softly at dinnertime. Some officers believed this to be completely inappropriate, but no one said anything. The formality of the mess could be stifling, the tone set by the rather aloof Harry Crerar; aides-de-camp, ordinarily very junior officers, usually suffered in silence.

Then there was water. In cities and towns, the water supply often had been destroyed, and there was a rational fear that the enemy might have poisoned reservoirs. Purification tablets were essential, though they left a foul taste. In the field, rivers and streams too often were full of the dead, both human and animal. More purification tablets were needed. The only safe supply of potable water was brought forward by the Royal Canadian Army Service Corps in water trucks, though this invariably tasted of the chlorine with which it had been laced to make it safe to drink. Soldiers, of course, always looked for beer, wine, and liquor, "liberating" alcohol from enemy caches or from farms and homes. This they drank straight from the bottle, passing it around to their mates. A few delicate souls could not bring themselves to swig from the bottle, and at least one soldier remembered that he carefully tucked a heavy glass tumbler into his pack, wrapping it in his extra socks, so he could drink with some propriety.

Naturally, soldiers also "scrounged" whatever they could—liberating jeeps from other units, stealing valuables from homes, and relieving enemy prisoners of their Zeiss binoculars, Luger pistols, medals, watches, money, and the loot they in turn had taken from the French, Belgians, and Dutch. Scrounging from others was tolerable and almost praiseworthy; stealing from comrades, however, was a detestable crime. Senior officers tried to control looting or dealing on the black market—cigarettes, especially Canadian or American cigarettes, which were vastly superior to British wartime brands, were a highly valuable commodity in France, Belgium, Holland, and later Germany—but it could not be stopped or even contained. When a few cigarettes could be traded for a good-quality camera or sex, controls were impossible to enforce.

Officer selection standards varied. In 1940, the defence minister told Parliament that different units had different standards—not a satisfactory situation—and he said that "for the future every candidate for a commission in the Canadian Army must first pass through the ranks." In all, of the 43,244 granted commissions during the war, only 20,723 did so.

Most of those commissioned were lieutenants who lived and died with their platoons in and out of action, and who had a short lifespan. If a battalion had heavy casualties, it would receive brand-new replacement officers who knew none of their men and who lived in hope that their sergeant and a section commander or two could help ease them into their job. Lieutenant William Smith, sent forward in late November 1944 as a reinforcement officer for the Calgary Highlanders, said, "When I went up to join the Highlanders I was accompanied by two other 'new' lieutenants, also replacing casualties … Their names were Brown, and Doakes, as I remember. We were along the southern edge of what became known as The 'Nijmegen Salient' which the Allies established as a fall-back from the Arnhem failure. There in early December, outside Groesbeek, on the edge of the Reichswald Forest, I was wounded on patrol. Brown was killed, shot in the kidneys by a sniper, and Doakes died of Diphtheria in a hospital somewhere in Holland."

Lieutenant Walter Keith of the Regina Rifles wrote an account of his time as a new platoon commander, beginning when he joined the regiment in March 1945. His company commander, the second-in-command, and his platoon sergeant were experienced, but most of his men had served only a few months with the regiment; he himself had been in the Royal Canadian Corps of Signals when he volunteered for remustering as an infantry officer. The men of his platoon were "mostly fairly small, very young, very quiet and most unwarriorlike," he said. But what impressed Keith was how well his platoon worked: "I now realize that I never once had to cajole or threaten or ever encourage them to do the job they were given, they automatically did it. The section commanders unhesitatingly led their small group of riflemen where they were told to go and the section followed them, stupid though the order may have seemed to be." These replacements, hardly grizzled veterans of the fighting since D-Day, fought well. If they were lucky, as Keith was, they survived.

Happily, medical care for wounded Canadians was superb. Ted Sills, another very young lieutenant in the artillery, who had graduated from the Royal Military College in 1942, wrote home that he was wounded in the knee in a mortar attack while acting as a Forward Observation Officer, directing his regiment's 25-pounder fire on the Scheldt: "I started down the lines of communication of the medical services … First, to the Regimental Aid Post of the Armoured Regiment to which I was attached, where the Medical Officer dressed the wound." Then he went to his own artillery regiment "where our own M.O. had a look at the leg and thought there might be shrapnel in it. So he re-dressed it with sulphanilimyde [sic] and gave me four pills and filled out more papers." Then Sills was taken by ambulance to a casualty clearing station (though he might have been taken to a field surgical unit), "where I was given food." He was then shipped to a general hospital, where "I was given a bed with sheets, and hot water for a bath—(you see, the five of us in the tank crew had had to sleep in the tank every night ... and we never had our clothes off for two weeks ...)." So, he added, "the whole thing seemed like heaven ... Every three hours I had a needle of penicillin. Then, this morning, I was X-rayed and visited by a major doctor—then ... to the operating room." Sills ended by telling his mother, "I am feeling fine and having a great rest."

No soldier wanted the folks at home to worry, and the hearty cheerfulness of Sills's letter obviously masked a good deal of pain and fear. But it was clear that with sulfa drugs, penicillin, X-rays, and plasma and blood transfusions, if and when needed, the odds for the wounded had greatly improved, giving them a far better chance of recovery than had been the case in 1914–18. In the Great War, 114 of every thousand men wounded died after initial treatment. In the Second World War, that figure dropped to 66 of each thousand. (By the time of the Korean War, 1950–53, deaths after surgery had fallen to 34 per thousand.) Abdominal wounds, very susceptible to infection, remained the most lethal.

The casualties treated were huge in number. The No. 12 Canadian General Hospital at Bruges had 1,200 beds, all of which were occupied by the end of October. The Royal Canadian Army Medical Corps' surgeons there, assisted by nursing sisters, completed 1,860 operations, one of them on Lieutenant Sills. In the 3rd Canadian Division, casualties numbered more than 2,000 wounded, with 400 more ill. One field surgeon wrote, horrified, about "trucks piled high with the dead" whom he had failed to save.

One nursing sister, Jean Ellis, wrote frankly about "slackers," those soldiers who had shot themselves to escape the front. "They were under guard" at the hospital, "but were considered innocent until proved guilty … If convicted, the boys got two years at hard labour, but some were acquitted. If acquitted, they were seldom sent back to the front, and instead were given jobs behind the lines." She and other nurses, she said, believed "these boys should not be judged harshly. Some men are cut out to be soldiers, others are not." But Ellis had no such sympathy for soldiers with venereal disease: "In a great many cases they had acquired infection deliberately in order to get out of action for a while." Preventive measures were available to every serviceman, but "many men admitted they had intentionally 'got a dose' and would say, 'You haven't seen the last of us, girls. We'll be back.' Sure enough they would be back, two and three times."

Then there were the men whose nerves had broken. In the 3rd Division, 421 battle exhaustion cases reached treatment centres during the Scheldt fighting; in the 2nd Division, up to 200. Men new to the front sometimes collapsed quickly, shocked by the noise and chaos of battle; the veterans of fighting frequently reached their limit, their reserve of courage used up, their breaking point reached. The Army psychiatrist in the 3rd Division, Major Robert Gregory, concluded that the experienced soldiers cracked because "for months they have had only the type of sleep one gets when eternally on guard. The gradually settling in winter weather without a roof over one's head plays a part; more important is the inability for the subject to see anything except misery and danger in the future … Most important of all, I think," the psychiatrist wrote, "he has had a feeling, ridiculous as it may be, that he will never actually die,

[but] he now begins to feel he is a marked man, that there is a bullet with his name on it."

The key to carrying on was morale strong enough to overcome the hopeless feeling that the war was going to run on until every man was killed. Worse yet, when men sent for treatment for battle exhaustion were returned to their unit, sometimes their fear, if it had not been dealt with, could infect others. One company commander wrote unsympathetically that his company had two such men brought back to the front lines: "Had those two nervous wrecks not been returned to us as reinforcements the morale of the company would never [have] been affected." But they were, and it was. "I found men crying," the officer wrote, "others vomiting. All felt dejected. All this was caused by [the] two men."

The soldiers, the vast majority of them, somehow kept going, not wanting to let down their friends and fearing the stigma of being called "yellow." New Brunswicker James R. Joyce recalled that "I would try to shoot [the Germans] if I could. That was what battle was all about. I had some reservations about shooting them, I didn't like to kill anybody … I didn't like the idea of having to kill a human being." But he did it. Joyce said that he especially feared house clearing: "I am not ashamed to say I was scared to death every time I did it. But, if I didn't do it I would have been branded a coward and that was something that nobody wanted … so I forced myself to go. That's why we were soldiers in the field of battle," he went on, "we could force ourselves to go and no matter how danger-ous it was we would go anyway, and trust in God that he would take care of us." Sometimes God did.

More often it was their section and platoon mates who took care of them. Who else would? They talked of women and sex frequently, they blasphemed and swore continuously, and they had their own language that was all but incomprehensible to civilians. They had trained at "Aldershit" in England, they hated the bloody Zombies, and they were fed up with painting blanco on their web belts. The Eyties had sometimes been hospitable with vino but the bloody Jerries weren't, and the Canadian Provost Corps' meatheads stopped their having a good time with local dames. The only needs they had were compo rations, ammo, and Sweet Caps—was that loud and clear?—and they all longed to go back to civvy street, if only they could last that long.

• • •

The task facing the soldiers on the Scheldt was far from easy. The weather in October 1944 was wet and cold; it would be worse still in November, the terrain indescribably muddy. The polders were below sea level, and the only way forward was atop the dikes. Company Sergeant Major Charlie Martin of the Queen's Own Rifles described the method of advance: "A section of men below the dike would slog along waist deep in water, watching their lead man near the top of the dike. He [was] the bait, the point man, as they sought to find the enemy. Sometimes he made it safely," Martin said, "sometimes he took a wound, often a bad one, and sometimes he was killed." The canals too were formidable obstacles, and even when troops made it across, their slit trenches all too often filled with water as soon as they were dug. The conditions were utterly miserable, the fighting bitter. "We were wet, always wet, always cold," one soldier recalled, shuddering still at the horror of the fighting in dreadful conditions.

Operation Switchback, the main task of which was the clearing of the Breskens Pocket, much of it the far western portion of the Netherlands, fell to Major-General Dan Spry's 3rd Canadian Infantry Division. The 11,000 men of the Wehrmacht's heavily armed 64th Infantry Division—a very good fighting formation with well-trained troops—and other units provided the opposition, hunkered down behind the Leopold Canal. Spry's plan called for heavy artillery support from over 325 guns, for his 7th Brigade to get across the canal, and for his 8th Brigade to exploit the opening to move north and west toward the towns of Breskens and Knocke. Meanwhile, the 9th Brigade would launch the first amphibious assault of the war using Buffalos and Terrapins—tracked water-going troop carriers that could carry thirty soldiers and a field gun—against the Pocket's northern shore. Spry sent his first attack across the canal on October 6, using the fire from twenty-seven Wasp flamethrowers, each carried on a Universal Carrier and loaded with eighty gallons of jellied fuel, to clear the way. The Wasps were positioned partway up the slope of the canal bank, then the searing flame was thrown onto the opposite bank and beyond it, where the enemy trenches were sited. This worked, temporarily frightening the enemy silly—the German troops feared the Canadian flamethrowers more than anything else, their general later told interrogators—and two battalions established bridgeheads, but, because of the mud and the high water table, the troops could not dig in.

The Germans, as ever, were resilient and well provided with artillery and mortars, counterattacking repeatedly; on one such attack they overran a company of the Canadian Scottish. But artillery concentrations and tactical air power provided by 84 Group, Second Tactical Air Force, of the RAF—the fighter bombers that had worked and continued to work closely with First Canadian Army—prevented the Germans from moving in daylight. The HQ of 84 Group was located side by side with First Canadian Army's HQ, providing every opportunity for joint planning and close cooperation. Nonetheless, it took a week before the Leopold Canal could be bridged so that tanks could cross. The brutal fighting lasted three more days before the enemy began to pull back. One prisoner of war told his interrogator from the Stormont, Dundas and Glengarry Regiment that the Typhoons had destroyed his unit's field kitchen. This hurt morale because all they could get was "cold food as a steady diet." Other Germans, as at Fort Frederik Hendrik on the Scheldt near Breskens, surrendered when threatened with heavy air attack. But this prisoner and such accounts were untypical: most of the Germans fought hard, retreating only when their position was hopeless and when ordered to do so.

Led by Brigadier John Rockingham, the 9th Brigade's water crossing had to cover some twenty miles before the assault began on beaches east of the town of Hoofdplaat, a site selected thanks to the reconnaissance by a Dutch Resistance fighter who had noticed a gap in the defences there. The troops got ashore, greatly relieved to be out of their "amphibs," which moved very low in the water and seemed vulnerable to everything that might hit them. Soon their bridgehead was more than a mile deep. Under a massive smokescreen, reinforcements arrived in the Buffalo LVTs operated by a British division, the 79th Armoured, that specialized in "funnies"—all the new armoured equipment designed for specific tasks ranging from mine clearing to bridge building. Then came the brigade's supplies of food and ammunition, brought over the beaches by 3rd Division's Royal Canadian Army Service Corps units. Artillery fire from a Medium Regiment soon smashed into the German positions, and the Wasps fired two squirts of flame. Surprised at the assault, the enemy surrendered in large numbers at once, and the German commander in the Pocket had to rush reserves to counter the 9th Brigade.

That gave General Spry the opportunity he was waiting for, and he ordered the 8th Brigade to move farther east and fight its way south. The conditions on the ground were dreadful, and the troops struggled to move forward. After one hard fight, the Régiment de la Chaudière tackled a water obstacle by driving a Bren gun carrier into a canal and then piling logs and dirt atop it. The resulting bridge was strong enough to let tanks cross. But the Germans resisted fiercely everywhere, even cutting down trees and laying them out in a herringbone pattern that soldiers had to remove by sawing the trees—while enemy mortars fired at them. "A fiendishly clever piece of work," the 8th Brigade commander said. Worse still, the Germans booby-trapped the bodies of their own dead, and the Canadians, burned once too often, thereafter left their enemies to bloat and rot.

The Canadian advance squeezed the Germans into an ever-shrinking perimeter. By October 19, the enemy territory consisted mainly of the town of Oostburg, which fell after being pounded by artillery and Typhoon attacks—and a fixed bayonet assault by a platoon of the Queen's Own Rifles. Knocke soon was taken, and the Breskens Pocket had been liberated, at a cost of 2,077 Canadian casualties.

The North Nova Scotia Highlanders had been in the final attack, and Captain Winfield, a company commander, took the surrender of the German divisional staff in a large bunker: "A dozen colonels and majors ... jumped to salute and offered Winfield a chair." After assurances that prisoners would be properly treated, "the General then indicated he wanted to surrender with all his staff … 100 in all." The officers were marched off by a corporal and two men, and the general was driven to Brigade HQ.

Most soldiers grew inured to the horrors of the front. Captain Hal MacDonald of the North Shore (New Brunswick) Regiment wrote his wife on October 24, "My Gawd we see terrific sights and yet we're so hardened to them—Horses tangled in wire & starving, animals badly wounded & necessitating shooting. Dead Huns in the ditches, groups of once well-kept farms now a mass of burnt-out rubble. Yes," he added somberly, "what we're fighting for is always clear in our minds."

Was it? The high-toned Allied aims mattered to some, but democracy and freedom were abstract ideas to most soldiers, who had lived through the deprivation of the Great Depression in Canada and the horrors of the front lines in France and Belgium. What they cared for most were their comrades, the men in their platoon, the men they lived and fought with and for. To let down their mates was the unforgivable sin, and men would kill to save their friends. They would die for them too.

The 2nd Canadian Division, meanwhile, was waging its own war for the Beveland peninsula. Since September 17 units of the division had been based in Antwerp, positioned along the Albert Canal, whose north bank was still held by the enemy because the British division that liberated the city had failed to cross the canal when the opposition was slight. The division remained in place for seventeen days, fighting a bizarre "streetcar war" that saw Canadians and Germans both commuting to the front on the Antwerp tram system, which continued to function. Out of the line, soldiers could take advantage of Antwerp's nightlife, which also continued to function, and "battle stained, unshaven troops found themselves being served by waiters in tails." October would prove to be much deadlier, as supplies for Montgomery's 21st Army Group, of which First Canadian Army formed a part, had begun to run short.

The divisional task was to get to the Beveland isthmus, cross it, clear South and North Beveland, and fight on to Walcheren. None of these phases was simple. The three brigades jumped off on October 2, 4th Brigade crossing the Albert Canal, clearing Antwerp's northern suburbs, and then heading north. The suburb of Merxem was held by an enemy "stomach battalion" made up of ill and injured soldiers, and the Essex Scottish, tasked with rooting them out, found the going easy. The Essex War Diary noted that the enemy soldiers, "having built the fortifications around Antwerp, were abandoned by the Nazis and told to defend what they had made. They were a uniformly miserable type," the diarist continued, "and were only too glad to give in." The 5th and 6th brigades, operating farther east, formed a flanking pincer. The Essex had a tougher time at Putte, a town straddling the Belgian–Dutch border. There they ran into determined defenders dug in along the main road with a series of machine-gun nests. B Company of the Essex took the crossroads in Putte, only to be driven out by a German counterattack. The town was not finally taken until the evening, but the company had by then lost some two-thirds of its 125 men, including 12 killed in action. The division made good progress, however, and was nearing Woensdrecht, the main town at the base of the isthmus, by October 6.

The German position was now threatened, and the enemy fought bitterly to stop further advances by deploying Battle Group Chill, a first-rate 2,500-man parachute regiment with many 88mm guns, commanded by Lieutenant-General Kurt Chill. For three weeks, one battalion after another tried to move forward over the wet ground, the Canadian positions under almost constant observation from a ridge on the edge of Woensdrecht. The Royal Regiment, the Rileys, the Calgary Highlanders, and the Black Watch either moved along the top of the dikes, under continuous fire, or struggled through waist-deep water. From October 6 to 24, the Canadians tried to cut the isthmus. On the thirteenth—Black Friday for the Black Watch—the Montreal unit launched a daylight attack north of Woensdrecht to capture a dike embankment that swung toward the South Beveland peninsula. Under cover of the guns of three regiments of artillery, as well as smoke, flame-throwers, anti-tank guns, and air support, the infantry moved forward in a mad daylight attack over 1,200 yards of sodden beet fields, came close to their objective, and then were destroyed by the dug-in German paratroopers. The Montrealers lost 145 men, including all the company commanders; one company had only 4 men left standing out of the 90 who had attacked. "The battalion seems to have horrible shows periodically," one officer wrote from a hospital bed, "and this was one of them." Black Friday indeed. Such attacks were fruitless.

On October 16, Field Marshal Montgomery finally concluded that Market Garden—the attempt to take the Rhine bridges and the Ruhr—had failed. Clearing the Scheldt now was his top priority. The same night, the Royal Hamilton Light Infantry, commanded by Lieutenant-Colonel Denis Whitaker, a Dieppe veteran who had been wounded in Normandy and returned to command the Rileys, tried its hand at cutting the isthmus once more with a heavily supported night attack. This made good progress until the inevitable enemy counterattack overran one company.

The company commander, Major Joe Pigott, called for artillery to shell his own position, and within moments the first of 4,000 shells all but wiped out the attacking Germans. "The fire caught the enemy in the open whereas our men were deep in slit trenches having been warned," the unit reported. "Our troops cheered; the slaughter was terrific." The regiment, however, had only 6 officers and 157 men after the battle, not including one company commander who had run away. "Unfortunately," Whitaker wrote later, "when men see their own leaders turn away from battle, it becomes a very natural choice that they should follow ... I had to watch this horrible sight, those wretched men running panic-stricken down the hill." Whitaker said he stopped the flight at gunpoint. Not until October 24 was the isthmus finally cut by the 5th and 6th brigades, and, assisted by a seaborne assault by British soldiers across the West Scheldt, Beveland finally was cleared.

The Scheldt battle was now entering its final phase. The 4th Canadian Armoured Division moved north of Antwerp toward the Dutch city of Bergen op Zoom, and the Germans abandoned part of the city. Civilians told the advancing Canadians from the South Alberta Regiment and the Lincoln and Welland Regiment that the city had been abandoned. The units' COs fretted that the reports might be incorrect, but the South Albertas' lieutenant-colonel, Gordon "Swotty" Wotherspoon, said to his Links and Winks counterpart, "Hell, Bill, let's take the damned place." They did, on October 27, but the enemy held on to the northern suburbs and had to be driven out, a task not completed for two days.

Meanwhile, Simonds had ordered a seaborne assault by British Commandos on Walcheren to take advantage of the flooding the RAF's bombers had caused. But to divert attention away from the landing thirty-six hours hence, the 2nd Division had to attack from Beveland to Walcheren over a 1,300-yard-long, 50-yard-wide causeway protected on both sides by a sea of mud. The Germans had the causeway covered by artillery, mortars, and machine guns, and they knew the Canadians were coming. The Black Watch, its ranks filled up with reinforcements since Black Friday, were the first Canadians to try to get onto Walcheren, on October 31. The regiment failed, and the CO wrote in the unit War Diary that "'battle morale' is definitely not good, due to the fact that inadequately trained men are, of necessity, being sent into action ignorant of any idea of their own strength, and ... overwhelmingly convinced of the enemy's." The Calgary Highlanders tried that night and also failed, suffering 64 casualties; they tried again on November 1 behind the barrage fired by two regiments of artillery on a 750-yard frontage. The Highlanders took their bridgehead and then suffered through very heavy counterattacks, including the enemy's employment of flamethrowers. The bridgehead contracted, and it was then the Régiment de Maisonneuve's turn in the meat grinder.

Understrength like all the French Canadian battalions because of a shortage of francophone reinforcements, the Maisies went into the line on the night of November 1–2, but only one company made it to the front, the others having been disrupted by a British artillery regiment's errant friendly fire. That company also came under friendly artillery fire and a German mortar attack, but amazingly made it to the end of the causeway. Lieutenant Charly Forbes's platoon had five men left of the twenty-one who had started out twelve hours earlier. They fired on a withdrawing German company, watched as a panzer was driven off by a

Typhoon attack, and finally withdrew under machine-gun fire, turning the struggle over to Scottish soldiers. Forbes had been wounded himself, and he carried one of his wounded men out of the bridgehead. He wrote that when the "weary, muddy" survivors came out of the fighting, "The men were indescribably dirty. They were bearded, cold as it is only possible to be in Holland in November, and wet from living in water-filled holes in the ground for 24 hours of the day. Their eyes were red-rimmed from lack of sleep, and they were exhausted." The shortage of trained reinforcements had begun to affect every unit in the 2nd and 3rd divisions.

The GOC of the 52nd British Division, a tough, highly trained formation new to battle, quite sensibly refused to put his men into attacks on the causeway; instead, his reconnaissance parties found a way onto Walcheren over the mud flats on November 2, outflanking the German positions. The Scots in the division were initially discomfited at working with the Canucks; some Scottish officers complained that "no one in Scotland would ask a pig to lie in the houses [recently vacated by Canadians] on the south side of the canal." They would learn to get along.

The seaborne assault on Walcheren was also making progress, the first landing by British Commandos having taken place on November 1. The island had been almost wholly swallowed by the sea, with the few acres of remaining land under heavy attack by naval gunfire, artillery, and air power. German guns inflicted casualties among the soldiers and heavy losses on the Royal Navy ships that carried in and supported the Commandos, but the island was soon cleared of the enemy. The Walcheren battle finally ended the efforts to clear the Scheldt. The real losers were the Dutch residents of Zeeland, whose memory of their liberation remains clouded by the disasters that fell upon them. It would take years of hard work to restore the farmland that had been ruined by seawater.

The Scheldt fighting ended on November 2 for the Canadians. Astonishingly, the entire 3rd Division received an invitation from the burgomaster of Ghent to spend almost a week there as guests of its liberated citizens. Everything that could be was provided; the soldiers were treated royally and, according to reports, behaved themselves. The 2nd Canadian Division took its respite in the fleshpots of Antwerp and Brussels.

At last, minesweepers could come in to get rid of the mines in the estuary, a job that took another three weeks. The first ship to reach Antwerp, the Canadian freighter *Fort Cataraqui*, arrived on November 28. Incredibly, no one in the Allied high command had thought to invite a representative from First Canadian Army to the ceremony that reopened the port to shipping.

The operations to clear the Scheldt were certainly First Canadian Army's greatest contribution to the Allied victory over Nazism. "In unimaginably foul conditions," Douglas Delaney wrote, "with too many tasks for the troops available, with shortages of ammunition and supplies, and with an enemy that was both fully cognizant of what the port of Antwerp meant to the Allied war effort and willing to fight for it, the First Canadian Army under Simonds did the near-impossible." Jack English stated that "Simonds distinguished himself" as Army commander in the Scheldt fighting. In his "innovative use of smoke screening, in his flooding of the island of Walcheren, and in his first use of amphibians in Europe, it was his finest hour." Even Montgomery—perhaps because Simonds had been in command, not Harry Crerar—told soldiers from the 2nd Division at an investiture that the Scheldt battle was the finest operation of the war, and Prime Minister Winston Churchill said to his House of Commons that the battle had seen "marvellous gallantry and great feats of arms." The Scheldt battle had shown Canadian soldiers at their best, overcoming the terrible conditions on the ground and the enemy's strong resistance with courage and skill. The long, hard-pounding battle of the Scheldt had cost 6,367 Canadian killed and wounded and almost as many British casualties. More than 41,000 Germans became POWs; their dead were uncounted.

• • •

The heavy Canadian casualties in France and on the Scheldt (not to mention those suffered in the severe fighting in Italy in late summer, when I Canadian Corps breached the Gothic Line) made the infantry reinforcements crisis acute. In 1956, General E.L.M. Burns, who in late 1944 was relieved of his command of I Canadian Corps in Italy, published a book called *Manpower in the Canadian Army*. His numerical analysis put the crisis of November 1944 into stark relief: that month "there were 465,750 men and women in the Canadian Army. Of these 59,699 were NRMA [home defence conscripts] and 16,178 were nurses ... leaving 389,873 soldiers and officers available for 'general service' [that is, volunteers who had enlisted for service anywhere]. Of that number, some 254,242 were in North-West Europe, Italy and the United Kingdom," Burns continued. "There were some 158,000 in the field formations; that is, divisions and troops of the 1st Canadian Army and the 1st and 2nd Canadian Corps, about 90,000 more in the base and lines of communications units in Italy and North-West Europe, and in the United Kingdom in reinforcement holding units and various other establishment." Maintaining a supply line to Italy and one to the United Kingdom and the Continent had absorbed many men. Burns went on: "The establishment strength of the [five] Canadian divisions was about 85,000 and that of the infantry battalions for which, as it was thought, reinforcements could not be provided was about 37,817. Those figures mean that with some 390,000 'general service' (GS) men on its strength, the Army could not find the bodies to reinforce the 38,000 infantry."

There was the heart of the difficulty, the nub of the conscription crisis of 1944. Lieutenant-General Kenneth Stuart, the Chief of Staff at Canadian Military Headquarters in London, had since August been aware of the infantry shortages, deficiencies he then believed could be resolved by transferring men from other trades to infantry and giving them some weeks of training. (As Farley Mowat described it, the Army was "forced to practice self-cannibalism in order to keep the fighting units in existence.") On October 18, Stuart wrote a long memorandum for Defence Minister Ralston in which he laid out the situation as it existed in the midst of the Scheldt battles. "Until about two months ago, I was satisfied with the general reinforcement position," he said, offering three main reasons for his optimism: "the general strategic situation; our overall reinforcement holdings and my expectation, based on 21 Army Group forecast of activity, that casualties for balance of 1944 would be intense and normal in alternative months." Every army plans for casualties and readies reinforcements to meet the needs of the front. British and Canadian planning assumed that intense or heavy fighting would not be continuous and that months of "normal" fighting would come more or less regularly, allowing reinforcements to replace casualties. "In early August every indication pointed to an early collapse of Germany ... before December 1944," Stuart wrote. But that no longer seemed likely. "Intelligent planning demands, therefore, that we must prepare for the prolongation of the war against Germany into 1945."

What did this all mean? There would be a shortage of infantry reinforcements of 2,000, Stuart said. But nothing was certain "because of what actually happened in the last two months. Our casualties in infantry have been greater than was anticipated." Infantry had absorbed three-quarters of all casualties, not the 55 percent forecasted, and the British scale of intense and normal casualties alternating monthly had turned out to be wrong. Instead, General Stuart said, our casualties "have been at an intense rate continuously."

Where, then, given the expectation that severe fighting was going to continue into 1945, could the needed reinforcements be found? "The only solution that I can see," Stuart said, "is to find an additional 15,000 infantry to add to our reinforcement pool on or before 31 Dec 44, and to ask that replacements sent monthly from Canada in 1945 shall be increased to 5300, of which 4300 should be infantry ... I recommend, therefore, if the numbers required cannot be found from General Service personnel in Canada, that the terms of service of N.R.M.A. personnel be extended to include service overseas in any theatre."

The NRMA soldiers—the "Zombies," in popular parlance—were by now well trained, almost all 60,000 of them. The first home defence conscripts had been enrolled in the summer of 1940, and many of these men had decided to volunteer for overseas service after their training. But there was a hard core who simply did not want to fight overseas.

They had manned divisions in British Columbia aimed at protecting the Pacific coast against a Japanese attack, and a brigade largely made up of NRMA soldiers had joined with American troops in an invasion of Kiska in the Aleutian Islands in 1943. The Japanese had withdrawn secretly before the troops landed, but the Canadian conscripts had been prepared to fight. By 1944, however, efforts to persuade Zombies to "convert" to General Service had been under way for years, and the home defence men could no longer be reached by appeals to their patriotism or the requirement to destroy Hitler and the Nazis. The NRMA men were a microcosm of the country—many English-speaking, many of "ethnic" origins, and many francophones—united only by their intention to remain in Canada or to force the government to order them to go overseas. Very few were cowards, in all likelihood, but the Zombies as a group had no desire to volunteer to fight. The politicians had created the situation in which they found themselves, and the government would have to force the Zombies to go overseas—if the prime minister and his Cabinet could summon up the political courage to do so.

Mackenzie King had to deal with this military and political situation, and his actions in late October and November 1944 have been the subject of debate for many historians. After hearing Colonel Ralston give his account of the overseas reinforcement situation when he returned from Europe in late October, King and his ministers grappled with the numbers of men available and not available for infantry service. Ralston grew progressively more adamant about the need to use the NRMA men. On October 31, Mackenzie King stunned the Cabinet by brutally firing him. The new defence minister was to be General Andrew McNaughton, the General Officer Commanding-in-Chief of First Canadian Army until late 1943, and the commander Ralston had sacked. As King recorded in his diary, "I said I believed he could get the reinforcements that were necessary … The people of Canada would say that McNaughton was the right man for the task."

McNaughton tried, but he was jeered when he gave speeches to Canadian Legion audiences calling for NRMA men to volunteer for overseas service, and his repeated efforts to persuade Zombies to convert—the term really did have almost a religious connotation by late 1944—to General Service fell flat. Only a trickle of soldiers came forward. Some senior officers began talking to the press about the hopeless task of persuasion of the intractable, and one officer, Major Harry Robinson, serving in Prince Rupert, BC, wrote privately that the NRMA men were not "no-good cowards. Eighty percent of them will go, & go willingly, when the Gov't tells them to." The real issue, he wrote, "is that the Gov't is the no-good collection of cowards in asking men to lay their lives on the line when it is not even prepared to lay its political future there" for fear of alienating Quebec voters. Others shared this view. A young officer, Lieutenant Joe Potts, went overseas in early 1945 with the first NRMA drafts and thought they were good soldiers. So did his father, a major-general in command of Military District No. 2 in Toronto, who sympathized with them in their refusal to make up the government's mind for them. The general attended one parade where an officer with the Victoria Cross asked why the men would not volunteer; an NRMA private stepped forward and said, "Why should we make up the government's mind?"

Wherever the blame should have been placed, on November 20 a shaken McNaughton reported to the Cabinet that he had been unable to find the necessary men. Conscriptionist ministers seemed on the verge of resigning, and King himself had indicated that he would quit rather than force the NRMA men to serve overseas. The Quebec Cabinet ministers and some others said they would go if King did. The government faced collapse because of a shortage of a few thousand of infanteers in the final stages of a great war in which Canadians had played a splendid part.

The way out of this morass came two days later, when McNaughton called King with news that, he said, had hit him like a blow in the stomach. "The Headquarters Staff here [in Ottawa] had all advised him that the voluntary system would not get the men," King noted in his diary. To King, looking desperately for a solution to the difficulties he faced, this sounded like a generals' revolt, and he saw at once that this fanciful interpretation could be used to persuade the anti-conscriptionist ministers to change their position. "Instantly, there came to mind the statement I had made to Parliament in June [1942] as to the action the government would necessarily take if we were agreed that the time had come when conscription were necessary." Not necessarily conscription, but conscription if necessary. Now conscription *was* necessary, and instructions to dispatch 16,000 NRMA men overseas could be put in place by order-in-council. King said to himself, and soon to the nation, "It will be my clear duty to agree to the passing of the order in council and go to Parliament and ask for a vote of confidence."

The political crisis in Canada had effectively ended. In Quebec there was much public and media fury at the government action, and a substantial number—6,000!—of the 16,000 NRMA men designated to go overseas as infantry reinforcements instead deserted or went

AWOL (absent without leave), while others staged "mutinies" in British Columbia camps—mutinies that were put down without much violence. In December, nonetheless, the NRMA conscripts, some of whom had decided to volunteer to get the extra benefits available to General Service soldiers, began to be shipped overseas. One soldier, later said to be unstable, threw his gear off the gangway, and this blew up into yet another media and political storm.

The conscription crisis in Canada infuriated many soldiers overseas. Montague Temple had been wounded in the leg and hospitalized, and he wrote home to say that "all the boys over here have been following the 'Conscription Issue' in Canada with great interest, and I can tell you from discussions, I doubt if McKenzie [*sic*] King gets a single vote from the soldiers now serving overseas. We all feel, as I know you do, that this is everybody's fight, and that all the young & fit men should be sent here if necessary. It's not fair that some should accept their responsibility to their own families and their country—while others sit back and take it easy, completely out of danger. I also know there are many boys ... willing & eager to come Overseas at any time, but for some reason or other are kept in Canada. Of course all able bodied men can't come overseas," Temple went on, "but if King had put in a system similar to that in the U.S.A; then nobody could have a finger pointed at them after this war & be called a zombie! Enough said on that subject, as I know you feel the way I do, but it's a darn shame a great country like Canada should get so much bad publicity just because of a stupid, cowardly politician."

Another officer, Major Joe Pigott of the Royal Hamilton Light Infantry, noted, "We had only feelings of disgust, of contempt for the prime minister and the politicians who were not facing the realities of the crisis," the realities of battle and casualties and understrength units attacking a stubborn enemy. Very often, men who had been wounded returned to the front, their too-quick "recovery" hastened by the reinforcement shortage. Frequently, they arrived at their regiment to find that almost everyone they knew was gone—killed or wounded. With trained men sitting in Canada, the soldiers' frustration and fury was evident. Captain Hal MacDonald, now the adjutant of the North Shore (New Brunswick) Regiment, wrote his wife on November 28, "We follow with interest the battle of the century—whether or not to send over the Zombies … If they do come over, my idea would be to put them into separate units because," he said, "they would never mix with the present fighting men. Life would be miserable for them. My gosh, I can't figure out why they should be so yellow." German propagandists made hay with the Canadian conscription mess.

The shortages of reinforcements were especially acute in the French-speaking infantry units. Henri Tellier, who ended his Army career as a lieutenant-general, served as a company commander with the Royal 22e Régiment in Italy and then in Northwest Europe. His regiment, much like every French-speaking unit, had trouble getting good, well-trained reinforcements, and he particularly remembered the ongoing difficulties by 1944 with what he called "second-raters": one draft of one hundred were all "bums." The best in early 1945, he said, were francophone NRMA men—at least they didn't have criminal records. As far as he was concerned, and he may have been untypical of French Canadian soldiers, the NRMA ought to have been sent overseas sooner.

The military crisis that had produced the infantry reinforcements situation soon eased. After the Scheldt campaign ended, the badly battered First Canadian Army had a respite of three months. "It was," Colonel C.P. Stacey wrote in his official history, "the Army's only such period during the campaign." There were no major operations; the Canadians took up positions on the river Maas, where they held the line into February 1945. That greatly helped the reinforcement situation. So too did the decision made by General McNaughton, the defence minister, and the rest of the Cabinet that as soon as it might be possible, I Canadian Corps should be pulled out of the line in Italy and moved to Northwest Europe to be reunited with II Canadian Corps in the First Canadian Army. The decision to move the corps to Northwest Europe was agreed to by the Anglo-American high command at the beginning of February. Thus, from February through to the middle of March 1945, I Canadian Corps was out of action, moving from north of Ravenna through Marseilles and then north to the Netherlands. The stasis on the main front and the move of I Canadian Corps let the reinforcement system catch up, even though First Canadian Army would be heavily engaged for three months from February 1945.

First Canadian Army had played a major role in liberating France and Belgium from Nazi tyranny. All that remained from the victory on the Scheldt to V-E Day was to defeat the enemy's Rhineland defenders, free the rest of the Netherlands, and conquer northwest Germany— none of these an easy task.

CHAPTER 4

Operations on the Maas and Rhine

Seven agonizing months passed from the clearing of the Scheldt to V-E Day and the end of the war in Europe. First Canadian Army had liberated Zeeland, the westernmost province of the Netherlands, during the battle of the Scheldt, and after the conclusion of that struggle, the Canadians spent three months of the bitterly cold winter of 1944–45 on the rivers Maas and Waal in southern Holland.

The main action of the early winter on the Western Front was the stunning surprise German assault through the Ardennes that began on December 16. Hitler sent a large force of panzers—secretly amassed, carefully masked by disinformation, and helped greatly by Allied overconfidence—through the weakly defended Ardennes forest and rough terrain. The Nazi aim was to recapture Brussels and Antwerp and surround 21st Army Group, including First Canadian Army, in a giant pocket. This Battle of the Bulge, the last major Nazi throw in the west, swept aside the American troops holding the Ardennes. While it reached within fifteen miles of Namur, the drive was checked by U.S. forces continuing to resist at Bastogne, Belgium, and by General George Patton's Third U.S. Army, which forced the Germans back. Casualties were heavy among the American forces involved, but First Canadian Army was not directly threatened or engaged, though the 6th British Airborne Division's 1st Canadian Parachute Battalion (its men inexplicably ill equipped and without winter clothing) was deployed on the British flank and fought some small actions. The Battle of the Bulge used up huge quantities of what remained in the west of the Germans' first-class troops and equipment.

The enemy had one additional trick up his sleeve: on New Year's Day 1945, a sudden air strike by a thousand Luftwaffe aircraft, the "Hangover Raid," caught napping the British, Canadian, and American air bases in Belgium and Holland and destroyed some 250 aircraft, most on the ground. It was a pyrrhic victory, however—the Germans lost 300 aircraft and 214 pilots killed, wounded, or taken prisoner in the operation, a loss that the Luftwaffe could never make up at this stage of the war.

For the Canadians, the watch on the Maas was their main task, a three-month period spent in the cold of a vicious winter in snowy, war-ravaged terrain. Fortunately, the troops of First Canadian Army had winter clothing, including camouflaged white outer garments. Patrolling was extensive, and there were small attacks, designed to keep up the offensive spirit that senior commanders always craved in their men, attacks that smacked of the Great War's trench raids. More usefully, infantry battalions and armoured regiments took time to ensure that reinforcement troops knew their jobs—throwing grenades, firing machine guns, and practising battle procedures. One infantry battalion CO wrote, "It took me all winter to get my battalion into shape to break out on the Rhine. If we had really got involved in another long-drawn-out, head-knocking operation again, we'd have been in big trouble."

The pause in operations permitted changes in senior officers. Much to Montgomery's frustration and disappointment, General Harry Crerar, now recovered from serious stomach complaints, returned from England to resume command of First Canadian Army. Ottawa decided to promote Crerar to the rank of full general, the usual rank of an army commander, but a rank that no Canadian had ever before held in the field. Field Marshal Sir Bernard Montgomery was not amused; the petty little commander told the Chief of the Imperial General Staff, "To arrange that announcement conveys impression that it is a normal promotion and NOT repeat NOT in any way for distinguished service in the field." But a Canadian promotion was beyond the War Office's or Monty's control.

Guy Simonds, Monty's favourite, returned to II Canadian Corps, and Charles Foulkes, General Officer Commanding the 2nd Division, who had been the corps' acting GOC, went to Italy to take over I Canadian Corps on November 10. He replaced the frosty Lieutenant-General E.L.M. Burns, who had not managed to create good relations with his Canadian division commanders, Chris Vokes and Bert Hoffmeister, or his British Eighth Army commander. Foulkes's personality was no warmer and his intelligence and tactical skills were weaker than those of the man he replaced, but he somehow did better as a corps commander than as a division GOC. Major-General Harry Foster, the commander of the 4th Armoured Division, went to Italy to become GOC of the 1st Division. Chris Vokes, a self-described "great rough red hairy bastard" who did not want to serve under Foulkes, took over the 4th. Vokes did not immediately endear himself to his new subordinates by telling them at once that he was "heartily sick" of hearing about their exploits on the Scheldt at "Bugger-off-Zoom, Sphitzen-on-the Floor and other places."

Brigadier Bruce Matthews, a gunner who had been the Commander, Corps Royal Artillery—the senior artillery officer for Simonds—was promoted to major-general to lead the 2nd Canadian Infantry Division. Matthews was the son of the lieutenant-governor of Ontario and came from a wealthy family. He had served in the militia artillery, and he rose steadily in England and in Sicily. Matthews, remembered Denis Whitaker, the CO of the Royal Hamilton Light Infantry, was very intelligent and had an excellent personality. He could delegate. He was solid and thoughtful, had the men's best interest in mind, and was level-headed. He wasn't a driver like Simonds, though he got on well with him. Why did he rise? He had luck, he was at Simonds's side at the right time, and he had the ability. Brigadier Stanley Todd, who succeeded Matthews as CCRA, was as good a gunner, but he didn't get the call. Matthews did.

When he was promoted to a divisional command, Matthews deliberately modelled himself on Simonds in some ways, but only some. He would go forward to brigades, he recalled, as he was constantly urged to do. And when an attack was on, he would try to go to the battalions near the start line to sense if the company and platoon commanders had a grip on their objectives. But, as he said, his problem was that there was never enough time for reconnaissance, and as a result there were always mines or obstacles that no one knew about. Because the Allies had air superiority, battalions could be trucked very close to the start lines.

His 2nd Division had had a hard time at Dieppe in August 1942, and then at Carpiquet in Normandy. Morale had dents in it, he said.

When he took over in November 1944, Matthews was told that the division needed careful handling to get its morale boosted, so he visited the units, speaking to all the men. He had good enough French to speak to his francophone regiments, the Régiment de Maisonneuve and the Fusiliers Mont-Royal, and he explained to all his men that he would work to reduce casualties. Fortunately, he had six to eight weeks on the Maas to do more training, working to integrate reinforcements into their new units and running company schools to give instruction on tactics and weapons handling.

Above all, Matthews was not Charles Foulkes. As W.J. Megill, one of Matthews's brigade commanders and one usually considered to be a troublesome subordinate, said, it was a banner day when Matthews took over because he asked for opinions as Foulkes and Simonds never did. Matthews was a consensual leader who looked for advice, took it, or explained why if he couldn't. He understood infantry–artillery cooperation, and he trusted his commanders and listened. He couldn't have been worse, Megill said, than Foulkes, who got all his advice from his staff. Simonds took little advice from anyone. Although the 2nd Division had crack units like the RHLI and the Calgary Highlanders, it may not have been the best in First Canadian Army. Matthews's achievement was that he made it into one that fought well.

There were changes in command in the infantry battalions too, many younger and battle-tested officers taking over their units. One such was the Fusiliers Mont-Royal's new Commanding Officer, Lieutenant-Colonel Jacques Dextraze, who had been a private with no military experience in 1940, and now, four years later, at age twenty-four, had become an experienced professional soldier well able to lead men into battle. Three decades later, Dextraze would be Canada's Chief of the Defence Staff. Another promotion was that of Lieutenant-Colonel Ross Ellis, a captain when he arrived in Normandy in July, who rose to command the Calgary Highlanders as a lieutenant-colonel at twenty-nine. It was a young man's war now.

In his memoirs, Major-General Chris Vokes ruminated on the way the war had pushed young men forward. "When the [1st Canadian] division had been mobilized in the autumn of 1939, all officers holding the rank of lieutenant-colonel and above, and many other officers and senior nco's had seen service in the 1914–18 War. Now ... the number of persons who had seen service in that war were few in number. None of these held unit command or above. I was 39, the brigade commanders were below 35, and the battalion commanders all below 30." He added that no one above lieutenant-colonel had held a rank higher than major before the war. "They had risen in rank through ability." First Canadian Army had become a combat meritocracy, and that fact accounted for its growing effectiveness in battle.

The war had also eased relations between the regular officers of the pre-war Permanent Force and the militia. Ability mattered, just as Vokes, a PF officer, had said, and most of his senior officers were militiamen. Brigadier William Murphy, newly placed in command of the 1st Canadian Armoured Brigade in Italy and then in Northwest Europe, wrote home of his promotion. "If there ever was a next step after this, it would be to command a division, or possibly go Brigadier General Staff on a Corps or Army HQ. Neither is in the least likely," he said somewhat grumpily, "and I feel I have got about as far as a militiaman can in this war." Able officer that he was, Murphy did not get another promotion, but he was wrong in believing that militia officers were being held back by the regulars. By the end of the war, three of the five division commanders in First Canadian Army were officers who had come from the militia—Major-Generals Hoffmeister, Keefler, and Matthews. They were just as good as the PF division commanders—Major-Generals Vokes and Foster—and Hoffmeister and Matthews were likely the two best of the five.

• • •

The main city in the Canadians' area was Nijmegen, a Dutch city that had been heavily damaged in September 1944. The city and its great bridge were key objectives in Field Marshal Montgomery's daring attempt to get into Germany in his "bridge too far" Market Garden operation in September 1944. "The Nijmegen bridgehead is the most important bit of ground along the front of 21 Army Group," General Simonds said in a directive issued just before II Canadian Corps moved into the city. "Here we hold the only bridge across the main course of the Rhine. If the Germans accept a decision west of the Rhine, the eastern face of the Nijmegen bridgehead between the Meuse and the Rhine forms a base through which an attack can be launched against the northern flank of the German battle line. If the Germans withdraw to the east bank of the Rhine," he went on, "the Nijmegen bridgehead forms a base from which an assault across the Neder Rijn [Lower Rhine River] turns the main course of the Rhine itself. Military bridging of the lower course of the Rhine is a doubtful possibility under winter conditions. Therefore, the Nijmegen bridge is of the greatest importance to us and must be protected against all forms of attack."

The Canadians were there in strength, but icy weather conditions forbade large-scale operations.

For those men at the front around Nijmegen, Simonds's corps staff tried to make the city a rest area for troops out of the line, and there were dances—Dutch girls in long dresses!—and even an attempt to open a swimming pool, which collapsed when the building was destroyed by bombing. One success was arranged by Major Gerald Levenston of the Deputy Assistant Adjutant and Quartermaster General's staff at Simonds's headquarters: Levenston opened a hotel for officers "practically in the front lines," he said, "but very nice," with a dining room where the waiters wore white tie and tails and served cocktails, sandwiches, and "French pastries (all made from Army rations) in the best Continental style."

Then Levenston built "the biggest Hamburger Café in Europe—I am calling it the White Spot and having the Engineers build it to my design out of Army huts—it will have a serving counter 90 feet long and is designed to serve 3000 troops a day." The café's name later was altered to the Blue Diamond, but this didn't bother Levenston. He told his mother in one of his regular letters that he had just taken over a bakery and butcher shop. "The bakery will turn out 2000 rolls, 100 pies and 4000 doughnuts daily—the butcher will mince enough meat for 2000 hamburgers daily, 700 pounds of onions are being used weekly." The Blue Diamond in fact served 6,000 burgers a day in its first month of operation, and all this only a thousand yards from the German border and the front.

At Christmas, the soldiers celebrated as best they could, every unit holding as gala a dinner as they could manage, with carol singing sometimes echoed by the Germans across the river. The officers of the Royal

Hamilton Light Infantry, wrote Lieutenant Gordon Holder, served the men a Christmas dinner with all the trimmings, and in their own mess were treated after dinner to a "long table ... set up to provide a crap shooter's paradise."

But if the Canadians ate well, the Dutch didn't. Operation Market Garden had led the Dutch government-in-exile in London to call for a nationwide rail strike; the Germans retaliated by forbidding all food transports to the western Netherlands. Nijmegen was not directly affected by the embargo, but food was terribly scarce that winter none-theless. Sergeant Red Anderson of the Calgary Highlanders recalled, "We had just arrived in Nijmegen, and we were staying in a school. This old man (70) came up to me and was pointing at the tables. Didn't know what he meant, so just nodded. He went to all our mess tins and ate the bacon rinds, took bread and cleaned out all the mess tins and ate everything. I grabbed him and took him to the cook house. Told Foggy DeBow the story. Foggy gave him some bacon and eggs and the old man washed dishes for four days. Every time I walked by the kitchen, he would come out and kiss me on both cheeks and rub my face with his soapy hands ... Poor old man. The Germans really starved the Dutch towards the end of the war."

The Nijmegen railway bridge and the large road bridge over the river Waal were vital to support the Allied bridgehead on the eastern shore of the Waal, the main branch of the Lower Rhine River. The Germans naturally grasped the importance of the bridges for future operations, and they tried to destroy the spans, employing air attacks, mines, frog-men, and even midget submarines. They had some limited success, but repairs were quickly effected. Equally serious was the threat of flooding the "island," the land on the enemy's side of the Waal occupied by First Canadian Army. In November, the Germans blew holes in the dikes, but British soldiers under General Crerar's command retained their foothold, driving off a German assault in the mud.

There were additional operations by First Canadian Army, ordinarily small in scale, and some less than successful by any operational or human calculus. In a waterlogged area northeast of Breda, a subsidiary channel of the Maas along the river's south shore forms a long island, in the midst of which is a ferry harbour called Kapelsche Veer. On this desolate spot the Germans established a tiny bridgehead in Canadian-controlled territory and dug themselves in thoroughly. Eliminating this foothold was a long, cold, and costly business, involving attacks across open and snow-covered ground in the face of a determined enemy. The Poles, serving under First Canadian Army, tried it twice without success. The British 47 Royal Marine Commando attacked the place on January 13 and 14, 1945, with no better result. Finally, two weeks later, the 4th Canadian Armoured Division mounted a considerable attack against the position with heavy artillery support and tanks, and there was thoroughly nasty fighting in miserable conditions.

The Lincoln and Welland Regiment, which assaulted in strength—including an attack on the harbour with a small force carried in fifteen Peterborough canoes!—bore the brunt of the attack, most of its men reaching the island aboard Buffalos, the Landing Vehicles Tracked (LVTs) that could swim and manoeuvre on mud or dry land, covered by a smokescreen. The enemy fired into the smoke, and the Links and Winks had a terrible hand-to-hand struggle in the snow. One Canadian tossed a grenade into a German slit trench then jumped in before it exploded. His feet were shredded, but the two Germans died. "He was about a foot shorter when he came out," one comrade recalled with unintentional humour, "than when he went in." Soon the Argyll and Sutherland Highlanders and South Alberta Regiment tanks came into the fray, and the worthless patch of ground was cleared. One German POW somehow had no socks and wore only Dutch wooden shoes, but he was alive. His comrades had lost 300 to 400 casualties, but the Canadian losses were also high: the Links and Winks had 50 killed and 129 wounded; the South Albertas, 7 killed; and the Argylls, 13 killed and 35 wounded. For ground of little importance, this was a very high price. The Dutch army today continues to study the action at Kapelsche Veer as an exercise in military futility.

As that small battle suggested, conditions on the Canadian front were hard: very cold weather, deep snow, and frozen ground, then mud everywhere when it thawed, and few comforts, beyond a hamburger at the Blue Diamond, when the units came out of the line for a rest. But what the winter on the Maas did do was to allow time for reinforcements to make their way to the infantry and armoured units, time for the new men to be trained to unit standards, time for them to begin to make friends with their mates.

Selected soldiers could also go on leave to Paris or Brussels or smaller towns. The Canadians had access to good hotels and rest facilities there, arranged by the army's leave centres, and Lieutenant David Marshall of the South Alberta Regiment wrote that in Paris, "our room was the biggest hotel room I had ever seen," including "a funny bathroom fixture that shot water straight up"! Troops out of the line could get their uniforms cleaned and a change of socks and underwear. They could eat without charge at the centres or get their meals on the economy. Prices generally were relatively reasonable, cigarettes could secure almost anything one desired, and there was entertainment galore. A few days of leave could change a soldier's outlook on life.

Men could also get a brief leave to England if they were very lucky, but there was almost never leave back to Canada. In September 1944, the Army had decided that men who were wounded three times could be granted six months' leave at home. Beginning in November, in addition, each month 450 men with five years' "satisfactory continuous service overseas" could be sent home on leave. The Americans had such a scheme; so too did the British, with a much shorter distance to travel. But most of Canada's soldiers must have felt as if they were Alexander the Great's men fighting half a world away from home with no end in sight. Major-General Bruce Matthews, whose wife had had twins in 1940, did not see his children for the first time until he came home after the end of the war. "Mommy, who is that man?" one son asked. War kills, and it also blights lives.

• • •

Ottawa had ordered 16,000 NRMA home defence infantry conscripts overseas in November 1944, and once they arrived in Europe, the Army's main concern was to ensure that they entered combat as quickly as possible. Headquarters in London and on the Continent agreed that the best way to deal with the new men would be to break up their units and place them in the reinforcement stream as individuals, with the goal of mixing them throughout First Canadian Army's ranks, rather than identifying

THE BEST LITTLE ARMY IN THE WORLD

them separately as conscripts. In early December, Brigadier W.H.S. Macklin, Deputy Chief of the General Staff at Canadian Military Headquarters in London, noted that the Army could be sure that most of the NRMA men would be relatively well trained, and many would probably be above the standard of some of the soldiers who had been produced by the bottom-scraping remustering programs in England in the autumn of 1944.

In General Crerar's words, the conscripts would "stand, or fall, in the eyes of the ranks now here, on how they prove themselves as soldiers." Crerar himself had not wanted NRMA men in his army of volunteers, preferring that they be sent to the Far East to fight against Japan. But the politicians in Ottawa had decided otherwise, and First Canadian Army's commander accepted the inevitable. Surprisingly, perhaps, according to a survey of the attitudes of unit commanders in all three Canadian divisions that were engaged in operations in Northwest Europe in early March 1945, the NRMA men proved to be as good as volunteers in general attitude, standard of training, fighting ability, and morale. In the 4th Canadian Armoured Division, "unit COs were not [even] aware that any NRMA personnel had been posted to their units," suggesting the NRMA conscripts were effectively indistinguishable from General Service volunteers. That was also the conclusion of the war diarist of the Loyal Edmonton Regiment, who wrote on April 30 that "in the few small actions they have engaged in so far, they have generally shown up as well as all new reinforcements do." Other accounts suggested that once the Zombies had seen some fighting, the distinctions between them and volunteers disappeared.

In the end, just under 10,000 NRMA conscripts reached the Continent, many after V-E Day. Only 2,463 saw duty in operational units of

First Canadian Army, and 69 were killed, 232 wounded, and 13 taken prisoner, or casualties of just under one in eight, a figure that suggests the severity of fighting in the last months of the war. By early April, the number of infantry reinforcements available to Canadian units in Northwest Europe was more than at any time since D-Day; even without the NRMA men, there were 8,500 men in the infantry reinforcement pool at the end of April. The move of I Canadian Corps from Italy and the winter on the Maas had reduced casualties and allowed the training system to catch up with the need for infantry reinforcements. Even so, "the NRMA seemed to have accomplished at least one of the goals of the army's administration of the program throughout the war," the historian of the NRMA, Daniel Byers, said, "by creating a force of well-trained, competent soldiers that could conduct themselves well in combat."

. . .

There was more killing and heavy fighting to come, but the Canadians now were at full strength again, as they had not been since they first went into action six months before. The Battle of the Bulge had delayed First Canadian Army's next big operation for six weeks. Operation Veritable, launched on February 8, 1945, put the Canadians onto German soil for the first time, fighting for the Rhineland. General Crerar led a thirteen-division force—the biggest force ever led by a Canadian, with a strength of over 470,000 men in the three Canadian and nine British divisions, and smaller forces from the Belgians, Dutch, Poles, and Americans. The British XXX Corps, commanded by the charismatic (but more than a little unwell because of wounds suffered earlier) Lieutenant-General Brian

Horrocks, effectively led the fighting, which aimed to take the ground between the rivers Maas and Rhine, necessary before the Rhine itself could be crossed.

First Canadian Army's task was to make a frontal attack against fortified zones firmly anchored on the Rhine River. The British and Canadians faced three heavily defended lines—an outpost line of trenches, anti-tank ditches, minefields, and strongpoints; the dugouts and concrete bunkers of the Siegfried Line, running through the heavily treed Reichswald; and the forested Hochwald, defended in depth. The defences included two and three lines of trench works linking strongpoints reinforced by anti-tank ditches. Small towns and villages between the second and third zones had been extensively fortified. The final objective lay forty miles beyond the start line.

Veritable had been planned as a three-stage attack, with enough time between each to regroup infantry and armour and to bring supporting artillery within range of their new targets. The initial assault would be made by the five divisions of XXX Corps (including the 2nd Canadian Infantry Division), and as the distance widened, the remainder of II Canadian Corps would join in on the left flank. Historian Bill McAndrew described Veritable as "the epitome of the Canadian way of war: large scale orderly preparation, accumulation of massive resources, and meticulous planning. It was another Vimy Ridge."

Such a huge operation posed an enormous logistical challenge. First Canadian Army's Royal Canadian Engineers had to build or harden a hundred miles of roads that threatened to collapse because of the number of tanks and half-tracks using them. They had to construct five long bridges requiring tons of stones, timber, and steel. The Army Service

Corps had to transport the fuel for the army's 35,000 vehicles, amounting in all to 1.3 million gallons of gasoline, along with all the food and ammunition. The artillery requirements for the 1,034 guns supporting the attack alone amounted to 11,000 tons. Air photographs numbered 500,000, and 800,000 maps were needed. And all this had to be done without tipping off the enemy to the "when" and the "where" the attack.

The Royal Air Force's Bomber Command supported the attack with 850 Lancasters and Wellingtons, which levelled the urban concentrations that lay before the attackers. Then a huge artillery concentration, the largest on the Western Front to that point in the war, preceded the assault, and counter-battery fire then followed, aiming to eliminate as many of the enemy's guns (outnumbered by 14 to 1) as possible. The tactical air support, free to operate because the skies were clear on February 8, hit every visible enemy position. But the weather had warmed, the ground and the dirt roads had turned to mud, and the enemy had flooded as much ground as possible. The battlefield was a morass.

Veritable jumped off at 10:30 in the morning on February 8 behind the barrage and bombs. The Sherman tanks then tried to clear the way for the infantry, struggling through the mud and water created when the enemy blew the dikes on the Rhine. The defenders of the outpost line, ersatz divisions formed by old men, stomach units formed from soldiers with ulcers, and Volkssturm units—literally a home guard of the too young and too old—folded quickly, completely demoralized by the concentration of artillery fire. The main difficulty came from mines, especially the hard-to-detect *Schu* landmines, set off by a misplaced foot that too often disappeared into a mist of blood, bone, and body parts.

Fighting was vastly more difficult on the Siegfried Line and in the

Reichswald. The Wehrmacht was not the force it had been four years before, but its professionalism was strong, it could still fight from fortified positions with great skill and determination, its resolve in defending German soil remained high, and the astonishing willingness of the soldiers to fight for Hitler was bolstered by SS units in the rear that were kept busy hanging deserters.

Attacking Canadian infantry had to wade through deep water, and Buffalos had to be called on to carry troops in what to many soldiers smacked of the misery of the Scheldt polders they had fought through the previous October. Major Gordon Brown of the Regina Rifles later wrote of this period that everyone knew the war was close to its end, "feeling quite naturally that it would be folly to lose one's life" then. "Those of us who had been with our units in England and since the invasion were near exhaustion," and "the gung-ho spirit of 1944 had been replaced with caution and apathy. We didn't want to take unnecessary risks or to suffer casualties through errors, either on our part or on the part of higher command. This malaise," Brown concluded, "affected all ranks." But the soldiers nonetheless carried on.

Contributing to this feeling of malaise, supplying the forward units became increasingly difficult because of the conditions, and the Royal Canadian Army Service Corps had to use DUKWs, amphibious tracked vehicles, to carry supplies of food and ammunition forward when roadbound trucks could not get through. Too often supplies ran short. But by February 10, the Canadians had cracked the Siegfried Line, and three days later, after brutal fighting, they had cleared the Reichswald.

Next was the struggle in Moyland Wood, a task that took a week despite better weather that allowed the Typhoons to operate. The enemy had fortified the small wood and entrenched some 800 first-class paratroopers to defend it. General Dan Spry, the GOC of the 3rd Division, told his unit COs that the Germans were "experts at forest-fighting. The troops will find it tough going; it will be up to the junior officers and NCOs to keep them moving." They tried, but there were limits to what soldiers could do. Heavily supported by their own artillery and well dug in, the Germans battered the 3rd Division's Canadian Scottish, Regina Rifles, and Royal Winnipeg Rifles at close quarters with mortars and machine-gun fire and with pre-registered artillery support from the far side of the Rhine. The shelling burst in the branches, showering the men with deadly splinters. The paratroopers, carefully camouflaged, let one entire Regina company move deep into the wood before cutting them off. An entire platoon was overrun, the survivors forced to surrender, while the others scrambled to dig in under mortar and machine-gun fire. "Many men," the Reginas' War Diary observed, "although not actually casualties are suffering from exhaustion due to continual shelling and the nature of the woods." The Canscots, trying to clear the eastern end of the woods, were quickly pinned down by heavy fire and saw one company reduced to 5 men, with 48 taken prisoner. The Regina Rifles lost 220 killed and wounded in the three-day fight. The Winnipegs suffered 105 casualties on February 11. But the Canadians used their own artillery and flamethrowers to clear the wood. The commander of the 7th Brigade, J.G. Spragge, was replaced during the struggle for Moyland Wood; the CO of the Reginas, who had been unhappy with the plans for the Moyland operation, temporarily took over and directed the successful final assault.

The war went on and on. The road from Goch to Calcar now had to be cleared, a task given to the 2nd Division's 4th Brigade. A two-battalion attack, launched with infantry in Kangaroos, the armoured carriers conceived by Simonds on the road to Falaise (the "defrocked Priests" had been replaced by Kangaroos built from Canadian-made Ram tanks), ran into 88mm guns, and enemy tanks from two panzer divisions caught the Royal Hamilton Light Infantry and the Essex Scottish without armoured support, the Shermans from the Fort Garry Horse having pulled back to rearm and refuel. One Rileys' officer wrote of the "dread [of] facing that awful feeling of nakedness when ... you must move forward across open country among the brutal sights and sounds of battle." The RHLI's Commanding Officer, Lieutenant-Colonel Denis Whitaker, described it as the "most vicious battle I remember"; one of his companies was overrun, all his soldiers in the rear were called up to bolster the defences, and a counterattack in the morning, supported by the Garrys, helped to restore the position. An Essex Scottish company had been feared lost, but on the afternoon of February 20, the unit discovered that its lost men had held their position—with only 35 men left standing. The Canadian anti-tank guns had knocked out seven panzers, and the Canadians hung on barely, casualties heavy: 204 in the Essex Scottish, 125 in the Rileys. After one more attack, the Germans, those still alive, then fell back and the road was cleared.

Then it was the Hochwald itself, a great state forest of trees planted in neat rows with carefully arranged trip wires and booby traps. On February 26, in what was called Operation Blockbuster, the 2nd and 3rd Canadian divisions led the way, attacking on a miserably cold, wet night on a 3,000-yard front behind a massive barrage. But German parachute infantry, supported by tanks, hit the 2nd Division's start line just before the H-Hour. They were driven back by the Rileys and tanks of the Fort Garry Horse, and the division's attack began on schedule at 3:45 a.m., the soldiers moving forward in Kangaroos under artificial moonlight created by bouncing searchlight beams off the clouds and with tracer fire that pointed the way.

The farm hamlet of Mooshof was heavily defended by paratroops, and Toronto's Queen's Own Rifles in the 3rd Division struggled to clear it. With his platoon officer killed along with many of his riflemen, Sergeant Aubrey Cosens sat in front of the turret on a 1st Hussars Sherman and directed the tank's fire. He pointed the tank into a group of counterattacking Germans and drove them away. Then, with the four remaining men of his platoon, he told the tank commander to ram one of the fortified two-storey farm buildings; covered by fire from his men, he cleared it. A second building was empty, and Cosens single-handedly cleared the third of its defenders. When he was on his way to report to his company commander, a sniper shot him in the head and killed him. One of his soldiers said that Cosens had told them, "I'm going to find the company commander and report to him ... I guess he got about 8 or ten feet from me and plink! Down he went—that was it." Cosens was awarded a posthumous Victoria Cross. He was twenty-three years old, and he was only one of the 101 members of his regiment killed or wounded that day.

The Régiment de la Chaudière, on the 8th Brigade's southern flank, attacked a series of strongpoints at the village of Hollen. One company saw the enemy raise a white flag, relaxed, and then came under machine-gun fire from three Panther tanks. That forced a withdrawal and embittered the survivors. In all, on February 26, Canadian soldiers killed in action numbered 214.

The CO of the 1st Hussars said a few days later that his unit had suffered serious losses during Blockbuster—40 officers and men and 21 tanks. "The troops fought till they were exhausted. I found two crews asleep in their tanks before the area they had helped to capture was mopped up." Then, the Commanding Officer added, tanks that had been repaired quickly and well by the 54th Light Aid Detachment of the Royal Canadian Electrical and Mechanical Engineers had been put back into action "manned by composite crews of knocked out tanks, regardless of Squadron or troop. The resultant teamwork, thanks to good training, was splendid. I have never felt prouder of the Regiment."

The Germans fell back to their next prepared position, fighting hard from concealed trenches. When the Canadians neared, planned heavy registered artillery and mortar fire hit them, followed by coun-terattacks. There were many casualties, but the Germans continued to be forced back, their own losses severe. Meanwhile, the 4th Armoured Division moved against the Calcar–Üdem ridge, with twenty-seven-year-old Brigadier Robert Moncel's "Tiger Group" leading. Tiger Group had three armoured regiments, a motorized infantry battal-ion, and two infantry battalions, supported by flame-throwing Wasps, self-propelled anti-tank guns, and flail tanks to blow up mines. The enemy resisted fiercely, but sheer weight of numbers—and courage—drove them back in a classic battle fought by tanks and infantry. Field Marshal Montgomery later described the barrage that hit Tiger Group as the heaviest "volume of fire from enemy weapons ... which had been met so far ... in the campaign." One Argyll recalled "the black haze that hung over the place after the shelling stopped, and the feeling you had of being absolutely dazed and in a stupor; while a sudden, unreal quiet descended, broken only by the feeble cries of the wounded."

One of the brightest young comers in the Army, Moncel described his 4th Armoured Brigade, most of Tiger Group, as splendid, tough, and efficient. A bad brigadier could lose in a day what he claimed his brigade lost in Northwest Europe under his command—some 350 men killed in action. Moncel was definitely a good brigade commander.

The Hochwald battle was almost as big as some of those in the Normandy fighting. Now, at dawn on February 27, the 4th Armoured Division's "Lion Group," consisting of the South Alberta and Algonquin regiments and two additional infantry battalions, attacked, the soldiers slogging through the heavy mud and German fire. The Algonquins breached the last prepared defences before the Rhine, and the Germans had to react. They did so in force, catching the attackers in a narrow defile, riddling a column of eleven Shermans and twelve Kangaroos with 88mm anti-tank fire, and inflicting heavy losses. One trooper in the South Albertas noted that the enemy "knocked out the front tank and the rear tank and when we had no place to go we were left with no alternative but to abandon the tank and run like hell."

A new attack, ordered by the GOC, General Vokes, went in the next day, this time led by the Argyll and Sutherland Highlanders and the Lincoln and Welland Regiment. Fighting on ground they knew well and having spent two weeks fortifying and digging tank traps, a fresh parachute regiment, aided by heavy artillery concentrations and a hundred panzers, smashed the Canadian attack, which was slowed by thick mud, reducing one Argylls company to fifteen men and shooting up the Shermans. The Germans held off the attackers for three days. The War Diary of the supporting South Alberta Regiment described the enemy shelling as "the most concentrated that this regiment ever sat under," including at Falaise in August 1944. The Germans somehow seemed to find countless guns and endless numbers of new or reconstituted regiments of highly motivated soldiers.

The 2nd Division's 6th Brigade moved into the line on March 1, the point company, led by Major Fred Tilston, provided by the Essex Scottish. The Essex had 500 yards of open country to cross; Tilston, wounded in the head, was nonetheless the first into the enemy position, where he knocked out a machine gun with a well-placed grenade. Hit a second time, he continued on and led his men to the next enemy position and cleared it. He then organized his few remaining men to drive off a counterattack. Repeatedly, he went back to get grenades and ammunition, until he was wounded a third time. Near death from the loss of blood, Tilston gave orders to the one surviving officer in the company to hold the position, which he did. Tilston, a thirty-eight-year-old pharmacist in civil life, lost both legs but lived. He received the Victoria Cross.

Moncel's 4th Armoured Brigade now drove for the Rhine with the Algonquins, the Lake Superior Regiment, and his armoured regiments leading. In miserable weather and heavy mud, the attack ground forward, the infantry carried in Kangaroos, until enemy counterattacks stopped it cold. "A terrific hail of anti-tank fire met the attacking force as it cleared the crest of the Hochwald Gap," Major P.A. Mayer of the Lake Sups said, "and within a few minutes the whole area became a veritable hell." Casualties were heavy, and there was little help from the air force, with anti-aircraft fire hurting the tactical air force's Typhoons and restricting the number of sorties. The Germans, although hopelessly outnumbered, continued to resist desperately. Not until March 8 was the Hochwald finally cleared and Xanten, the historic town beyond it, taken. The Germans had employed ten divisions and lost 22,000 prisoners and at least 70,000 killed and wounded. British losses in Veritable were some 16,000, American casualties 7,300.The Canadian toll was 5,304 killed, wounded, and captured.

Crerar's Army had done its difficult job with efficiency and great effectiveness. The Allies noticed. General Eisenhower was very complimentary. So too was Lieutenant-General Sir Brian Horrocks, commanding XXX British Corps, who wrote later that Crerar was "always very well-informed because, in spite of the bad weather, he made constant flights over the battlefield in a small observation aircraft." Crerar, he went on, "has always been much underrated, largely because he was the exact opposite to Montgomery. He hated publicity, but was full of common sense and always prepared to listen to the views of his subordinate commanders." Moreover, as historian Terry Copp wrote, Harry Crerar "managed a highly effective staff that proved capable of meeting the most difficult challenges." He, like the soldiers of his Army, had grown into the job, even if Monty continued to grumble about him.

• • •

The conclusion of Veritable provided an opportunity for reinforcements to come up to the armoured regiments and infantry battalions, and for some command changes. General Simonds had become unhappy with the way the 3rd Division had tackled its task at Moyland Wood, and he wanted the GOC, thirty-two-year-old Major-General Dan Spry, sacked. When 3rd Division put in a brigade attack, Simonds was at the start line and Spry wasn't. The attack was a mess, recalled Stanley Todd, Simonds's Commander, Corps Royal Artillery and previously Spry's CRA, and Simonds went back to Spry's headquarters, where he found him asleep, apparently after an all-night poker game. Simonds sacked him on the spot. Spry, said the corps commander in his official letter, lacked "quick tactical appreciation and robust drive in … urgent tactical situations." A reluctant Crerar eventually agreed, and the 3rd Division's new commander, Holley Keefler, a colourless but competent pre-war militia officer, took over on March 23. Spry went off to head the Canadian Reinforcement Unit in England, more than slightly bitter. He said later that his superiors "seemed to feel that the pace of battle could be carried on regardless of the realities of the situation … When troops are wet, cold, miserable, bloody-minded, scared, and tired, it takes time to move and assemble, re-assemble, and deploy them … Everything slows down." The senior commanders, he claimed, "really didn't understand the sharp end of battle" as he did from his time in Italy. "They'd never been there." That was harsh, but likely true; still, a first-rate GOC would have been at the start line when his men attacked.

To replace Keefler at the 6th Infantry Brigade, Crerar selected Lieutenant-Colonel Jean-Victor Allard, the CO of the Royal 22e Régiment. French Canadian senior officers had to be given their chance if public opinion in Quebec was to be satisfied. There was a widespread sense in Quebec that French-language units had fought well, as they had, but that francophone officers had not been promoted as they deserved. The only high-ranking francophone officer in a theatre of war in mid-1944 was Brigadier Paul Bernatchez, commanding a brigade in the 1st Division in Italy. One French Canadian officer, Major T.L. Bullock, wrote angrily in June 1944 that because they had proven themselves, francophone officers "must be given full and equal recognition *in the field*. That means they must command Divisions and, before the war is over, a Corps." That was not to happen—no French Canadian would rise that far—and it was simply unrealistic to expect that the few francophone regulars and relatively few French-speaking militia officers would have field marshal's batons in their knapsacks. There were few enough anglophone senior officers with real talent, and anglophones outnumbered the francophones in the Army by more than six or seven to one. But Allard was a good choice for brigade command, and two decades later he became the first francophone Chief of the Defence Staff in Ottawa.

By this time, I Canadian Corps had begun to arrive in Northwest Europe to rejoin First Canadian Army, Crerar taking command of his nation's two corps on April 1, 1945, while the British corps that had long fought as part of First Canadian Army left. Lieutenant-General Charles Foulkes had commanded the corps for some months in Italy and had, some observers thought, done well. Brigadier Elliot Rodger, Simonds's Chief of Staff, had visited Italy in January and wrote in his diary that "Foulkes was in particularly good form and had apparently taken charge and was running the show with a firm hand—and the Div[ision]s were happy about it." Douglas Delaney observed shrewdly that Foulkes flipped the Peter Principle on its head: "The higher he went, the more comfortable—and competent—he got." He was never popular with his officers and men, but he had performed well enough.

When they arrived in the Netherlands, the soldiers and their commanders in I Canadian Corps soon realized three things. First, no one was sorry to have got out of Italy—"Italy was dirty. Italy was battered. Italy was wet and cold in the winter and Italy in the summer was a mélange of heat, flies and dysentery," wrote a trooper in the Governor General's Horse Guards. "We were glad to see the last of it." Second, they could not miss seeing that their war in Italy had been fought on the cheap. There, they had little air support, even second-rate equipment was scarce, and they received too few supplies of all kinds. The war in Northwest Europe was much different—there were tanks and trucks aplenty and supplies in immense quantities. There were specialist units providing radar warning, gun-laying radar, air survey units, and a vast array of workshops, salvage units, specialized transport companies, and the like. There was more of everything.

Finally, the soldiers of I Canadian Corps quickly understood that the relatively relaxed disciplinary standards of the British Eighth Army, under which they had fought since July 1943, were gone forever. First Canadian Army had more formalized, more rigid standards set by the GOC-in-C, Harry Crerar. In Italy, operation orders had sometimes been verbal; in Northwest Europe, they never were. Other formalities also had to be observed. On April 12, Crerar told all commanders of his concern with "slovenly turnout" and "poor saluting": "The standard, or customs, of personnel of other Services or the soldiers of other countries, is not my particular concern. I am, however, vitally interested in the reputation of those who serve in the Canadian Army."

Crerar was correct, but the reaction of the men, heavily engaged against desperate resistance, can be imagined. Soldiers never liked what they called "chickenshit." Nor did generals, Chris Vokes remarking that "I felt, militarily, having just been separated from my competent British superiors, as though I was in the position of a boy whose loving mother had just died and who is then put under the control of a cold-hearted and ignorant stepmother. I didn't like it." Harry Crerar's Army, he complained, "stood for shining buttons and all that chickenshit." Ouch. Still, as Captain Sydney Frost of the Princess Pats in the 1st Division wrote later in his memoirs, "The more I saw of the orderly, deliberate way the [First] Canadian Army went about its tasks, the more I liked doing business with them."

The armoured regiments of the 5th Canadian Armoured Division and the 1st Armoured Brigade received new tanks, many being the Sherman Firefly, the upgunned version of the standard Allied tank, equipped with a 17-pounder main weapon that could penetrate the armour on the enemy's panzers. Their obsolete Honey reconnaissance tanks disappeared, replaced by the better Stuart. The one area that was more difficult was air support. In Italy, the air force, though small, was always on call; in Northwest Europe, while there were many more aircraft, the demands on them were greater, and units in the field sometimes had to wait their turn.

• • •

The next big operation was Plunder, the crossing of the Rhine, which began on March 23. First Canadian Army had a large role, but in the initial plan the Canadian participation was to be limited to the 1st Canadian Parachute Battalion. Brigadier Rodger described in his diary how Crerar told General Simonds "of the plot for 21 Army Group's next battle—30 [British] Corps to do it through 2 Canadian Corps striking into [the] Reichswald Forest and thence South between [the] Waal and Maas [rivers]—all to be timed to strike into [the] top of [the] German armoured reserves just when they are being committed against the Americans." General Simonds wrote General Crerar a note pointing out the repercussions and bad taste that would come out of this "from our Canadian soldiers—to be left out of THE battle—probably the one that ends the war," Rodger noted. "General Crerar saw Monty the following day and apparently as a result 3 Canadian Division was included in the 30 Corps attacking divisions." Whether the men of the 3rd Division would have been shattered if they had been held out of Plunder is doubtful.

Canadian initial involvement was still relatively light: 475 men of the 1st Canadian Parachute Battalion, part of the British 6th Airborne Division, participated in the huge air drop that preceded the water crossing. The parachutes of 1945 were nowhere near as accurate as those of the twenty-first century, which can land jumpers on a dime, and the wind and errant aircraft trying to avoid anti-aircraft fire scattered the Canadians widely. They nonetheless took their objectives against very tough opposition. "They were young and full of fight," one airborne Canadian recalled, and another said the Germans "fought like tigers." The battalion killed or captured some 600 Germans, despite losing 20 percent of its strength. The CO, Lieutenant-Colonel Jeff Nicklin, a well-known football player with the Winnipeg Blue Bombers and a very tough disciplinarian, was killed in the initial drop when he got caught in a tree directly above entrenched Germans and was riddled with machine-gun fire before he could get loose. One of the unit's medical orderlies, Corporal George Topham, won a Victoria Cross for carrying a wounded comrade to safety despite being wounded in the face; later he pulled wounded men from a blazing carrier, risking his life again. "I didn't have time to think about it," he said later. "I was too busy."

One brigade of the 3rd Canadian Infantry Division, the 9th, crossed the Rhine on Buffalo LVTs in the early hours of March 24. The Highland Light Infantry, leading the brigade, faced German paratroopers who resisted fiercely, but, using flamethrowers and supported by massive artillery concentrations, they took their objectives north of Rees. The two other battalions in the 9th—the Stormont, Dundas and Glengarry Highlanders and the North Nova Scotia Highlanders—battled with paratroopers and panzer grenadiers who fought to the end. The North Novas, in particular, had to struggle fiercely at Bienen on March 25 against superior German forces that were better armed and defending a fortified village with its flanks secured by water obstacles. Lieutenant Donald Pearce led his North Novas' platoon at Bienen and wrote in his fine memoir that his men "assaulted in a single extended wave over the dyke-top and down the other side. Ten tumbled down, nailed on the instant by fire from two or maybe three machine-guns; we had gone broadside into their central defences." One soldier stood up in the open and tossed grenades into two of the German positions before being shot. Finally, Pearce and the one other unwounded survivor took the position. Pearce wrote that he then reported to his CO "weeping inarticulately, unable to construct a sentence, even to force a single word out of my mouth." Pearce was sent back to the rear to recover, but his battalion had done the job, at a cost of 112 killed and wounded, 30 percent of its strength. Despite the casualties and Pearce's understandable breakdown, there was no obvious sign in the North Novas of the malaise that some officers had earlier reported.

By March 27, the entire division was across the Rhine, capturing Emmerich and the nearby high feature, Hoch Elten. Once it had been cleared, the Royal Canadian Engineers threw a 1,373-foot bridge across the great river. Two more soon followed.

"Probably no assault in this war," wrote General Eisenhower in a congratulatory note to Harry Crerar on March 26, "has been conducted under more appalling conditions of terrain than was [yours]. It speaks volumes for your skill and the valor of your soldiers, that you carried it through to a successful conclusion." In his reply, Crerar gave the credit to his men: "I believe that no troops could have put up a finer exhibition of enduring gallantry and determination than was demonstrated during those weeks of bitter, bloody and muddy fighting." First Canadian Army's commander was more restrained in private, noting that despite the atrocious conditions and cost, "we have accomplished the task … and … enabled other Armies to achieve striking advances with a minimum of enemy to contend with." Slandered in Normandy, forgotten on the Scheldt, the best little army in the world was getting some overdue recognition even as the tough tasks it had handled tended to be somewhat overlooked then—and after—by historians.

Much of Germany had been devastated by Bomber Command, the Canadians discovered, but not everything was ruined. Artillery officer Elmer Bell, a lawyer from a small village in Wellington County, Ontario, wrote home on April 7 "from a nice German town across the Rhine. This one never got a bomb and hasn't been evacuated. We drove in here in tanks at 25 miles per hour and didn't fire a shot." Bell went on to say that "this is a war of knifing deeply now and leaving thousands of Jerries behind. The result is that every corner is a puzzle, are there Jerries

25. Two Germans taken prisoner at Falaise are escorted by Canadian infantry.
CANADIAN WAR MUSEUM

26. Infantrymen follow a Sherman tank on the road to Falaise in August 1944.
LIBRARY AND ARCHIVES CANADA

27. Soldiers from the Highland Light Infantry wait to get their mess tins filled in August 1944. The grub was substantial, but never fine dining.
KEN BELL/LIBRARY AND ARCHIVES CANADA

28. Royal Canadian Engineers building a pontoon bridge during the gruelling Scheldt campaign, October 1944. LIBRARY AND ARCHIVES CANADA

29. The flooded terrain and the all-pervasive mud during the Scheldt battle forced tanks and men to move on narrow roads. LIBRARY AND ARCHIVES CANADA

30. Moving heavy artillery pieces in thick mud was back-breaking work for gun crews, and accurate aiming was hampered by the lack of a firm foundation. LIBRARY AND ARCHIVES CANADA

31. Near Nijmegen in January 1945, a patrol from the Queen's Own Rifles moves out wearing snow camouflage. BARNEY J. GLOSTER/LIBRARY AND ARCHIVES CANADA

32. Looking almost glamorous, a Canadian sniper carried his rifle with a scope, binoculars, a grenade and a pistol, his camouflage netting wrapped around his neck and over his hair. LIBRARY AND ARCHIVES CANADA

33. Toronto dentist Harry Jolley served in Italy and Northwest Europe; his letters home offered shrewd insight on the war's impact. AUTHOR'S COLLECTION

34. The Canadians were hailed as heroes as they liberated Dutch towns and cities, as here at Deventer and Utrecht in the spring of 1945. LIBRARY AND ARCHIVES CANADA

35. Soldiers of the Régiment de la Chaudière of the 3rd Division scramble aboard a raft to cross the Ijssel River in Holland, April 1945. DONALD I. GRANT/LIBRARY AND ARCHIVES CANADA

36. Fighting in Germany continued to V-E Day. Tanks of the Fort Garry Horse pass infantry of the Fusiliers Mont-Royal at Munderloh on April 29, 1945.
DANIEL GURARICH/LIBRARY AND ARCHIVES CANADA

37. Infantrymen of the 3rd Division's South Saskatchewan Regiment under fire on their way to Groningen in the Netherlands in April 1945. LIBRARY AND ARCHIVES CANADA

38. The fighting in the Hochwald in February 1945 was brutal in the cold and mud, but the Canadian material superiority was overwhelming. LIBRARY AND ARCHIVES CANADA

39. The 1st Canadian Parachute Battalion moved rapidly east in May 1945, successfully blocking Soviet troops from advancing into Denmark. This Canadian para shook hands with a Russian trooper at Wismar, Germany, on May 4. CHARLES H. RICHER/LIBRARY AND ARCHIVES CANADA

40. The government marked V-E Day with a grand celebration on Parliament Hill. LIBRARY AND ARCHIVES CANADA

41. The Ontario Regiment (11th Armoured) returns to a snowy Oshawa, Ontario, on November 29, 1945.
CITY OF TORONTO ARCHIVES

42. Repatriation was a complex operation, but these soldiers landing in Halifax were happy just to see Canada again.
LIBRARY AND ARCHIVES CANADA

43. War brides—and war babies—began arriving in Canada early in 1946. These somewhat apprehensive mothers arrived in Toronto not knowing what to expect.
CITY OF TORONTO ARCHIVES

44. Receiving little sympathy and less care from the victors, German soldiers after the surrender had to scramble to survive. LIBRARY AND ARCHIVES CANADA

45. The Allies had bombed Germany into ruins, as this dense destroyed city showed in 1945. LIBRARY AND ARCHIVES CANADA

there or not[?]. The civvies are queer. They act almost glad to see us. They organized surrender and assisted us to round up German soldiers hiding here and Hitler Jugend." But only a few miles from this cowed, almost friendly town where everyone hoped to escape the war with their lives and possessions intact, Bell continued, there was a prison camp "where all the Russian women in the camp starved to death and many of the men. The brutality of these people when they are up is beyond understanding; their kindness and demeanour when beaten, just as ununderstandable." Bell did not comment, but everywhere in Germany civilians claimed not to know anything of the nearby POW or concentration camps.

Certainly that was true of Belsen, a camp in Lower Saxony liberated by the British. RCAF officer Ted Alpin went there and wrote of "the still of death and the sweet sickly scent of human flesh. When the Army arrived here there were 10,000 unburied bodies on the ground and 13,000 more have died here since then." Belsen was not a death camp like Auschwitz, where millions were gassed, but it was nonetheless horrific, and an estimated 50,000 men and women had died there. The British forced the former SS camp personnel to help bury the thousands of dead bodies in mass graves. Some local civil servants were then brought to Belsen and confronted with the crimes committed on their doorstep, which, they said in unison at once and ever since, had been unknown to them.

At newly liberated Cleve, Rabbi Sam Cass, a chaplain in First Canadian Army, presided at a Passover seder. The service was held in a bombed-out building—there was little else in Cleve that had not been destroyed by Bomber Command—and it attracted a considerable number of Jewish soldiers. Ralph Allen, reporting for the *Globe and Mail*, wrote that "until today the feast had not been observed publicly in Germany since 1939, but in Cleve there was no one who could say for sure. In the entire community, not a single Jew was left to testify." Word of the extermination camps liberated by the Red Army in Poland had begun to reach the west, and the seder on German soil created some satisfaction.

CHAPTER 5

The Liberation of the Netherlands

To liberate a nation from a long, brutal occupation is a great and good act. The Netherlands suffered just such an occupation from 1940 to 1945, and it fell to First Canadian Army to finally drive the Germans out in the spring of 1945. The close relations between the Dutch and Canadians began then and continue into the twenty-first century.

In March 1946, the Dutch weekly *Vrij Nederland* (*Our Free Holland*) published an open letter to mark the departure of the last remaining Canadian soldiers for home—a letter addressed to "Jimmy, Jack, Harold, Reggie, Tom, Bill and Harry and the thousands of other battle-dressed boys of the Canadian Army!" The weekly paper expressed Dutch gratitude movingly, and it ended by saying that someday "our grandchildren will ask us who liberated us and then we will say, many brave, gay boys with caps on their heads; we shall tell them all—much and much more than that Montreal and Ottawa are two big cities in Canada! Godspeed, boys, and welcome home!"

• • •

Fresh from clearing the Rhineland and crossing the Rhine, First Canadian Army turned in early April 1945 to the liberation of the northern Netherlands and the conquest of northwest Germany. General Harry Crerar's orders for II Canadian Corps directed it to cross the Ijssel River south of Deventer to reach the Otterlo–Apeldoorn Line and then head into the northeast of the country. Lieutenant-General Charles Foulkes's I Canadian Corps was to clear the Lower Rhine, cross the river to the west of Arnhem, take that much-fought-over city, and then free the heavily populated western provinces of Holland.

The advance into northern Holland and northwest Germany proceeded quickly, with Deventer, Zwolle, Emden, and Wilhelmshaven being taken easily, as were Arnhem and Apeldoorn. Everywhere in the Netherlands the Canadians met cheering crowds. Resistance fighters assisted where they could, pointing out enemy positions and giving directions through the countryside. At Deventer, after the North Nova Scotia Highlanders liberated the city on April 4, "the people ... poured into the streets in throngs, surging this way and that, demonstrating their freedom," wrote Lieutenant Donald Pearce. Soon, "nearly all the soldiers had found girls, or were found by them; and Deventer spent its first day and night of liberation in a kind of mad Elysium."

But at Leesten on the same day and at Warnsveld on April 6, the Stormont, Dundas and Glengarry Regiment and the Régiment de la Chaudière, of the 3rd Division, faced strong resistance from what seemed almost crazed German teenagers in a parachute training unit. The war diarist of the Chauds noted that even in April 1945, the captured soldiers believed "Germany would win" and "their belief in Hitler and Nazism [remained] unshaken." The para trainees were at most sixteen years old, the product of a decade of Nazi indoctrination, and they fought fiercely. A few young soldiers taken prisoner without firing their weapons cried in frustration at their fate.

The Glens had taken heavy casualties at Leesten and were exhausted by the struggle. One Dutch boy recalled years later that his father woke him up at their farmhouse. "Quiet, come and have a look, but don't make a sound!" his father said. "He opened the door into the cattle barn area. It was quite a sight. The floor was covered with wall-to-wall bodies: snoring Glens. Even on top of the potato-sorting machine, a most uncomfortable piece of equipment, a soldier was sleeping soundly."

Meanwhile, the 1st Division, having been switched to serve under General Guy Simonds's II Canadian Corps, moved north in secrecy to stage an assault crossing over the Ijssel River. On the afternoon of April 11, using amphibious Buffalo LVTs carrying up to thirty men and swimming the river under cover of smoke, with heavy artillery fire and air support, the division achieved total surprise. Small enemy battlegroups, made up of sluggish occupation troops for the most part but with numbers of better-trained and well-equipped soldiers, were handled relatively easily, and when the Germans staged the usual quick counterattack mandated by their battle doctrine, they walked into heavy fire. The division took Apeldoorn without a fight; the local citizens went wild with joy at their liberation.

But from April 14 to 16, the 2nd Division had a difficult struggle at Groningen that cost it more than 200 casualties. A Dutch SS battalion, one of many units formed by right-wing fascists in the nations conquered by the Nazis, fought with great ferocity, its men knowing that they had no future in a liberated Dutch nation. Some of the SS dressed in civilian clothes and sniped at the Canadians, and the soldiers soon had orders to kill them on sight. The fighting was house to house in this city of 150,000, the Canadian artillery having been forbidden to shell the town for fear of inflicting too many casualties on civilians. Thus there were odd moments. A Calgary Highlander recalled that "one of our machine gunners set up his Bren gun in a kind of bay window in the front of [a] living room. He had the bipod of the Bren resting on a small hardwood table and he was firing through the bay window at a German vehicle down towards the end of the street ... [The lady of the house] must have been so bewildered that she wasn't really aware of what was going on around her. Seeing this Bren gunner in the process of ruining her little hardwood table with his wretched Bren gun, she handed him a little cushion and asked him to put it under the legs of the gun, which he obligingly did." Then, the soldier went on, "she handed him a cup of coffee which he graciously accepted and then continued to fire on the German vehicle down the street. Unbelievable!" Most unbelievable, perhaps, was that the woman had coffee, worth its weight in gold in 1945 Holland.

At the same time, an officer of the Black Watch peered through a hedge at a bunker and watched as enemy soldiers moved in and out. He ran unobserved to a nearby house, then decided to act alone. "I ran down the stairs and right out into the middle of the street," recalled Russell Sanderson. "I hollered in German for them to surrender, with a few obscenities," and to his surprise and relief, some forty soldiers did. He double-timed them back to his lines.

In another incident in the fight for Groningen, Major Sandy Pearson of the Calgary Highlanders recalled, "In the early evening, I had a visit from the postmaster, a distinguished man in a morning coat, silk hat, etc. He explained that the Germans were concentrated in the post office which he did not want burned. He wanted me to walk to the post office with a white flag and persuade them to surrender peacefully. I said 'Fine, I'll tell you what I'll do, I'll walk down the street if you walk down the street.' He said, 'Oh, no.' I told him I'd much sooner burn the post office [with our Wasp flamethrowers] than risk any Canadian lives and he left in a bad mood. Next morning we attacked and the Germans tumbled out in a hurry to surrender."

The Cape Breton Highlanders of the 5th Armoured Division took Barneveld, west of Apeldoorn, on the night of April 16–17. The Resistance leaders in the town contacted the battalion CO "and asked him," one Dutch man told an Army historical officer, "if the liberation was permanent or whether there was any chance of them withdrawing and the Germans re-occupying the town. He said that it was permanent … The Underground immediately took over command of civil affairs. [The Resistance leader continued:] 'The mayor and the chief of police, though not collaborators, had been weak … and were dismissed and replaced by people of our choosing. Most of the civil police,'" he went on, "'were old time accomplices of ours … There has been absolutely no break down in law and order. Unauthorized executions are forbidden … About one hundred collaborators have been arrested, and eight or ten girls have been gathered up and will have their heads shaved [for sleeping with Germans]. This last is an expression of public indignation and, although not an official punishment, is tolerated by us.'" Similar events occurred in almost every liberated Dutch town.

There was another fierce melee, at Otterlo, the next night. Fleeing from Apeldoorn, German troops, many said to be drunk, tried to break out of the Canadian net and reach the Grebbe Line, their still-intact main positions defending western Holland. The enemy overran units of the 5th Canadian Armoured Division, with the 17th Field Artillery Regiment, the 24th Field Ambulance, and the Irish Regiment of Canada bearing the brunt of the attack. Private Sam Doggart of the Irish remembered that "we were heading north of Arnhem to go to the Zuiderzee and liberate the north end of Holland when we had a counter attack of about one thousand Germans coming in … We had liberated the town at about 11 o'clock in the morning. Sent out a patrol because some civilian said there was some enemy down in one of the farm houses, patrol went out and run into an ambush. Two of the guys got killed and then two come back. Then all of us went down, took the whole company, cleared the brush where the attack took place and ended up taking another 58 prisoners there. And that counter attack," Doggart said, "came in about 11 o'clock at night and it came in because the First division which had taken Apeldoorn were squeezing the enemy and they were facing towards us without us knowing it … I was with B Company and they came right through where we were and there was only about 35 of us there … We fought all night," he said, "and it was all over about 5 o'clock in the morning and there was 200 enemy dead and we only had lost 7. That was pretty good for that one fight."

The gunners had as difficult a struggle, the Germans burning the command post and running through their vehicle lines. The Regimental Sergeant Major shot two Germans with his Sten gun, and when it jammed (as the unreliable Stens always did), he used his bare hands. It took tanks from the Canadian Grenadier Guards and the Irish Regiment's Wasp flamethrowers to clean out the enemy. The War Diary of the Field Ambulance recorded that the unit's Service Corps drivers had defended the position successfully until the flamethrowers did their work. The surgeons of the 24th treated 146 wounded, a third of them German POWs. The diarist summed up: "At 0830 hrs [when] the battle had ceased 400 German dead lay in the fields, ditches and roads and 250 had been taken prisoner from a force estimated to be 1000 strong."

Sergeant Major Gord Bannerman of the 17th Field remembered that in the morning, "standing up in, I guess, a large armoured car was our divisional commander Major General [Bert] Hoffmeister. He was speaking to the Irish group probably a company. The general said what a terrific fight that the Irish had put up last night and how well all personnel had performed. 'So I thank you all for a job well done.' Up spoke an Irish major," Bannerman said, "and his views were expressed to a man. 'It was not us Sir who broke the German attack it was those darn artillery men who did not know enough to run but stayed and broke the attack.' General Hoffmeister then said 'who can lead me to the gunners' and Darcy Spencer and I said 'we can. We are from the 17th.' 'Climb on the armoured car and show me where,' was his reply!" Hoffmeister knew how to fight and to lead; he was said to have come out of his caravan wearing pyjamas when the enemy came close to his HQ during the fight, but this is apocryphal. He left his caravan in the middle of the night, quite sensibly, for an armoured command vehicle that had good communications and provided overhead cover.

Over the border in Germany, the 4th Canadian Armoured Division was pressing toward Oldenburg. One armoured trooper, Lieutenant David Marshall, wrote, "Funny thing, when we passed the border into

Germany, all the waving and the smiling and the laughing [from civilians] stopped. Our greetings were somber, hateful looks. Well, we didn't like them much either." And the Wehrmacht wasn't quite finished yet. At Sögel, the Lake Superior Regiment cleared the town on April 9 and then had to withstand a vicious counterattack the next day. About twenty-five to thirty Germans, some of them seventeen-year-olds with only a few weeks' military experience, reached the town centre where the Lake Superior Regiment, the Lincoln and Welland Regiment, and the 12th Field Ambulance had laagered. Captain Harry Jolley, a dentist from Toronto in his late thirties, found himself fighting to survive—and was surprised he did so well in action. He hoped in vain that he might get the Military Cross, but he did get a Mention in Dispatches and later the British Empire Medal. In his next letter home, he said nothing of Sögel, only mentioning that he was reading *Forever Amber, the* sexy novel of 1944, and it was "not very exciting." Not as exciting as fighting off the enemy, certainly.

A few days later, Major-General Chris Vokes, commanding the division, heard that one of his battalion commanders, Lieutenant-Colonel Fred Wigle of the Argyll and Sutherland Highlanders, had been killed by a civilian in Friesoythe. Furious, Vokes ordered the town razed to the ground. The town was systematically set on fire by Wasp carriers. When the fire burned out, armoured bulldozers razed the remaining walls, and the rubble was loaded on trucks. "We used the rubble to make traversable roads for our tanks," Vokes wrote much later in his memoirs. The information he'd been given was incorrect—the CO of the Argylls had been shot by a German soldier when the battalion headquarters came under attack by paratroopers—but Vokes said, "I confess now to a feeling still of great loss" over the officer, a good friend, "and a feeling of no great remorse over the elimination of Friesoythe." Harry Crerar, antipathetic to the Germans, felt much the same. In a letter to his brother, he spoke of "the fanatics and crazy men," of whom, "for the good of the future, the more . . . that are killed off, the better." Crerar was not wrong.

Lieutenant Marshall observed that even the old or young Germans who had been pressed into military service could kill if they were behind a machine gun. As a result, "as we moved through the country we did not leave a haystack or barn unburnt, and if the house did not have a white flag, then it went too." Most Canadians tried to play by the rules in their treatment of POWs and enemy civilians, although all the frontline troops were stunned by the brutality they saw, the worst excesses certainly those committed by the SS and Wehrmacht in their concentration and POW camps. Still, after ten months of fighting in Northwest Europe, the soldiers had no sympathy at all for any of the German soldiers or civilians they faced, and no Canadian was willing to take the chance of being killed by allowing a barn that might be fortified to survive unburned.

Groningen, Sögel, and Otterlo were aberrations in the fierceness of their combat, however; many of the Germans now ordinarily rolled over without much fighting. Brigadier James Roberts of the 3rd Division's 8th Infantry Brigade said in his memoirs, "We marched through Friesland like Napoleon's troops through Austria in 1805." Most of the 3rd Division's advances were as easy, but Roberts' 8th Brigade had hand-to-hand combat on April 8 at Zutphen and had to employ Crocodiles—flamethrowers mounted on Churchill tanks—to get ahead. The Crocs projected jellied chemical flames that stuck to any German they hit. The disorganized enemy soldiers fled screaming, their uniforms and flesh burning.

To the east, also in Germany, the 4th Armoured Division took the town of Meppen, where Matthew Halton of the CBC went to a Russian POW camp, one of eight in the area. "We came too late to save them," he said in a broadcast. "They're diseased and starved and beaten. They're skin and bones. Quite literally there's no flesh on them. They are just bags of bones with swollen, ghastly heads." Halton had reported from the Reich for the *Toronto Daily Star* in the 1930s, and he had warned Canadians repeatedly about the Nazi goals. Now he said that Germany was a "country of unspeakable evil," and people needed to understand "what a gang of homicidal maniacs ha[d] been let loose on Europe these last few years." Like Harry Crerar, he too was correct.

First Canadian Army itself did not liberate any death camps, but on April 12, armoured cars of the 14th Canadian Hussars and infantry of the South Saskatchewan Regiment did find a transit camp at Wester-bork, north of Apeldoorn in Holland. The camp had been used over the years of Nazi occupation to gather 107,000 Dutch Jews, including Anne Frank and her family, for transport to Auschwitz or Treblinka; there were under a thousand Jews left there when the Canadians arrived. One survivor wrote that he heard the shout "They are coming, they are coming," and saw the armoured carriers. "A soldier looked over the top and I grabbed his hand and all I could say was 'Thank you, thank you!' He grinned and said 'It's okay. It's okay.'" The liberated Dutch began to sing their national anthem. "Our liberators started singing. We didn't know the song, had never heard it, but … they sang it with such pride, standing there with their dirty faces beaming … They sang

… O Canada … and we were free." That night the soldiers and the freed inmates celebrated the triumph of life over death together.

• • •

At Utrecht, in the Netherlands, on April 12, the Canadians had begun preparing to attack the defences of the Grebbe Line when word came that Arthur Seyss-Inquart, the Nazi Reichskommissar for the Netherlands, had offered a truce to permit First Canadian Army to provide food for the starving civilians in the heavily populated Dutch cities. Seyss-Inquart clearly hoped to avoid the gallows for his years of abuse of the Dutch, but he would be hanged nonetheless. The Nazi food embargo, put in place after a rail strike was called by the Dutch government-in-exile in September 1944, had been relaxed in November, but the harshness of the winter had frozen the canals, stopping barge traffic. Food stocks in the Nazi-occupied areas, especially in the large cities of The Hague, Utrecht, Rotterdam, and Amsterdam, quickly ran out, and official daily rations during what the Dutch called the "Hunger Winter" fell from 1,400 calories in August 1944 to 500 calories in April 1945. A single potato, a piece of bread, and a sugar beet amounted to that 500 calories. Many families had been driven to eating tulip bulbs, and the shortage of fuel, the collapse of transportation in the cities, and the failure of the electricity system compounded the misery. An estimated 20,000 Dutch men, women, and children died from malnutrition or the cold, while hundreds of thousands more were desperately ill. People burned furniture or books in their effort to stay warm. Meanwhile, the well-fed Germans and Dutch fascists continued to hunt down members of the Resistance. Many were executed right up to the final capitulation in May.

After consultation with Field Marshal Montgomery of 21st Army Group and General Dwight Eisenhower, the Supreme Allied Commander, and with negotiations with Seyss-Inquart under way, First Canadian Army ceased all fighting throughout the western Netherlands on April 28. The details of what was called Operation Faust were worked out between representatives of 21st Army Group, General Foulkes of I Canadian Corps, and General Johannes Blaskowitz, the German commander in the Netherlands. Starting on May 3, 300-truck food convoys began to roll each day on safe corridors through the lines, while Bomber Command aircraft, including those from No. 6 Group of the Royal Canadian Air Force, dropped parachute-loads of food. Rooftops near The Hague had signs painted on them: "Thank You, Canadians." Special rations, including vitamins, were directed to pregnant women. The Dutch rejoiced as the food went to a central depot near the German lines; unfortunately, the distribution of the rations was slowed by an overburdened Dutch administration, a ruined rail system, and gasoline and truck shortages. Apparently, little food reached the hungry until May 9.

Still, everyone knew the war was fast drawing to a close—and German officers intimated as much in the course of the negotiations over the food convoys—but fighting continued in northeastern Holland and northwestern Germany. Many German leaders tried to propose surrendering in the west if they could continue fighting against the Red Army. The Americans, Soviets, and British had agreed on unconditional surrender, refused the Nazi entreaties, and vowed to continue to maintain the pressure on the enemy until all resistance ceased. This meant that fighting had to be continued to the end, and there was also the political and humanitarian necessity of ensuring that the Soviets did not liberate Denmark in the same way they had exacted revenge on Germany, raping and pillaging without let. The Soviets had fought the Wehrmacht and SS since June 1941, and had flattened most of the German war machine in four years of brutal conflict, the Russian people and armies absorbing huge punishment and at least 20 million dead in doing so. In May 1945, no one cared much about Soviet savagery against the Germans, who had behaved with shameless brutality in the east, but there was genuine concern that the blameless Danes be protected.

The 1st Canadian Parachute Battalion, part of the 6th British Airborne Division, faced a tough fight at Minden in Germany and then raced east, hoping to reach the advancing Soviets before they could move north from Lübeck and up the peninsula into Denmark. At Wismar on the Baltic, the Canadian paratroops met the Red Army and were greeted warily, but politely, for being much farther east than expected. The Danes had been saved from "liberation."

Many of the enemy continued to fight hard in their lost cause. The 5th Canadian Armoured Division, now under command of Simonds's II Canadian Corps, had been moving toward the Netherlands port of Delfzijl, on the Ems estuary across from the German city of Emden, and it relieved the 3rd Division—but not before the 3rd's Canadian Scottish ran into a stubborn defence at Wagenborgen. A company attack failed, and it took a stronger effort to dislodge the enemy troops. Among the sixty-four casualties was the company commander, Major Anthony Compton-Lundie from Duncan, PEI. Ten days later, his brother-in-law, Royal Canadian Artillery Major Jim Else, also from Duncan, was killed when his jeep ran over a land mine on German soil. "My grandmother lost her husband and her brother within 10 days of each other at the end of the war," a relative said sadly in 2014.

Hoffmeister's 5th Armoured Division had been ordered to minimize civilian casualties in attacking the large town of Delfzijl and could use only its normal support weapons, tanks, 25-pounders, and mortars. The GOC, worried about the reaction of his soldiers being sent into action without full fire support, asked his brigade commanders to get the soldiers' opinions. Hoffmeister recalled saying, "I think this is something that can't morally be decided by me or by you." The soldiers' response, he said, was "'Let's go.' There wasn't the slightest bit of hesitation ... They were prepared to lay it on the line for the Dutch people." And they did. Beginning on April 23 in miserable wet conditions, the 11th Infantry Brigade attacked Delfzijl, its 4,000 defenders, and their heavy guns with four battalions of infantry and two armoured regiments. German heavy artillery at Emden, across the estuary, pounded the Canadians, there were mines and road demolitions everywhere, and the mud and cold made for hard going over flat terrain that offered little cover.

For nine days the fighting continued, until the Cape Breton Highlanders and tanks of the 8th Hussars launched the final assault on April 30. The day before, the Canadians had fired psychological warfare leaflets into the German lines, telling the enemy that Gestapo chief Heinrich Himmler "has today offered unconditional surrender to the Allies ... We Canadians assume that up to now you don't know about this. The war is practically over. You have done your duty." Unfortunately, enough fools wanted to die in the *Götterdämmerung* of the Third Reich to waste more lives of "the beautiful young men" that Barney Danson, badly wounded in Normandy with the Queen's Own Rifles and later the Minister of National Defence in the Trudeau government, always called his lost wartime comrades.

On May 1, Adolf Hitler, his capital besieged by the advancing Red Army, shot himself in his bunker under Berlin. With his corpse already burned outside his bunker, the Capes, the Nova Scotia regiment that had fought its way north through Italy, now faced what some called its hardest battle of the war. Twenty men died trying to seize the town, along with uncounted Germans. The liberation of Delfzijl in all cost the lives of sixty-two beautiful young Canadians. Between May 1 and May 5, 114 Canadians died in action in the Netherlands and Germany, including 12 on the last day of fighting in Germany, on the fifth. Two were officers of the Canadian Grenadier Guards, killed while trying to help enemy wounded.

After the Germans capitulated at Delfzijl, General Hoffmeister set the captured troops to clearing the minefields around the town. "There were a few grisly sights because they insisted they had no plans or maps of the mine fields and I said, 'OK you can go in and pick them up anyway.' So they did." Their scruples dulled by six years of horror, neither the general nor his soldiers felt any regrets.

On May 4, at last, the Nazis surrendered all their forces in the Netherlands. General Crerar had called off operations as soon as the Germans began the final parleys, and all the German armies everywhere gave up on May 7. V-E Day—Victory in Europe Day—was May 8, 1945.

Over the CBC Canadians heard Matthew Halton say, "The German war is over—five little words that one hardly dares to speak ... Now that the nightmare is over, one has to wonder if it isn't a pleasant dream from which we will wake to find the usual mad mornings of war and blood. Young men," he said, "have grown old in a morning. Gentle men have grown callous at slaughter … And then someone tells you it's over and your first thought is, 'No more Canadians will die.'"

• • •

Canadians held prisoner by the enemy were now beginning to be freed by advancing Allied troops. Private Gerald Dow, a soldier in the Essex Scottish, had been captured south of Caen in Normandy during Operation Atlantic on July 20, 1944. Like his fellow Canadian POWs, he could receive personal parcels from Canada—parcels which, thanks to special ration coupons, included two pounds of sugar, one pound of coffee, and four ounces of tea. The Canadian Red Cross also sent POWs food parcels with canned meat, biscuits, chocolate, powdered milk, raisins, and other necessities that kept the prisoners going when German rations were especially thin. One Red Cross parcel was supposed to be provided each week, but this was often not possible—or the parcels were looted by the German guards. Other parcels, sent by various "Prisoners of War Relatives' Associations" in Canada, contained clothing and other necessities—shirts, drawers, pyjamas, socks, toothpaste and toothbrush, razor and blades. The cost of one such parcel was $16.

In his first letter home to his parents in rural Quebec after liberation, Dow wrote that the rail trip from France, where he had been captured, to Germany had "lasted from twelve to fifteen days. We had very little to drink and were given very little food." He and his mates arrived in Germany, where they were registered with the International

Red Cross, then were sent to Czechoslovakia, "another hard trip in box cars" for ten days. Then it was on to Poland, where the POWs worked in a coal mine for four months. "The food was mainly potatoes … and we … were forced to finish our work before coming to the surface."

The worst was yet to come. In late January 1945, with the Red Army moving quickly west, the Germans began to march the POWs on foot ahead of the Russians in the middle of the very harsh winter. Dow wrote that they "started the march and the first eleven days was almost starvation. Many of our boys who had not worked because of sickness had to be left behind along the road" to die. The guards, he added, "were SS and would not let the civilians feed us," shooting any who tried. Most of the POWs "had no winter clothing or gloves and suffered frostbite." But at the end of April, American troops arrived to free the men "and we are being well fed and getting the best of everything … We can hardly believe yet that we are free." For Dow and the rest of the Canadian POWs who had been in German hands, soon it was England and then Canada.

• • •

Harry Crerar had fought the Germans in two great wars, and he had seen members of his family, his friends, and his soldiers die at their hands. He could not bring himself to meet the surrendering Germans to accept the capitulation of their forces in Holland and Germany—"I saw no purpose in meeting any German generals," he said; "I have had them in adjoining fields … That was enough"—and he assigned his two corps commanders, Generals Charles Foulkes and Guy Simonds, to do it. For the same reasons of dislike, he would order that the Canadian soldiers killed on

German soil be reburied in the two cemeteries eventually established in eastern Holland, at Holten and Groesbeek. He wanted his men to lie in friendly soil, and the Commonwealth War Graves Commission cemeteries are still visited regularly by Dutch schoolchildren and ordinary citizens who remember who freed them and liberated their nation.

The discussions with the Germans that preceded the surrender were detailed, laying out responsibilities and giving the enemy clear instructions and warnings. On May 3, General Foulkes told the Wehrmacht representative, General Paul Reichelt, that while there would be no further Canadian attacks, any incidents started by the Germans would "be retaliated tenfold." Reichelt agreed to consider disarming the Dutch members of SS units, hated by the local population, and, according to the Canadian account, Foulkes showed him "a map of Europe which had marked on it what remained of the Third Reich and informal talks on the question of surrender were carried on. Gen Reichelt expressed the opinion that he and the German soldiers in HOLLAND were prepared to flood the country and, if necessary, die in HOLLAND sooner than to submit to surrender which meant being transported to Russia as slave labour." Foulkes replied "that as far as he knew there was no such arrangement and that there seemed to be little object and very little to be gained, except the destruction of Holland, by flooding the country and attempting to hide behind the Dutch people. It was also pointed out to Gen Reichelt in no uncertain terms ... [that] this act would be considered a war crime and those responsible would be considered war criminals and would be dealt with as such." The Dutch had suffered enough in five years of occupation; they would at least be spared this final act of ruination by the Germans.

With General Foulkes presiding at the Hotel de Wereld (the World

Hotel) in Wageningen, General Johannes Blaskowitz signed the capitulation document on May 6. The Nazis had sung, "The morning will come when the world is mine / Tomorrow belongs to me," but that world had come to its end appropriately enough at a second-rate hotel in a small town in newly liberated Holland. General Crerar reported to Ottawa that he was told that the enemy generals "looked like men in a dream, dazed, stupefied and unable to realize that for them their world was utterly finished."

The manifold details of the surrender still had to be worked out. The Germans quickly provided the information they had on the location of their minefields and obstacles, and they indicated the quantities of supplies in their warehouses. They also accepted responsibility for disarming survivors from among the 8,000 Dutch SS men based in western Holland. Foulkes wrote later that Blaskowitz and his staff were upset at the terms of capitulation: "In the first place they thought that they would be accepted by us as prisoners-of-war and therefore would be fed by us ... However," he went on, "as the stocks of food available were very short" and the needs of the starving Dutch very great, "I decided that the Germans would have to fend for themselves and that if there was any further shortage of food it would be the Germans who had to go short." Letting the disarmed Germans "fend for themselves" had consequences in the next months—the American and French armies let "Disarmed Enemy Forces," as the Allies characterized them, starve and die of disease in huge numbers in rudimentary camps. The British and Canadians did better by their defeated enemies.

There were other incidents, personal in nature, around the end of the war. Brigadier Roberts of the 8th Infantry Brigade wrote in his memoirs that when he escorted a German general and his aide to meet his superiors at 3rd Canadian Division's HQ, the general asked if Roberts was a professional soldier. Roberts replied that he was a citizen soldier, like most Canadians. What had he been in civilian life? the German asked. An ice cream manufacturer came the reply, which clearly offended the enemy officer: to surrender to a "common civilian," an ice cream maker, was humiliating.

There were additional shocks in store for the enemy. General Simonds's II Canadian Corps delegated two officers to deal with the Wehrmacht on surrender details in their area. The Deputy Assistant Adjutant and Quartermaster General, Brigadier H.D.V. Laing, selected the Corps' General Staff Officer, Grade 1, Lieutenant-Colonel Robert Rothschild, an RMC graduate of Jewish origin, and Major Gerald Levenston. When the major asked why he had been selected, Laing replied, "Let them surrender to a Jewish officer." Levenston himself wrote home that he had enjoyed "telling [the enemy officers] curtly what they would and would not do—(the culmination of my army career—it gave me some satisfaction, I can tell you)."

For the soldiers, the end of the fighting was met with little jubilation. Captain Harry Jolley, in Germany, heard the announcement of V-E Day on the unit wireless. "None of us shouted, threw hats in the air, nor anything of that sort," he said. He felt "practically nothing. If anything what I felt most was surprise … for failing to react in a manner more in keeping with the moment." He added, "We're tired—physically & emotionally." And because he ended his war in Germany, they "lacked the civilian spark to set the flames dancing" as they did in Britain and Holland. Gerry Montague of the Canadian Scottish wrote home on May

7 to say, "I should be happy but I find it very hard because so many of my Comrades that should have been here are lost and will not return." Gunner J.P. Brady of the 4th Medium Regiment, Royal Canadian Artillery, noted in his diary, "Our crew ... are silent and thoughtful. Anticlimax. There is no feeling of exultation, nothing but a quiet satisfaction that the job has been done and we can see Canada again."

Brady's regiment, much like many other units, held a parade the day after V-E Day and, as he wrote, "the Colonel begins to read the 36 names of our fallen. Tears are in his eyes. He falters and hands the paper to the Adjutant who calmly folds the paper and puts it in his pocket and quietly says: 'It is not necessary. They were comrades. We remember.'"

First Canadian Army's casualties in Northwest Europe from D-Day to V-E Day were 44,339, of which 11,336 soldiers were killed. In the fighting from the crossing of the Rhine on March 24, 1945, to the final liberation of the Netherlands, Canadian losses numbered 6,298, with 1,426 fatalities. When the dead in Italy and at Hong Kong and Dieppe were included, Canada's Army had lost 17,682 killed in action and 5,203 dead from other causes. The RCAF had 13,498 killed in operations and 3,603 from other causes. The Royal Canadian Navy suffered 1,533 killed in action and 491 dead from other causes. The total of more than 42,000 Canadian dead was a terrible price for a small nation. "They were comrades," Brady's adjutant had said. "We remember."

• • •

Only now, after the end of fighting in the Netherlands, were the Canadian soldiers able to move their truck and armoured columns freely into the large cities. For most of the Dutch population, this was *de bevrijding*, the liberation. An officer in the 1st Canadian Division wrote in a report that "whatever their routes, the convoys were greeted with the wildest of enthusiasm by hysterically happy crowds lining the roads ... Thousands of country folk and burghers ... lined the roads and blocked the way through the towns, to laugh, to wave, to shout, to weep ... Each Canadian private," he said, "was a Christ, a savior." That was no exaggeration. One woman, Marian Haayen, remembered her reaction thirty-five years later: "I saw a tank in the distance, with one soldier's head above it, and the blood drained out of my body, and I thought: 'Here comes liberation.' I had no breath left," she went on in an almost scriptural cadence, "and the soldier stood up and he was like a saint. There was a big hush over all the people, and it was suddenly broken by a big scream, as if it was out of the earth. And the people climbed on the tank, and took the soldier out, and they were crying. And we were running with the tanks and the jeeps, all the way into the city."

John Gray, an intelligence officer and later a noted Canadian publisher, was one of the first of the Canadian liberators to enter Rotterdam after the German surrender. He came out of the city hall, having inquired where he could find the city's Resistance leaders, and saw a dozen or so Dutchmen around his jeep. "As I was about to climb in I saw the cardboard box with the remains of our lunch—sandwiches and pie. If these men were hungry—would it be resented?" Gray then asked one man if the food was of interest. The Dutchman "stared at me incredulously—any use? He climbed onto the bonnet of the jeep and began to break the sandwiches into little bits and to give each man a small handful. The men ate slowly, relishing every crumb, licking at their hands to get the last taste. Some got sandwich, some pie, but all had something, relishing it, smacking their lips … Many soldiers," Gray went on, "had a similar experience that first day … and to many Dutch people the very taste of liberty remained for a long time a mouthful of good bread or pastry such as they had almost forgotten."

First Canadian Army's victory parade took place on May 21 at The Hague. Crerar, Simonds, Foulkes, and Prince Bernhard of the Netherlands took the salute as the troops marched past, accompanied by sixteen pipe and five brass bands. Major-General Harry Foster wrote in his diary that there was "heavy rain … a miserable showing by the troops … The men looked slovenly and were out of step … Discipline will become a problem. I can't blame the troops. The war is over and they want to go home." The army of warriors was eager to leave war behind. The best little army in the world, an army of civilians who had become fine soldiers in the fires of battle, now simply wanted to get back to Canada.

CHAPTER 6

Aftermath

The 5th Canadian Armoured Division had fought in Italy and Northwest Europe. Its thirty-eight-year-old General Officer Commanding, Major-General Bert Hoffmeister, was arguably the most successful division commander in First Canadian Army, with many battles fought and won, three Distinguished Service Orders, and a host of other decorations. On May 23, 1945, "Hoffy's Mighty Maroon Machine" assembled— every man and every tank, self-propelled gun, carrier, truck, mobile workshop, ambulance, and jeep—on an airfield near Groningen in Holland. General Harry Crerar took the salute as the entire division rolled past. One soldier, Sergeant Gordon Bannerman, recalled that "the men were able to see for the first time what a whole armoured division looked like concentrated in one spot. They were able to move around in their own time before and after the inspection, just to marvel at what they'd seen, and take pictures with their own cameras ... They could take back to Canada an impression of this great division of which they were a part."

Before leaving Europe to take command of the infantry division that Canada had pledged to the war against Japan, Hoffmeister sent a message to his men: "Thank you, one and all, for your loyal co-operation and support during the tenure of my command. You were magnificent both in battle and out.

"Of 5 Canadian Armoured Division it can be truly said: we have fought the good fight with all our might. Other battles are ahead. For some it will be against the Japanese. For others it will be the battle to earn a living. Fight these battles as well as you fought for me, and you cannot possibly lose."

Hoffmeister had taken his division and made it into the "Mighty Maroon Machine," and every trooper was conscious of the tag. Morale among the men had been weak when Hoffmeister took over in Italy—they had first had the incapable Bud Stein as GOC, then Simonds briefly, then E.L.M. Burns for a short time, and then Hoffmeister. But the newest GOC had established himself very quickly. The division was training in late March 1944, before attacking the Hitler Line, and, having done mainly static defence, had to learn how to move like an armoured division. The infantry soldiers were practising an advance behind a barrage when Brigadier "Sparky" Sparling, the 5th's Commander, Royal Artillery, had to locate Hoffmeister; he was told he was with the leading infantry battalion teaching them how to "lean into a barrage"—in other words, how to follow a rolling artillery barrage. "Obviously that went around the division just like a flash," A.E. Wrinch, the Commander, Royal Signals in the division, said. "Everybody knew that the new GOC really knew what he was doing and was not afraid to show the boys precisely how to do it himself regardless of the danger." When the word got around, morale began to soar, and "Hoffy's Mighty Maroon Machine" was in formation. He created a division-wide esprit de corps, the only division commander who managed this, and he accomplished it because of his charisma and his battlefield courage, and because every soldier understood that Hoffmeister would not ask him to do something that he himself would not do.

Brigadier Jack Christian, the Commander, Royal Engineers in the 5th Armoured, said that the only major problem with Hoffmeister—one the senior staff officers had to talk to him about—was his habit of going off to the frontline battalions in action. That left the division headquarters staff to try to fight his battle. But Hoffmeister knew that he was responsible for his soldiers' lives, and he insisted on being seen by the men and sharing their risks. "When soldiers see the boss," Hoffmeister's biographer wrote, "they can at least feel that they are not alone or unappreciated or dying for nothing." He added that in the hell of Christmas at Ortona in 1943, Hoffmeister came to the dinner the Seaforth Highlanders, his old regiment, managed to put on in a ruined church just behind the front. The troops cheered, Doug Delaney wrote. "That says something."

Hoffmeister became absolutely first class as a division commander; he listened to and took advice, and his Orders Groups were preceded by discussion. On one occasion in the Netherlands at Arnhem, instead of issuing his orders and then asking his subordinates to comment, Hoffmeister began by asking Brigadier Christian to give the orders for the division's units of the Royal Canadian Engineers and then he followed, knowing that the engineers' equipment would determine the attack. "You could work in a team with him," Christian said. "Lots of guts, a good leader."

Major-General Desmond Smith, who had commanded an armoured brigade in 1944 and might have expected to get command of the division, did not know his new GOC until Hoffmeister took over the 5th Armoured

Division. Hoffmeister won over Smith at once: "Des, I know sweet bugger all about armour and I'm going to depend on you." That started a great relationship, Smith said, and that was why Hoffmeister was successful. He also had a great appearance and personality, and he was technically competent, though in Italy the tactical skills required for armoured divisions were limited by the terrain. He studied the ground, worked out his fire plan, and didn't get mesmerized by it all. And he was innovative: he and Smith found that by welding old #9 wireless headsets on the back of a tank, they could greatly improve infantry–armour cooperation. That type of charismatic, intelligent commander is rare in any army; certainly it was unequalled in the Second World War in First Canadian Army. Hoffmeister was one of the leaders who created the best division in the best little army in the world.

When, in February 1944, Lieutenant-General Guy Simonds took command of II Canadian Corps in England, he wrote a paper on "Essential Qualities in the Leader," a memo for his officers—and himself. To Simonds, a military leader needed both acquired and inherent skills, the former gained through study and training, the latter including innate resolution and determination. "A man who originates good ideas and intentions but who is unable to get them put into practice may be useful in a pure research or in an advisory capacity, but is quite useless in any executive command." That was surely correct. So was Simonds's comment that a commander "must know how to command—how to delegate to his subordinates and his staff, how to control, how to position himself on the battlefield and make use of his communications, and, most importantly of all, he must have an understanding of human nature and how to 'get at' men."

Simonds was certainly good at seeing the problem and deciding how best to tackle it. But he was less able to understand what his subordinates and his soldiers were able to accomplish. In Normandy, his corps was green, the divisions either lacking battle experience or badly bruised by it. There, as historian Terry Copp wrote, his "overwhelming self-confidence and a degree of arrogance which did not encourage expressions of dissent" meant that Simonds commanded, but did not attempt to lead. He was, said Major-General Harry Foster, "a hard man to work for." The reason was that "Simonds used fear," whereas Bert Hoffmeister, wrote his biographer, Douglas Delaney, "built teams." So did Bruce Matthews, GOC of the 2nd Division, in sharp contrast to his predecessor, Charles Foulkes. Still, while he may not have been a consensual team builder, Simonds was a success, and his conduct of the battle of the Scheldt was unquestionably superb. Copp properly concluded that he "lacked the human touch that distinguishes great leaders, but no other corps commander displayed such technical competence and flexibility."

• • •

After V-E Day, after the German armies in the Netherlands had capitulated, the Canadians had a host of problems to handle. First, the enemy had approximately 150,000 troops in western Holland and some 30,000 in the Emden–Wilhelmshaven area of northwest Germany, and they remained a powerful if demoralized and defeated force. They controlled large sections of the communications, transportation, and administrative systems of the Netherlands, and under the surrender agreements,

General Blaskowitz was "responsible for the maintenance and discipline of all German troops" in the western Netherlands. The newly liberated Dutch were more than a little surprised to see armed Canadian soldiers going up the street while armed Germans passed the other way. And the Dutch Resistance fighters sometimes had to be restrained from trying to kill any stray German soldier they came across. In Germany, II Canadian Corps dealt with General Erich Straube, and orders were passed to Straube's staff in daily conferences.

The Canadian goal was to concentrate the defeated enemy into manageable areas, disarm them, and return those in Holland to camps in Germany as expeditiously as possible. The German high command assisted in this process, with some units simply dropping their weapons and moving to a designated concentration area. These "Surrendered Enemy Personnel" or "Disarmed Enemy Forces," as they were called, were not granted prisoner-of-war status; they were to be self-sufficient and organizationally intact, and, to the extent practicable, were required to administer and maintain themselves. This was dubious international law, to say the least—a violation of the Geneva Conventions—but in the circumstances of Europe in May 1945, it seemed all the Allies could or would do.

In fact, the Canadian and German commands worked efficiently together, the Canadians issuing orders to the Germans, and the Germans carrying them out. But within the concentration areas, the Germans ran their own show, each area having a commander. As Chris Madsen, a historian of the period, noted, "a parallel German leadership existed beside the Canadian military hierarchy. German troops in Holland maintained, with Canadian approval, allegiance to the larger German armed forces."

Here was where difficulties of a particular kind began to arise. Some German soldiers and sailors had deserted their units in Holland, found shelter with relatives or girlfriends, and waited for the end of the war. With the capitulation, they were picked up by Canadian units or Dutch Resistance elements. During the war, the Allies had encouraged Germans to desert, but now Canadian policy—deserters from any military being seen as bad for discipline—was to hand them back to the German military, where severe punishment awaited them. The Canadians would not interfere.

On May 12, members of the Dutch Underground brought two deserters to the German detention camp at a factory that was guarded by the Seaforth Highlanders of 1st Canadian Division. Bruno Dorfer and Rainer Beck were sailors in the Kriegsmarine, and the Seaforths turned them over to the Germans. The next morning, the German commandant informed the Seaforths that the two would be tried and, when found guilty, shot as deserters. The fifteen-minute trial took place before the entire German population in the detention camp, and the guilty verdict was quickly pronounced. In an Allied policy vacuum, the decision to carry through with the execution was made by General Blaskowitz.

The Seaforths duly arranged for a truck and issued eight rifles with sixteen rounds of ammunition to the Germans, and astonishingly, the Seaforths' acting Commanding Officer sent soldiers to ensure that the firing squad was not interfered with by Resistance fighters. On May 13, Dorfer and Beck were lined up against the wall of an air raid shelter and shot. Apparently as many as eighteen other deserters had been or were subsequently turned over to the Germans by Canadian units to suffer the same fate. "Order and discipline," Madsen wrote, "overrode claims to justice."

But soon, some Canadians began to question their army's acquiescence in the executions, and the policy quickly changed; within a few days of the killing of Beck and Dorfer, it was decided that Germans who had deserted after the surrender would be turned over to their own authorities, but wartime deserters would be treated as POWs and handled differently.

The executions were a shameful episode, but one that was quickly forgotten in the general obscenity of the war. The Canadians now wanted to get the Germans out of the Netherlands as quickly as could be managed, through the process detailed in what was called Operation Eclipse, and that evacuation required the cooperation of the German military. The operation began on May 15, the Seaforths moving their camp inmates to a larger concentration area. General Blaskowitz's staff planned the march of German units back to their homeland, and the Canadians simply accepted the German plans. Beginning on May 25, the "Surrendered Enemy Personnel" marched in large and extremely orderly formations of approximately 10,000 men by road. Canadian troops went along to hold back the Dutch. It was, said General Hoffmeister, "obvious right from the start that we were going to have to deploy practically the whole division because the Dutch people would have wounded a lot of them and maybe killed a few." The enemy troops and vehicles were subject to search, and Canadian troops took more than 15 million guilders from the Germans, some of it hidden in ambulances or carried by female soldiers. Searches were carried out several times en route, and the goods retrieved ranged from fur coats to jewellery.

The Germans completed their return to northwest Germany on barges or landing craft, and once they arrived, more transport was seized and returned to Holland. Bill Boss, a Canadian Press correspondent, flew over the landing craft loaded with Germans. "We were," he reported, "cheered by several thousand Germans ... They were in good spirits as they waved and shouted at the aircraft." Boss added that that Dutch civilians sometimes threw stones at the marching columns, "but so far there has been no serious incident. This is probably due to the fact the Canadian escorts have orders to open fire immediately the German troops attempt to start trouble." More likely, it was because the Germans had been disarmed. By June 15, the evacuation from Holland and concentration on German soil had ended.

Ten days earlier, First Canadian Army had ordered Blaskowitz to reorganize and consolidate units within his 25th German Army—the unstated but nonetheless real rationale being that, in case the Red Army made aggressive moves, the hundreds of thousands of surrendered Germans constituted a force that might be needed. The Cold War was in creation. It was not until 1946 that the German forces in the British zone of Germany began to be demobilized. In the meantime, thousands of German soldiers died of hunger and disease in squalid camps. European civilians too, both the liberated and the defeated, were short of food, but prisoners of war, even German POWs—whatever they were called by Allied military policy-makers—ought to have been entitled to decent treatment. So too should the German deserters executed because of Canadian naiveté.

• • •

Once the Canadians had escorted the defeated enemy out of the Netherlands, First Canadian Army became the occupying army. That states matters baldly, but correctly. The Dutch had been liberated and were grateful, exceedingly so, showering kisses on the liberating troops and taking them into their homes and frequently into their beds. But the Canadians, while allies, were nonetheless foreigners, and they had the food, fuel, and power to offer or deny to a population that had suffered five years of brutal occupation and was now short of everything. The Germans had sent 550,000 Dutch men to Germany for forced labour, and most of these men were still trying to get home, if indeed they had survived; 30,000 had not. Others were in German or Japanese prisoner-of-war camps, waiting on repatriation or V-J Day. At least 16,000 Dutch men, women, and children had died of starvation; 70,000 more died of disease after liberation, and thousands more were desperately ill. In all, the Netherlands government estimated in 1948 that the enemy, Allied bombings, the deportation and killing of Jews, and starvation and disease had claimed 271,900 lives out of a population of 8.8 million.

Food and clothing were scarce in Holland and, if available, very expensive. In June, for example, butter was $12 Canadian a pound (approximately $190 in 2015 dollars) on the black market, but that was a bargain compared to the price of $61 during the German occupation; tea was unobtainable, and a woman's dress that had been valued at $9 before the war could be had only for $200. The bus and streetcar systems in the cities scarcely operated, and the railways were broken. The black market had functioned during the war—and still did. Wrote Michiel Horn, a Dutch-born Canadian historian who has written on the liberation period, simply surviving had placed "a premium … on deceit, theft and ingenious mendicancy." Very simply, authority had broken down, and in the dislocation of the spring and summer of 1945, it seemed unlikely to reassert itself quickly.

The basic task of the Canadians in the Netherlands immediately after V-E Day was to feed the Dutch. Vast quantities of foodstuffs and other necessities came into the country for distribution to the population—in all, the Canadians said, 242,000 tons of food, coal, gasoline, stores, and equipment by June 22. In addition, the Canadians seized goods from the Germans, including radios, bicycles, horses, automobiles, and trucks, all of which was turned over to the Dutch authorities. But why was this detailed list collected? Because Dutch newspapers complained bitterly that the Canadians had shipped food and supplies from Holland to Germany for the maintenance of the German civilian population. General Crerar had to produce an explanation, which verified the precision of his figures, and a statement that the Germans had been permitted to take from the Netherlands only 450 tons of the food, fuel, and stores, which they required for their immediate needs. But as this episode suggested, the liberators were beginning to be viewed with suspicion.

The soldiers in Holland were allowed and encouraged to have a good time. Discipline relaxed, and the men took courses on farming or academic subjects or simply began planning their futures and celebrating the end of the war with parties, dances, liquor, and sex. Captain Hal MacDonald of the North Shore Regiment wrote home on May 29 from Doorn that he had gone to a dance that was "swell ... Everybody got drunk or happy." After another all-night party that concluded with a drunken ride in a scout car, MacDonald wrote that "the locals think we're crazy. Sometimes I wonder."

Public buildings, schools, and factories had been turned into

Canadian barracks, while clubs and sports grounds were reserved for soldiers' use; this created some resentment, burgomasters pressing to be told when these facilities would be returned to them. There were tensions in the first weeks and months after liberation, but every effort was made by the grateful Dutch to see that *onze Canadezen,* "our Canadians," were well cared for. Fraternization was encouraged, home visits were frequent, and the troops regularly brought along canned meat, tea, coffee, and chocolate, all items in short supply for the Dutch.

(At the same time, a young Captain Farley Mowat of the Hastings and Prince Edward Regiment received orders to begin collecting German equipment in the Netherlands and Germany for shipment to Canada. The Canadian War Museum in Ottawa and other institutions across the nation wanted their trophies. Mowat gathered tons of materiel, even including a V-1 rocket that had room for a suicidally inclined pilot, a Jagdpanzer anti-aircraft armoured vehicle, and a "beetle tank," a remote-controlled tracked demolition vehicle that had been used against Canadians in Normandy. Some of this German materiel remains on display in Ottawa's new Canadian War Museum.)

Unfortunately, the occupation provided the Canadians plenty of opportunities for illegal money-making. Although soldiers were forbidden to sell goods to civilians or to barter, the orders were essentially not enforceable. Cigarettes were plentiful for the soldiers (gratis or from Canada for $3 per thousand) but very scarce for civilians. A few cigarettes could buy sex; a pack or two of twenty could sometimes be traded for a Leica camera. Liquor was available to officers, but it was as scarce as tobacco for civilians; not a few Canadian officers took advantage of the deals that could be made by trading whisky for luxury goods. And virtually every kind of military stores—from boots and soap to typewriters and radios to jeeps—found its way onto the black market. The corruption and misappropriation of Army supplies was widespread and led to the courts martial of several officers, including Brigadier J.F.A. Lister, the Chief of Staff of the occupation forces, who had lived very high on the hog. Lister was acquitted (and treated the officers who had tried him to champagne in the officers' mess) despite accusatory testimony by General Guy Simonds. And while Major Gerald Levenston, stationed in Holland in September 1945, helped in the rescue and return of some two hundred works of art belonging to the Kröller-Müller Museum in Otterlo, including priceless paintings by Vincent Van Gogh, other Canadians disappointingly looted whatever they could find. One gunner wrote in April 1945, while fighting was still fierce, that one of his battery mates "got stuck in Holten while looting before it had been taken. Had to lay down a heavy barrage to get him clear. Result—loss of 60 days pay & w[ee]k's guard" duty at Regimental Headquarters. Queen Wilhelmina actually felt obliged to protest to General Simonds about the looting of art, a complaint that led to the courts martial of two officers.

The greatest irritant in relations between the Dutch and the Canadians was the way women swarmed around the liberators. This was understandable—the soldiers were fit young men with access to scarce commodities, while Dutch males, if they were even in the country, had been weakened by privation. Dutch men had been beaten militarily by the Germans in 1940, wrote one journalist, and beaten again sexually in 1945. "Let's face it," one Dutch war bride said in 1980, "after what we had been through the Canadians looked delicious." The proper

Dutch worried about this, as did their clergy, and girls were warned that the Canadians would eventually go home and leave them behind, perhaps with a baby (6,000 babies were fathered by Canadian soldiers, and there are still organizations of Dutch men and women looking for their fathers, "Private Jones from Toronto"). Dutch comedian Wim Kan had a routine, Michiel Horn wrote, in which he described the liberation as the time "when the Canadians threw out the Germans and supplied Dutch men with cigarettes, Dutch women with chocolate, and Dutch children with little brothers and sisters." It seemed to be so, and some towns saw illegitimacy rates increase tenfold from pre-war years. "We will do anything for the Canadians," a newspaper editorialized in August. "But our girls must stay away from them. We can't accept the risks. And we will praise God when the Canadians have gone back to Canada." The Canadians wanted to go home too, but they took along 1,886 Dutch war brides and 428 children, their passage paid by the Canadian government. Many more presumably married a year or two after the Canadians had returned to Canada.

One of those Canadians who fell in love in the Netherlands was Brigadier James Roberts, who had commanded the 8th Infantry Brigade in the 3rd Division with great distinction. Roberts had been away from Canada for six long years when he met May Ruys de Perez in Doorn in late May. She was the widow of a Dutch air force officer who had been executed by the Nazis, and had a young son. Roberts secured compassionate leave to return to Canada to inform his wife—who had also moved on to other relationships—that he wanted a divorce. There was no objection, and Roberts and Ruys de Perez soon married.

By the autumn of 1945 it was becoming clear that the Canadian occupation had gone on too long. Resentment was growing at the perceived lavishness of the Army's officers' clubs, at the plenitude of food and drink available to the Canadians but not to the Dutch, and at the truck parks full of vehicles that seemed to stay unused when transport for civilian purposes was unavailable. The situation was such that Queen Wilhelmina told General Simonds that he should take his Canadians home. "Including the dead, Your Majesty?" was the general's perhaps apocryphal reply.

The developing bad feeling was understandable. The Dutch wanted their lives—their nation—back, and any occupation force, even a friendly one, was hard to bear. The Canadians too wanted to go home, and by March 1946, almost all the soldiers had departed. But before he left the Netherlands for repatriation, Edmund Fitzgerald, an NCO in the North Novas, went to call on the Dutch families he'd got to know. "[T]here were three piles of coal in the schoolyard" where his unit HQ was, and he told them, "'You can have two of those piles. You have to take them after midnight and they have to be cleaned up afterwards' … The next morning the two piles were gone and the cement was as clean as ever."

Now, almost seventy years later, every trace of resentment is gone and only the immense gratitude for liberation remains. The emotional victory parades in Apeldoorn every five years will come to an end very soon as the last Second World War veterans finally succumb, but they were amazing displays of affection, with young mothers holding up a baby to a Canadian vet so that the child could be told a decade hence that he or she had been kissed by one of the liberators. In Apeldoorn in 1995, one banner hung over a neighbourhood street by local residents read, in English, "Bless You, Boys," and that seemed a particularly appropriate phrase that made eighty-five-year-old Canadian vets sob openly.

The Dutch-born writer and scholar Ian Buruma wrote of that same parade in his fine book *Year Zero: A History of 1945*. He described "elderly Canadian men … saluting the crowd with tears in their eyes, remembering the days when they were kings." But what struck Buruma most was "the behavior of elderly Dutch women … in a state of frenzy … stretching their arms to the men in their jeeps … 'Thank you! Thank you! Thank you!' They couldn't help themselves. They too were reliving their hours of exultation. It was one of the most weirdly erotic scenes I have ever witnessed."

• • •

There was no such gratitude expressed by the locals to the Canadian Army Occupation Force (CAOF) in Germany. Ottawa had approved Canadian participation in the eventual occupation of Germany in December 1944 with a force of approximately 25,000 men organized as an infantry division. The division's units were to be formed from soldiers in reinforcement units in England, from volunteers in the divisions that had fought the war, and from "low point" men—that is, soldiers who were not likely to be quickly repatriated to Canada because their time in service was short. Major-General Chris Vokes was named commander of the 3rd Canadian Division, Canadian Army Occupation Force, and the force began its move from the Netherlands to northwest Germany in the Oldenburg region.

Aside from the Canadian Berlin Battalion, a composite unit that spent a month in the destroyed German capital in the summer of 1945 to represent Canada during the Potsdam Conference and the Berlin Victory Parade, the CAOF's task was to impose the will of the Allies on the defeated enemy, to care for displaced persons—of whom hundreds of thousands roamed through Germany trying to get home or to Palestine or anywhere safe—to regulate relations between German groups, and, gradually, to acquiesce in the breaking down of the "no fraternization" policy that had forbidden Allied soldiers from having any relations with the German population. The orders actually stated, or so one RCAF non-commissioned officer, Stanley Winfield, recalled in a memoir, that "you must not have anything whatsoever to do with German nationals and this includes smiling or giving gum or chocolate etc. to any child regardless of age."

There was no difficulty with the locals, militarism having been completely blasted out of them by bombing and crushing defeat. Winfield noted that the Germans "were still bowing and scraping, doffing their hats and saluting every private just to be sure of not making any mistakes." But they were amazed that the Canadians were not permitted to have anything to do with them. "The frauleins took definite advantage of this order and saw only the wonderful opportunity of 'getting even.' They would go for a stroll where they knew Allied soldiers would be ... and appear as vivacious and desirable as they possibly could. They knew if a soldier was caught talking or even smiling at them it would mean a heavy fine ... for the soldier involved." A young officer wrote home in July that "the non-fraternization policy has not been too hard to deal with so far, because we don't go out much and there isn't much in town anyway. At least nothing has caught my eye so far! It may be better that way anyhow. But the policy is ridiculous! It is we who are being punished," he went on, "not the Germans, who couldn't care less and who just laugh at us. They would be willing to make friends and cooperate. But if this non-fraternization policy lasts too long, they will end up being difficult and crazy." In fact, the *frauleins* had all the cards, and Canadians soon succumbed, the no-fraternization policy be damned, securing sex in return for providing the women with cigarettes and food, items of huge value on the local economy.

Another soldier, Captain Hal MacDonald, wrote that the German civilians "can't take gentleness. Treat them like slaves or swine & they'll do as you order them. In other words they will accept orders meekly but do not know how to accept gentleness." Later he talked of "sullen people who doff their hats as we pass." Behind every house, he said, "we have come across buried loot & goods—chattels, silks, liqueurs, SS equipment—anything & everything—shoes, suits."

Inevitably, the occupation of Germany soon turned out to be a party, with local wine and women, and song from visiting military entertainment troupes. General Vokes ruled his area as a personal fiefdom and took up hunting, and his ample wine cellar was well used by visiting Canadian dignitaries. During the no-fraternization period, Major-General James Tedlie later recalled, Vokes set up leave centres in nearby Denmark so officers and men "could get fucked." Senior officers and sergeants alike soon had mistresses, and one member of the Berlin Battalion observed that "troops evacuated by our Medical Officer generally suffered, not from shrapnel, but from VD."

Sergeant Winfield gave his estimates of what cigarettes could be bartered for in Celle, southeast of Oldenburg, where he was based: a Leica camera went for 500 to 1,500 cigarettes; watches for 500 to 800; binoculars, 300 to 500; silk at 10 cigarettes per metre; jewellery and precious stones, 100 to 500 cigarettes. "Our boys," Winfield wrote, "are acquiring articles worth hundreds and hundreds of dollars for practically nothing."

The CAOF began its return to Canada in late March 1946. By late June, all the men were gone, their duties turned over to the British.

• • •

The repatriation of the 280,000 or so soldiers and nursing sisters of the Army overseas—on the Continent and in Britain—was a colossal task. The plan, derived at First Canadian Army Headquarters in consultation with Ottawa, was initially organized roughly on the basis of "first in, first out." Each soldier had a points score based on when he enlisted and where he had served. One month's service in Canada was worth two points, while a month's service overseas was worth three; twenty additional points were added for married soldiers, widowers, or the divorced with dependent children. Those with high point scores were to be the first to go home, and some began leaving in May 1945. But the Army also sought volunteers for the occupation force, securing some 10,000; they would remain in Europe. Simultaneously, it sought men to go to the Pacific, where the victory over Japan had still to be won. Some 25,000 soldiers volunteered to serve in the Canadian division, organized and equipped along American army lines, that was to form the Canadian Army Pacific Force and to participate in the invasion of the Japanese home islands. As an encouragement for volunteers, the Army offered thirty days' leave in Canada. The atomic bombs on Nagasaki and Hiroshima ended the war in the Pacific in August, and the Canadian Army

Pacific Force was disbanded. Those who had volunteered were among the first to return from overseas and the first to be demobilized.

The process of repatriation was too slow for men awaiting their return to civilian life. "We all have one thing in mind," Gunner Ted Loney wrote from his camp in England, "and that is to get out of here as fast as possible, if possible." From the Netherlands, Captain Hal MacDonald told his wife on June 11 that his brigadier had briefed him on repatriation: "Those with up to 100 pts are put into Occupation & remain there until their turn comes. Then, as a rough guide, 110 to 180 pts return with their b[attalio]ns on a territorial basis—over 180 points are now posted to 1st or 2nd Div who go back before 3rd Div. It is anticipated that 3rd Div goes back in September … It def[initely] put me into a funk," he wrote, contemplating his 174 points. "Had been planning on being back by August." Major Harry Jolley, the dental officer with 12th Light Field Ambulance, had moved from Germany to the Netherlands by July 18 and wrote that he was "browned off" because "there's so very little to do that seems worthwhile & any entertainment provided seems to be only something that helps fill in a few hours … Work & monotony," he said, in a small Dutch town without any real recreational facilities.

Other soldiers, waiting in the United Kingdom for "ships that never come in," grew unhappy enough to riot in Aldershot on July 4 and 5, 1945, furious at the delays and angry that some NRMA conscripts somehow managed to get repatriated before long-service volunteers. Oddly, Major-General Dan Spry, commanding the Canadian Reinforcement Units in England, had to deal with the rioters; his father, Lieutenant-Colonel D.C.B. Spry, had had the very same task in 1919, when Canadians ran amok at Kinmel Park camp near Liverpool for similar reasons. Remembering the Aldershot riots of 1945, General Spry's wife said she feared for his life, as he insisted on driving his jeep into the rioting mobs. Spry was unhurt, and there were no serious casualties, though nearly 800 windows were broken in the town. Six rioters received prison sentences ranging from eight days to seven years, and, General Spry said, their "schoolboyish action" threatened to "undermine the good reputation Canadians have built up on the battlefield."

General Crerar could see that First Canadian Army was caught up in a process of "repatriation by disintegration," losing qualified officers and trades specialists at a high rate. If this went on, the Army would soon cease to function, so the first in, first out principle was adjusted. Repatriation now was to be on "a selected sequence of Divisional Groups, units and sub-units," as MacDonald had been told, instead of only drafts of high-point soldiers. The points for repatriation were lowered in mid-June. Then there was a sudden and unexpected availability of shipping—the war with Japan had been ended by the A-bombs on Nagasaki and Hiroshima—and repatriation sped up. MacDonald learned on August 16 that his number had come up, and he proceeded to England. He was made the adjutant for his draft of men, and had to organize "documentation, parades. Forms, travel warrants for Eng[lish] leave, and ration cards." Then, after some shopping and theatre visits in London, he spent the morning of September 14 "putting the men through their last Medicals and Pay, etc." Finally, he boarded ship for Canada on September 15.

Overall, there had been 281,757 men in First Canadian Army in Northwest Europe on V-E Day; by New Year's Eve, 184,054 had been returned home. By October 1946, as many as 343,000 Army, RCAF, and RCN personnel and 45,000 dependents had been repatriated from overseas, and a grand total of 713,000 men and women had been discharged from the armed forces.

On the Continent, the headquarters of First Canadian Army closed down on July 30, 1945; the next day, General Simonds took command of the Canadian Forces in the Netherlands (CFN). Simonds's command gradually shrank: by the end of August, some 59,000 had been repatriated; by the end of November, 101,575. The headquarters of the Canadian divisions closed down in succession, and the HQ of CFN ceased operations on May 31, 1946. All that remained were some 500 Canadians building war cemeteries, helping soldiers' war brides get to Canada, arranging transport, and completing other duties. Even these duties concluded on November 30.

The war artist and, later, iconic Canadian painter Lieutenant Alex Colville wrote that he had remained overseas until early October 1945. "I came home on the Ile de France with 11,000 other people. We sailed into Halifax harbor on a Sunday morning, the 21st of October. It was a very beautiful morning, clear and sunny. I had never thought of myself as a patriot or even a sentimental person," he said, "but I was very moved by this experience."

In mid-December 1945, 645 officers and men of the Queen's Own Rifles of Canada reached Halifax aboard the *Monarch of Bermuda*, in time to be home for Christmas. Only three officers and nine men of those who landed were with the regiment when it first left Canada. A total of 385 QORs had been killed in action or died of wounds, two of them on V-E Day. The six years of war had taken a very heavy toll, and the surviving members of the regiment—and all who served in Canada's armed forces—would carry its scars for the rest of their lives.

...

Who fought Canada's war against Hitler and the Nazis? Trying to calculate which groups of Canadians provided the men and women who served in the Canadian armed forces in the Second World War is no easy task. We know that 1.1 million, or 10 percent of the total population of 11 million, donned a uniform at some point in the war. Of those, almost a million men and women, or more than 90 percent, volunteered to serve in the armed forces, an astonishing statistic that demonstrates the nation's resolve to defeat Hitler and the Nazis. We also know that roughly 750,000 served in the Canadian Army, 250,000 in the Royal Canadian Air Force, and 100,000 in the Royal Canadian Navy. Some 50,000 of these enlistments were women. But there is no genuinely hard data on how long men and women served, and on whether men were called up under the National Resources Mobilization Act and then volunteered—or not—for service before enrolment, or if they joined the RCAF or RCN on receiving call-up notices for the Army. The best information, from a Cabinet committee set up in the midst of the conscription crisis of 1944, indicates that from March 1941 until then, 150,000 men had been conscripted under the NRMA. Of this number, 42,000 had gone "active," 33,500 had been released, 6,000 had transferred to the RCAF or RCN, and 8,676 were on extended leave.

The task of identifying service in the Canadian forces by ethnicity and religion is even more difficult. We do know that the Canadian-born made up a substantial majority of enlistments. The best estimates are that French Canada saw 150,000 or so of its sons and daughters join the forces, or about one in seven of all enlistments, a much higher ratio than in the Great War. This took place notwithstanding marriage courses offered by parish churches in Montreal in the summer of 1940 to help young single men avoid being called up under the NRMA by getting married. The very powerful *nationaliste* rhetoric in French Canada created and continuously fed the sense that the Second World War was only another British imperialist war, and that Canada had no real stake in the fight. Major T.L. Bullock, a French Canadian officer, wrote in 1944 that "we must begin with the realization that the French-Canadians who have volunteered for active service overseas are those among our young men who ... have the broadest minds, the most tolerant views and the greatest aptitude to become leaders." But, Bullock continued, "because of the political atmosphere in French Canada, it takes more courage for a French-Canadian to enlist ... Our boys have to defy public opinion to enlist." This was surely correct. Even a highly intelligent young man like Pierre Elliott Trudeau, a *nationaliste* in the early 1940s, completely missed the necessity of stopping Hitler and the Nazis, viewing the war as merely another eruption of British imperialism, and treated the Canadian Officers' Training Corps at the Université de Montréal as a joke; Trudeau left Canada in 1944 to attend Harvard University in the United States. Those francophones who volunteered to fight for Canada and against Hitler flew directly into the teeth of an anti-war, anti-British, anti–de Gaulle and his Free French public opinion.

We also know that in late 1944, the remaining 60,000 NRMA "Zombies," the diehard group of home defence conscripts who resisted service overseas until the King government compelled 16,000 of them, were mainly French-speaking and "ethnic." Of NRMA men conscripted in 1944, 47 percent (62.6 percent in 1945) listed Quebec as their place of residence. Also worth note is that in 1944, of the 60,000 NRMA men in the ranks, 6,000 had been called up in 1941, 25,000 in 1942, 17,000 in 1943, and 10,000 earlier in 1944. The Zombies who resisted repeated calls to volunteer to fight overseas were mainly men with relatively long service.

One senior officer who had grappled with the question of trying to persuade NRMA men to volunteer for overseas service was Brigadier W.H.S. Macklin. He noted in May 1944 that he had had almost no success in persuading francophones in the Régiment de Hull to volunteer, and he added that "the great majority [of NRMA soldiers in other units] are of non-British origin—German, Italian, and Slavic nationalities predominating. Moreover most of them come from farms. They are of deplorably low education, know almost nothing of Canadian or British history and in fact are typical European peasants." The NRMA men included a large number of English-speakers (37.5 percent) whose ethnic origins remain unclear; many were likely of British origin. Daniel Byers's detailed research on the composition of the NRMA men generally supports Macklin's observations on ethnicity, though not necessarily his commentary.

It is also important to note that several ethnic, religious, or racial groups—in some cases despite the fact that Canada was at war with their nation of origin—claim that their men enlisted in very high proportions. Italian Canadians apparently served in large numbers, even though the Fascist Mussolini regime had had substantial numbers of supporters in Canada before 1940 (some of whom were interned). Ukrainian Canadians were badly divided between Communist and anti-Communist leanings, and the former had little incentive to serve when Hitler and Stalin were allied between August 1939 and June 1941. Large but indeterminate numbers nonetheless enlisted, although Ukrainian Canadian organizations that campaigned for a "yes" vote in the April 1942 conscription plebiscite were badly embarrassed when constituencies with large Ukrainian populations voted "no." Polish Canadians, with many good reasons to enlist if they had old-country ties, also apparently served in substantial numbers. "Hundreds" of blacks are said to have joined and served alongside their white comrades, as did 3,090 Status Indians, or 2.4 percent of males, a figure that does not include non-Status or Métis men. About 600 Chinese Canadians served, or so Chinese cultural groups claim, even though racist attitudes meant that they were not called up under the NRMA until 1944, nor allowed to join the RCAF until October 1942 or the RCN until March 1943. Some 200 Japanese Canadians enlisted, most leaving the camps in the British Columbia interior to which they had been forcibly evacuated in early 1942 to do so. We also are told that, while Mennonites and Hutterites were excused military service, some 3,000 Mennonites did enlist. But all this information is fragmentary, and none is based on anything more than self-collected material and much propagandistic, breast-beating hearsay. It can be nothing more until all the personnel records are searched.

Jewish Canadians have been particularly assiduous in speaking of their record of service. Gerald Tulchinsky, much the most reliable interpreter of the data, cites the Canadian Jewish Congress's figure of 16,441 men and 279 women who served, 39.1 percent of Jewish men of military age. This, he observes, did not compare favourably to the 41.4 percent of eligible Canadian men who served. Tulchinsky noted that Jewish participation in the Army, especially its combat units, and in the navy was below national levels. Jews constituted 1.5 percent of Canada's population in 1940, but provided 2.6 percent of its airmen, 1.4 percent of its soldiers, and 0.7 percent of its sailors.

Tulchinsky was also the first to venture into the reasons why Jewish enlistment varied by service and corps. The RCN, where anti-Semitism was rampant, initially appeared to refuse to enlist Jews, and the RCAF's physical and education standards were very high at the outbreak of war. Except for a few regiments, the Army took almost anyone, it appears, but Jews, apparently with more education than the norm, tended to be pushed toward—or perhaps chose—non-combat roles. Many served in frontline units, however, and some—like the later backroom politico Eddie Goodman in the Fort Garry Horse, Canadian historian Joe Levitt in the Governor General's Foot Guards, and businessmen Ben Dunkelman and Barney Danson in the Queen's Own Rifles—had distinguished records. Nonetheless, the death rate for all Canadian servicemen was 4.08 percent; for Jews in uniform, it was a much lower 2.61 percent. In his unsparing but sympathetic account in *Canada's Jews*, Tulchinsky added that of the 16,441 Canadian Jewish men enrolled, 21.2 percent were home defence conscripts—2.2 percent of the total of all who served in the NRMA. This compared to Jews' 1.46 percent of the total population, and was, he notes, the highest percentage for any religious denomination.

As far as one can tell, therefore, it was English-speaking Canadians of British origin who made up the bulk of those who served in the Canadian Army in the Second World War. But all who volunteered to fight Nazism and those conscripts who served overseas, whatever their origin or ethnicity, did their bit in a good, just, and necessary cause.

It was a just cause, this last good war, but that was only small compensation for those the dead left behind. Gregory Clark, a Great War officer, war correspondent, and well-known columnist for the *Toronto Star*, lost his son, Murray, killed near Boulogne in September 1944. Seven years later, he visited the Commonwealth War Graves Cemetery at Calais, where Murray, a twenty-three-year-old lieutenant in the Regina Rifles and an aspiring poet, lay. "He sleeps in a garden," he wrote his wife, "on a high and remote hilltop with six hundred and eighty-nine more of his Canadian comrades, amid roses, hydrangea, golden mimosas." The emotion of the visit overwhelmed Clark: "I fell down to my knees and simply let go ... And I found myself saying: 'Thank you, God, for letting us have him for the years we did ... for the years we were blessed by having him.'"

• • •

For a month before and a month after V-E Day, Canadians were in the midst of an election campaign, the national vote taking place on June 11. The Progressive Conservatives were led by John Bracken, a stiff—indeed, wooden—former Liberal-Progressive premier of Manitoba who had been selected as leader at the end of 1942. The Co-operative Commonwealth Federation, the social-democratic party, had the intelligent, able Major J. Coldwell—Major was not a military rank but an unusual first name—as its chief.

The Liberals, as they had been since 1919, were headed by Mackenzie King, and the party's program was forward-looking: social welfare and Keynesian economics. During the war, the government had brought in unemployment insurance and family allowances, the hugely popular baby bonus that, beginning on July 1, 1945, would put money in the hands of many women for the first time. While there were no promises of great new social programs in the campaign, the Liberals did make clear that they were spending heavily on veterans' benefits, housing, conversion of industry to peace, and a host of plans to ensure that the Great Depression did not resume after the war, that the transition from war to peace was smoothed by huge dollops of government cash.

The CCF, heavily attacked by business groups as the next thing to Communists and simultaneously as "national socialists," were Liberals in a big hurry. Their social-democratic program pitched social welfare, high spending, and an eventual end to the miseries and inequalities of capitalism. Bracken's Tories, however, went against the direction of its opponents, calling for conscription for the war in the Pacific and lambasting the Liberals for their many wartime sins.

For only the second time in Canadian political history—the first was the 1917 election during the Great War—the military vote mattered. There were approximately 750,000 military voters, a huge segment of the electorate in a total Canadian population of 11 million. The soldiers' vote was taken early in June and the results delivered to Canada to be added to the constituency totals released on June 11. Each of the parties eagerly sought the military vote, the Conservatives especially working hard. Party polling had discovered very high CCF sentiment—perhaps as much as 90 percent in the RCAF, for example—and the Conservatives in consequence had deluged the forces with literature and gifts of cigarettes. The troops who had served in or passed through England—where Winston Churchill, the saviour of civilization and the British Isles, would be crushingly defeated in July—had seen the sentiment for

Labour growing. The soldiers in Europe and Canada had heard and read of the Tories pushing conscription for the Japanese war, a policy for which there was almost no support in the military.

On the other hand, all the serving men and women, soon to be veterans, could see what the Liberals were promising them: the Veterans Charter, which included rehabilitation grants; a clothing allowance; out-of-work grants; a generous gratuity based on length and theatre of service (the average payment was $700 at a time when the weekly wage was some $40); pensions for the disabled and for dependents of those killed; free education, including university (by 1947, 35,000 vets were enrolled in university programs); a farm, if desired; help in starting a business; and perpetual medical care for the wounded and injured. Moreover, the 50,000 women veterans received exactly the same benefits as men. This Charter was astonishingly generous, the initial estimate of its cost to the treasury being $1.2 billion (the total federal budget in 1939 had been $550 million), a clear attempt to ensure that justifiable grievances over the treatment of Great War veterans after 1919 would not be repeated. There was some cynicism—one RCAF flight lieutenant said, "I don't know a great deal" about the Charter "except that every man is going to be a millionaire and be given a home and a cushy job. Somehow or other, that doesn't sound right to me." But as the historian of the veterans' programs, Peter Neary, wrote, "There had never before been a social welfare scheme of such scope and magnitude in Canada, and it unquestionably delivered much to many. The Veterans Charter truly was a nation-building initiative by the Government of Canada." None of this hurt the Liberals.

What the Charter did completely guarantee was the rehabilitation of the wounded. Stewart Bull, a company commander in the Essex

Scottish, was wounded in Operation Totalize in August 1944; he lost an eye, and his face was badly damaged. He spent much time in hospital in England, had repeated plastic surgery, and gradually recovered. But the war had a permanent impact on his life. "Today I bear three evidences of the war," he wrote much later. "One is, of course, that I have no right eye. I have an artificial eye, which is replaced annually ... The second thing is that I have no sense of smell. Ever since my time in the hospital I've felt that I could not tell what food was before me ... The third thing is that in my face, from my nose across to my cheekbone, and down to my jaw line, and over to my lips and mouth, there's no feeling. There has never been any feeling for the last 60 years." Bull was philosophical about his wounds: "That's not a serious thing." He had survived, and he received medical care as long as he lived, thanks to the Veterans Charter and the Department of Veterans Affairs, which ran more than thirty medical facilities across the country, initially with beds for 17,000 patients.

But the impact of the benefits for veterans was yet to be felt by the soldiers who would cast their votes in the general election. Certainly nothing helped to change their perception of the prime minister. The troops detested Mackenzie King, wrote Kurt Loeb of the Argyll and Sutherland Highlanders, "his prissy walk and manner of speaking and his evident discomfort at being in the company of such vulgarians" as common soldiers. But it was the failure to reinforce the Army in France that truly agitated soldiers. Elmer Bell, a lawyer from Wellington County, Ontario, and an artillery officer, expressed the feelings of many after the Falaise Gap battles: "Our tanks and infantry really bore the brunt. It makes me mad every time I think of those fellows here who go on and on and on without a week's rest even and 75,000 Zombies [stay] in Canada. It is," he said bluntly, "building up a hatred that won't be erased in a generation. It is criminal to keep those reinforcements at home."

Still, General Crerar was probably right when he privately told a friend in March 1945 that "there is a general feeling of resentment … and no political party, or person or political life in Canada, stands high at present in the eyes of the Canadian Army Overseas." Perhaps that attitude explained why only 342,907 men and women in uniform voted and almost 400,000 did not. That was one surprise. The other was that Mackenzie King's Liberals won the most votes from the troops, 118,070, compared to 109,679 for the CCF and 87,840 for the Conservatives. The anger expressed by many soldiers fighting on the Scheldt or the Rhineland that the government had not had the courage to enforce full conscription apparently had dissipated with victory. Or, perhaps, the civic education lectures given the troops by junior officers had created interest in making a better world that would not send their sons off to war again. Another possibility is what military historian Lieutenant-Colonel Dr. Jack English called the "de-Canadianization" of the soldiers, "the outright antagonism of many troops toward Canadian policy and Canadians at home." Army researchers at the end of 1944 reported that the "only consistent and pervasive object of Canadian interest to the majority of … personnel … overseas was their family." Certainly this attitude—and the fact that soldiers had been away from Canada for up to five and a half years!—must partially explain the low turnout among military voters overseas.

Whatever the reasons, among the soldier voters in Northwest Europe, the CCF took the most votes, in round numbers 37,000 to 28,000 for the Liberals and 24,000 for the Conservatives. The CCF also led in the vote totals in Britain (and on the Prairies and in British Columbia), but King's party scored heavily among uniformed voters in Quebec, Ontario, and the Maritimes.

Still, the military vote did cost Mackenzie King his own seat in Prince Albert, Saskatchewan. It was "cruel," King told his diary in a self-pitying, self-deluding tone, that "it should be my fate, at the end of the war, in which I have never failed the men overseas once, that I should be beaten by their vote." If his own loss hurt the feelings of the prime minister (who soon found a safe seat in Glengarry, Ontario), he was nonetheless returned to power, his party winning some 45 percent of the civilian vote. The Conservatives took only 67 seats, the CCF 28, and the Liberals from 125 to 127 seats (depending on the voting intentions of Independent Liberals). It was a bare majority in a Parliament of 245, and King had been saved by Quebec, where, despite the fury over conscription in 1942 and 1944, he won 53 seats and 50.8 percent of the popular vote. In the eyes of the Québécois, it seemed, Mackenzie King had resisted the conscriptionists as long as humanly possible.

First Canadian Army's initial commander, General Andrew McNaughton, had lost a by-election in Grey North, Ontario, to a Progressive Conservative on February 5, 1945. Nominally, his views on conscription were the issue, but in fact his wife's Roman Catholicism had seemed to matter greatly in an Orange riding. Despite the loss, McNaughton somehow stayed in Cabinet, and in the general election, he ran for the Liberals in Qu'Appelle, Saskatchewan, where he had been born. He lost badly, finishing third with only 29.6 percent of the vote, but again the rules were bent, and he remained as defence minister into August 1945. The leader of the Canadian soldiers overseas from 1939 to the end of

1943 had discredited himself in the eyes of many Canadians, likely by joining King's government—and by resisting conscription until he, like King, had had to implement a limited version of compulsory service for 16,000 NRMA men.

• • •

The best little army in the world? Among military historians in Britain and the United States, the sense persists strongly that First Canadian Army was something of a disappointment. In the First World War, the Canadian Corps had established a great reputation as a wonderfully effective fighting force, its stature recognized by generals at the time and later by scholars of all nationalities. But the verdict on the fighting capacity of Canadian troops in the 1939–45 conflict has been much more tepid. Max Hastings, the very successful British historian and journalist, was only one who wrote harshly in 2004 that "the Canadian Army was a weak and flawed instrument because of the chronic manning problems imposed by its nation's politics."

The official historian of the Canadian Army in the Second World War sometimes seemed to agree with the critics. Colonel Charles Stacey, the country's greatest military historian, wrote of the failings of the officer corps in Normandy, pointing at the errors not of the generals, but of battalion and company officers. In particular, Stacey was very harsh in assessing what he saw as the failure of II Canadian Corps to close the Falaise Gap before thousands of Germans were able to escape to the east to fight again. Historian John A. English, one of the sharpest critics of the Canadian performance in Normandy, disagreed in 1991, arguing that the blame properly lies at the feet of the generals because they failed first in training their men and then in leading them in battle in Normandy. Yet the same Colonel English wrote in 1998 that "by the end of the war, having paid a steep price in blood for the peacetime neglect of military professionalism, it was probably the best little army in the world. Certainly in the performance of the Canadian Army overseas the government of Canada got much more than it deserved." So which is it?

The first point that must be said is that English was right: Canadian training was sadly flawed for the first two years and more of the war. General McNaughton and his hand-picked commanders either had little interest in training or didn't know how to train well. The learning curve was slow, almost stagnant. It took a British officer, then lieutenant-general Bernard Montgomery, to pick up the Canadian divisions, brigades, and battalions by the scruff of the neck and shake them. "The soldiery in the Canadian Corps are probably the best material in any armies in the Empire. And they are fit and tough. But they are going to be killed in large numbers," Montgomery said, "unless [their] commanders can learn to put them properly into battle." Monty duly got rid of the ineffective leaders; eight of twenty-two major-generals and above who commanded divisions, corps, or the First Canadian Army overseas were fired before they saw action and two more were relieved after their first battle. The Chief of the Imperial General Staff, General Sir Alan Brooke, got rid of McNaughton (with much Canadian help) in late 1943. By then, two Canadian divisions were in Italy, and good commanders and battle-tested soldiers had emerged. In battle, commanders, like their men, learned quickly, or they died. Guy Simonds was the ablest Canadian commander of the war, and he learned to lead in action in Sicily and Italy. Chris Vokes was an effective if unimagina-tive division commander, and Bert Hoffmeister, who rose from major to major-general very quickly, was superb.

Simonds became II Canadian Corps' commander a few months before Normandy and, however able and imaginative a tactician he was, his senior commanders in the first months were flawed indeed. Rod Keller of the 3rd Division was popular but weak, mistrusted by his staff, and properly considered ineffective by British senior officers. Charles Foulkes, the commander of the 2nd Division, was equally uninspiring, yet, protected by his patron General Harry Crerar, he survived. Too many of his soldiers did not.

But within the nine months remaining of the war in Europe, the Canadian commanders improved mightily. The division commanders at the end of the war—Vokes, Harry Foster, Bruce Matthews, Holley Keefler, and Hoffmeister—were very good, and Matthews and Hoff-meister were first-rate. Simonds was a fine corps commander—"a first-class commander with a most original brain and full of initiative," British general Sir Brian Horrocks said—and his creation of armoured personnel carriers revolutionized armoured warfare. Charles Foulkes, commanding I Canadian Corps, turned out to be much better as a corps commander than as a division GOC. (Foulkes, a careerist political animal and master bureaucrat, would be the dominant military figure in the postwar Canadian forces, rather than the more able but politically inept and much less smooth Guy Simonds.) As the Army commander, Crerar was no Napoleon, but he did his job in ensuring that Canadian interests were as well protected as they could be in a military alliance in which Canada was destined to be nothing more than a junior partner.

And as the Canadian commanders improved, so too did their tactics and their soldiers. There were more attacks at night, more Kangaroos, Buffalos, and flamethrowers, more engineers to speed the advance, and superb heavy and field artillery. By late 1944, there were anti-mortar radars, chemical smoke generators, rocket batteries whose fire demoralized the enemy, and the closely coordinated tactical air power that made enemy movement difficult and destroyed vehicles and men. Like their American and British comrades, the soldiers of First Canadian Army also developed their skills in the stress of battle and took advantage of the equipment they had, and the infantry and armour took their objectives. The war was as bloody near its end as it had been at its beginnings; the infantry paid a heavy price, worsened by severe reinforcement difficulties from August to November 1944. But the training system, the move of I Canadian Corps from Italy to Northwest Europe, and the shipping of home defence conscripts overseas in early 1945 largely fixed the manpower problems. Max Hastings's criticisms were uninformed and much overblown.

But yes, First Canadian Army did not get the renown of its Great War predecessor. One reason for this was that Harry Crerar was not Sir Arthur Currie, generally considered by Canadian historians to be Canada's greatest military leader. Crerar was a competent Army bureaucrat, a skilled soldier-politician, but he had not the slightest spark of military genius. He deserves to be remembered primarily because he commanded the first—and last—field army ever deployed by Canada.

The main reason for the absence of kudos, however, is completely different: the combination of time in action with accrued battle experience and expertise. In the 1914–18 war, the 1st Canadian Division went into action in early 1915 and passed what it had learned to the 2nd Division; the 1st and 2nd contributed to the 3rd Division; and the first three gave their accumulated expertise and some of their experienced commanders to the 4th Division, which went into the line in late 1916. By August 1918, when the Canadian Corps began its triumphant Hundred Days, which smashed the German army in the field, the leaders and soldiers had learned how to manoeuvre on the battlefield, and their organization and equipment were first class. The experience gained by each division was shared in a Canadian Corps that saw itself as and was a learning institution.

Matters were different in the 1939–45 war. Hong Kong and Dieppe aside—two disasters that provided little useful battle experience for the few survivors who would later fight in Northwest Europe—no Canadian soldiers saw action in strength until the invasion of Sicily in July 1943. The two divisions that fought in Italy stayed there until early 1945, and although some battle-tested soldiers returned to England to help the 2nd, 3rd, and 4th divisions and the 2nd Armoured Brigade prepare, these formations and the corps and Army headquarters that led them were effectively untested when they landed in France. The 3rd Division saw eleven months in action (and spent more time in "intense combat" with more casualties in Normandy than any British division); the 2nd Division (second in both categories in Normandy) had ten months in action; and the 4th Armoured Division had nine months' combat experience. This was vastly different from the First World War, when even the 4th Canadian Division fought for two years.

This mattered. Experience in battle was the key to effective performance, the critical measurement that separated good officers from bad, fine soldiers from the rest. In the period from June 6, 1944, to the end of August 1944, the men of the Canadian divisions in France learned how to fight and suffered terrible casualties as they did so. By the time of the Scheldt battles—arguably Guy Simonds's ugly tactical masterpiece—they were on their way to greatness, even with their infantry ranks understrength. And when they fought in the Rhineland, northern Germany, and the Netherlands, they were a tough, experienced, well-led, and well-supplied army that had earned and deserved comparison with the best. General Horrocks wrote of working with the Canadians in Operation Veritable that "this was the first time I had come into close contact with the Canadians … I was more and more impressed … They were not only well trained but also seasoned troops … All the plans went very smoothly." General Sir Oliver Leese, who led the British Eighth Army in Italy, also observed that the 1st Canadian Armoured Brigade, which moved to Northwest Europe in February 1945, was "acknowledged by all as the best brigade out here and every division asks for them." Leadership and the battle experience of both officers and men were the keys.

We ought not forget that Canada's Great Power partners also had to get the right leaders and battle experience as they learned how to fight the Germans. Both the British and Americans suffered their debacles in the North African desert and in Northwest Europe, and both armies replaced generals and colonels in action in wholesale lots. Two British armoured divisions were all but destroyed in a day of battle in Operation Goodwood in July in Normandy, losing almost two hundred tanks, and the troops intended to reach the Rhine bridges to relieve Operation Market Garden's airborne troops in September were perhaps less aggressive in pressing forward than they might have been. The British also had their own reinforcement problems and had to cannibalize divisions to keep fighting. For their part, the Americans too had to learn to fight. The Yanks were badly beaten by Rommel at the Kasserine Pass in 1943, and Lieutenant-General Courtney Hodges's First Army of mostly experienced troops battered themselves senseless in the Hürtgen Forest in September, October, and November 1944, while other American divisions were almost wiped out in the Battle of the Bulge in the Ardennes in December. The U.S. Army also had to scramble to find enough reinforcements for its infantry and armoured units. General Jean de Lattre de Tassigny's French First Army ended the war bigger than First Canadian Army, but it was nowhere near as effective in battle, not least because it was notoriously unwilling to follow the Supreme Allied Commander's orders. Allied combat effectiveness varied dramatically, just as much as the Canadians' proficiency sometimes did. All one can say with confidence is that the British, American, French, and Canadian soldiers learned that beating the Germans was never easy.

The Canadian divisions had their difficulties, to be sure. But the problem with First Canadian Army was never the men, Lieutenant-General Robert Moncel said forty-five years later: they were superb, eventually becoming the best-trained army ever put in the field, and all of them volunteers until a few thousand NRMA men arrived in the last days of the war. There was, Brigadier Stanley Todd said, no soldier like the Canadian for initiative. He was amenable to discipline if properly led and if he could be persuaded that discipline would help save his life in action. What you had to do was to instill pride and get him away from his civilian attitudes. General Simonds said in late 1943 that Canadian soldiers were "the best in the world *bar none*," and he said much the same in July 1944: "If you explain to the Canadian soldier what is required of him and give him a good reason for it he will produce the goods every single time and do it twice as well as any other individual." Simonds had it right—the soldiers did produce and deliver the goods time after time, even against fierce opposition.

The problem initially was that the officers—especially the general officers and unit COs, who had been training for about the same length of time as their soldiers—were untried in battle, which was understandable, and unable to train their subordinates, which was much less so. Bert Hoffmeister, commanding a company in the Seaforth Highlanders in 1940, recalled that he "didn't have anything by way of a training manual. I went down to Aldershot and into a store where they sold these things and bought pamphlets." Then, when he was ordered to prepare an operation order for an exercise, "I hadn't a clue as to what an operation order looked like, or how to write one." There was, he said of his higher-ups, "a distinct lack of professionalism there." Hoffmeister learned his job in three years of training, but some officers, regrettably, did not. General Chris Vokes said flatly that the 1st Division "was not ready for battle until the end of 1942 ... It had taken three years to train the officers to train the NCOs to train the soldiers." Even so, some officers who had done well in big exercises in England suddenly became terrified of making decisions on the battlefield for fear of making the wrong ones and causing too many casualties to their men. They had to be replaced.

General Simonds understood the problem. "We have the material to provide the standard of leadership required," he said in December 1943 to Harry Crerar, his superior officer, who sometimes seemed to believe in seniority above all. "Only outworn prejudices prevent it being used to the best advantage … seniority, position on 'lists,' the fact that so and so has done such and such a job for a certain time and 'hasn't done anything wrong' (probably because he hasn't done anything at all!) … I consider," Simonds stated bluntly, "that before going into action it is not sufficient to remove only the 'bad' C.O. The 'indifferent' must be replaced by the 'better' and the 'not quite good enough' by the 'best.'" In action, Simonds was ruthless, and he acted as he had written, sacking the commanders who didn't push hard enough until he found those who would. Canadian soldiers deserved the very best leaders, and as the war went on, they got them. Donald Tansley, a private in the Regina Rifles and later a distinguished civil servant, wrote in his fine memoir how impressed he was with his platoon and company officers: "They were involved in the front lines of battle as were we. They led, they fought, they endured the same shit, mud, lack of sleep, danger, irregular food and casualties as the men they commanded." And, he added, most were in their early twenties, just as were their men.

The officers who succeeded, men like Lieutenant-Colonels Denis Whitaker of the Royal Hamilton Light Infantry, Jacques Dextraze of the Fusiliers Mont-Royal, and Sydney Radley-Walters of the Sherbrooke Fusiliers, knew that they had to do everything possible to ensure success—make a good plan, arrange fire support, and use the available equipment and manpower to get the best result. One of the great advantages such officers had was that they could call on the artillery. German guns were likely better and had longer range, but the Canadians, with their centralized artillery control, could in minutes bring the fire of half a dozen regiments or even more to bear on a single town or enemy concentration. "You knew there would be casualties but you had to make yourself go ahead," Whitaker said. He did, and so did his men.

The same process of finding the best went on with the staff. At the beginning of the war, there were very few officers with staff training, but as time passed and experience accrued, brilliant planners and organizers came to the fore. Simonds's Chief of Staff, Brigadier Elliot Rodger, was one such; his GSO1, Lieutenant-Colonel W.A.B. Anderson, was another. Crerar's Brigadier General Staff, Ted Beament, was a third, and at the 3rd Canadian Infantry Division, for example, the GSO1, Lieutenant-Colonel J.D. Mingay, was excellent; the Commander, Royal Artillery, Brigadier Stan "God" Todd, was first-rate; and the A&Q (administrative) side was handled very well by Lieutenant-Colonel Ernest Côté. Only Rodger and Anderson of these officers were regulars; all the others, and many more, were militiamen who had learned on the job.

It was the same throughout First Canadian Army. "It took seven or eight months for the army to get it together" in Northwest Europe "and get rid of all the drift and dead wood," General Moncel said. "They were then probably the best force on the continent." Historian Douglas Delaney wrote that "by the spring of 1945, commanders from brigade to army level could trust their staffs in a way that was not possible a year earlier. Ten months of combat had done much to hone collective skills. It had also done much to weed out the old and the incompetent and replace them with the young and the capable." First Canadian Army, I and II Canadian Corps, and the five infantry and armoured divisions were well run and well led, without doubt the equal of any formations on the Continent. General Anderson said long after the war that "by the time that we had got up to Antwerp"—in other words, by the time First Canadian Army had been in the field for two or three months or so—"I think that we had just as good, if not better, logistical staff as the British." Indeed, the Canadians had more and better of everything.

But in truth there is no way of comparing apples to oranges or Canadian to British and American divisions. How does one measure military effectiveness in a war with almost infinite variables of terrain, opposition, and available support? All we can say with confidence is that First Canadian Army did everything that was asked of it, and the Canadian divisions, brigades, and battalions were at least as capable as, if not more so than, any of those they fought alongside. On the Scheldt, for example, the Canadians did more than they should have been expected to do—and did it very well, though at a terrible cost.

Canada was not a great power—no nation of 11 million could be. But its navy and air force were the third and fourth largest in the world by the end of the war, and its First Canadian Army made a greater contribution to the Allied victory over Germany than the armies of all but Britain, the United States, and the Soviet Union. This was almost a miracle of biblical proportion, an astonishing act of creation from not quite nothing, certainly the creation of a great host from very little.

By the end of the war First Canadian Army was unquestionably superb. "It could move instantly," Moncel said; "it was magnificent, and it had taken five years to build it." That was a long time, and too many Canadians died while the Army struggled to learn how to master the enemy. The price of the interwar neglect of the military had been very high; so had the nation's manpower policies. But the Canadians, generals, unit COs, and soldiers, learned how to fight the Germans in Normandy.

Many died, while many others were wounded or had to be replaced, but the quality continued to improve. The Germans of the Waffen-SS and Wehrmacht with their Panthers and Tigers, their Nebelwerfers and deadly mortars, were often superb soldiers and formidable foes, but the Canadians emerged victorious. They had more tanks and guns, yes, but they also had courage and increasing skill as the months of battle continued, and they prevailed. They studied the enemy tactics and learned how best to effectively counter them, and they beat the Germans.

Field Marshal Montgomery could never have conceded that First Canadian Army was very effective. How could it be any good if Harry Crerar commanded it? "The Canadian soldier," the Field Marshal said, "is such a magnificent chap that he deserves, and should be given, really good generals." That was not Crerar, in his fixed opinion, and Monty remained unforgiving, sometimes blaming First Canadian Army for the failure of his plans. British and American historians have tended to be cool too, pointing to slowness in Normandy and elsewhere and citing Stacey's official histories, almost always the only Canadian books they had read.

But the critics who look only at the Canadian performance in June, July, and August 1944—and too often overstate II Canadian Corps' flaws there, as Terry Copp's fine revisionist books have demonstrated—always neglect the way First Canadian Army improved out of all recognition over the next months. Charles Stacey himself noted this. In private letters to John A. English some two decades after his official history of the Canadian campaign in Northwest Europe, *The Victory Campaign*, appeared, he wrote, "It is a pity perhaps that we focus our attention so much on Normandy, for in the nature of things our troops appear to better advantage … in the post-Normandy stages of the North-West Europe campaign." He also said somewhat ruefully, "I almost regret having written the rather severe comment on Canadian regimental officers" because of "the use that UK and US writers" made of it. "They use my stuff as a basis for assuming the superiority of their training and work in the field to ours," and this, he added properly, remains completely unproven. It still does.

Stacey's later comments are surely correct. The Army that fought on the Scheldt under Guy Simonds was different from and far better led at all levels than the same corps in the Falaise Gap. Without the Army's victory on the Scheldt, the Allied armies that ground to a halt by the end of 1944 for want of supplies would have been unable to move well into the spring of 1945; the war might have lasted much longer. But just as Monty forgot about the importance of the Scheldt in September 1944, so have the war historians tended to overlook the Canadian success there for the Field Marshal's glamorous failure of Operation Market Garden. Similarly, they have not noticed that the II Canadian Corps that battled through the Passchendaele-like battleground of the Rhineland was better than the Army that cleared the Scheldt. And the reunited First Canadian Army—now including the 1st Infantry and 4th Armoured divisions from Italy—that liberated the Netherlands and conquered northern Germany was probably the best little army in the world. "It was magnificent," General Moncel maintained, and he was surely correct. And, one should add, First Canadian Army was not so little—the Army headquarters, two corps headquarters, three infantry divisions, two armoured divisions, and two independent armoured brigades with the full panoply of support services at corps and army made up a good-sized force of some 185,000 men in Northwest Europe, one that could fight and win battles anywhere against any and all opposition. Certainly, it was the largest force Canada has ever put in the field, and likely the largest force it ever would.

There is a lesson in the story of First Canadian Army in the Second World War. The Army did not spring fully formed from the land and people in 1939. The Canadian government had paid very little attention to the military since 1919, and it had allowed its army, navy, and air force to shrink to almost nothing, and equipment and skills to moulder. The Permanent Force's officers were few in number and most were too old for the tasks ahead. Its leadership was flawed and largely untrained, as were the soldiers of the PF and the militia. Long training was essential, and so was battle experience. It took five years and more to turn the raw levies of 1939, 1940, and after into the best little army in the world of 1945—five years of casualties and death and loss. Canada paid a high price for its political leaders' neglect of their nation's interests and their basic duty of protection and preparation.

Nations should learn from experience, but most do not, and Canada is no exception. In the 1950s, when postwar rearmament was in full flight, Canada spent more than 7 percent of its gross domestic product on national defence and fielded well-equipped professional armed forces of 120,000 men and women who played an important role in defending Western Europe, Korea, and North America against the militaries of the Soviet Union and its satellites. Today, with the world in disarray in Europe, Africa, and Asia, we spend 1 percent of GDP and field just over 65,000 men and women in the increasingly ill-equipped Canadian Forces; only some 20,000 of them are soldiers.

The lesson of the Second World War should be clear: a small, well-trained, well-equipped professional army is a national insurance policy. If we fail to pay the monetary premiums today, we will surely pay them tomorrow in treasure and with the lives of our sons and daughters.

APPENDIX 1

Table of Ranks

Private/Gunner/Sapper/Trooper

Lance Corporal

Corporal

Sergeant

Quartermaster Sergeant

Company/Battery/Squadron Sergeant Major

Regimental Sergeant Major

Second Lieutenant

Lieutenant

Captain

Major

Lieutenant-Colonel

Colonel

Brigadier

Major-General

Lieutenant-General

General

Field Marshal

A corporal or lance corporal usually led a section of up to ten men.

A sergeant was usually second-in-command of a platoon/troop.

A sergeant major (WO2) was responsible for discipline in a company or squadron.

A regimental sergeant major (WO1) was responsible for discipline in a battalion or regiment.

A second lieutenant or lieutenant ordinarily commanded an infantry platoon or armoured troop of some thirty men.

A captain was usually a company/squadron commander or battalion/regiment adjutant.

A major usually commanded a company/squadron of four platoons/troops, or 120 or so men. Or he was a battalion/regiment second-in-command.

A lieutenant-colonel commanded a battalion/regiment of some 900 men.

A colonel was usually a senior staff officer.

Brigadiers commanded brigades of three battalions/regiments (roughly 4,000–5,000 men).

Major-generals commanded divisions of three brigades plus supporting arms and services (approximately 17,500–21,000 men).

Lieutenant-generals commanded a corps of two or more divisions.

Generals commanded an army of two or more corps.

Field marshals commanded two or more armies in an army group.

APPENDIX 2

*Organization of the Canadian Army Overseas**

Unit	Components	Make-up	Command	Strength (men)
Army		2 or more corps	General	100,000–190,000
Corps		2 or more divisions	Lieutenant-General	35,000–60,000
	Division	2 or more brigades	Major-General	10,000–18,000
	Brigade	3 or more battalions	Brigadier	3,500–5,000
	Battalion	4 or more companies	Lieutenant-Colonel	600–1,000
	Company	2 or more platoons	Major	100–150
	Platoon	2 or more sections	Lieutenant	16–40
	Section		Corporal	4–12

FIRST CANADIAN ARMY
Headquarters: Defence Battalion, Royal Montreal Regiment

I CANADIAN CORPS
1st Corps Defence Company, Lorne Scots

1st Canadian Infantry Division

- *1st Canadian Infantry Brigade*
  - Royal Canadian Regiment
  - Hastings and Prince Edward Regiment
  - 48th Highlanders of Canada
- *2nd Canadian Infantry Brigade*
  - Princess Patricia's Canadian Light Infantry
  - Seaforth Highlanders of Canada
  - Loyal Edmonton Regiment
- *3rd Canadian Infantry Brigade*
  - Royal 22e Régiment
  - Carleton and York Regiment
  - West Nova Scotia Regiment

The 1st Canadian Infantry Division also included the 4th Reconnaissance Regiment (4th Princess Louise Dragoon Guards); Saskatoon Light Infantry (machine gun); 1st, 2nd, 3rd Field Artillery Regiment, RCA; 1st, 3rd, 4th Field Companies, RCE; 1st Anti-tank Regiment, RCA; 2nd Light Anti-aircraft Regiment, RCA; 1st Infantry Divisional Signals, RC Sigs; 1st Infantry Divisional Troops Company, RCASC; 1st, 2nd, 3rd Infantry Brigade Companies, RCASC.

5th Canadian Armoured Division

- *5th Canadian Armoured Brigade*
  - 2nd Armoured Regiment
    (Lord Strathcona's Horse (Royal Canadians))
  - 5th Armoured Regiment

(8th Princess Louise's (New Brunswick) Hussars)

- 9th Armoured Regiment (British Columbia Dragoons)

- **11th Canadian Infantry Brigade**
  - 11th Independent Machine Gun Company
  - Perth Regiment
  - Cape Breton Highlanders
  - Irish Regiment of Canada

- **12th Canadian Infantry Brigade** *(disbanded in March 1945)*
  - 11th Independent Machine Gun Company
    (Princess Louise Fusiliers)
  - Westminster Regiment (Motorized)
  - 4th Princess Louise Dragoon Guards
    (from 1st Canadian Infantry Division)
  - Lanark and Renfrew Scottish Regiment
    (created from Corps anti-aircraft assets)
  - 3rd Armoured Reconnaissance Regiment
    (Governor General's Horse Guards)

The 5th Canadian Armoured Division also included the 17th Field Regiment, RCA; 8th Field Regiment (Self-propelled), RCA; 4th Anti-tank Regiment, RCA; 5th Light Anti-aircraft Regiment, RCA; 1st, 10th Field Squadrons, RCE; "G" Squadron, 25th Armoured Delivery Regiment (Elgin Regiment), Canadian Armoured Corps; 5th Armoured Divisional Signals, RC Sigs; 1st, 2nd, 3rd Infantry Brigade Workshops, RCEME; 5th Armoured Divisional Troops Company, RCASC; 5th Armoured Divisional Transport Company, RCASC; 5th Armoured Brigade Company, RCASC; 11th Infantry Brigade Company, RCASC.

- *1st Canadian Armoured Brigade*
  - *11th Armoured Regiment (Ontario Regiment)*
  - *12th Armoured Regiment (Three Rivers Regiment)*
  - *14th Armoured Regiment (Calgary Regiment)*
  - *1st Armoured Brigade Workshop, RCEME*
  - *1st Armoured Brigade Company, RCASC*

II CANADIAN CORPS
2nd Corps Defence Company (Prince Edward Island Light Horse)

2nd Canadian Infantry Division
- *4th Canadian Infantry Brigade*
  - Royal Regiment of Canada
  - Royal Hamilton Light Infantry
  - Essex Scottish Regiment
- *5th Canadian Infantry Brigade*
  - Black Watch (Royal Highland Regiment) of Canada
  - Régiment de Maisonneuve
  - Calgary Highlanders
- *6th Canadian Infantry Brigade*
  - Queen's Own Cameron Highlanders of Canada
  - South Saskatchewan Regiment
  - Fusiliers Mont-Royal

The 2nd Canadian Infantry Division also included the Toronto Scottish Regiment (machine gun); 8th Reconnaissance Regiment (14th Canadian Hussars); 4th, 5th, 6th Field Regiments, RCA; 2nd, 7th, 11th Field

Companies, RCE; 2nd Infantry Divisional Signals, RC Sigs; 4th, 5th, 6th Infantry Brigade Workshops, RCEME; 2nd Infantry Divisional Troops Company, RCASC; 4th, 5th, 6th Infantry Brigade Companies, RCASC.

3rd Canadian Infantry Division

- ### *7th Canadian Infantry Brigade*
  - Royal Winnipeg Rifles
  - Regina Rifle Regiment
  - 1st Battalion, Canadian Scottish Regiment
- ### *8th Canadian Infantry Brigade*
  - Queen's Own Rifles of Canada
  - Régiment de la Chaudière
  - North Shore (New Brunswick) Regiment
- ### *9th Canadian Infantry Brigade*
  - Highland Light Infantry of Canada
  - Stormont, Dundas and Glengarry Highlanders
  - North Nova Scotia Highlanders

The 3rd Canadian Infantry Division also included the 7th Reconnaissance Regiment (17th Duke of York's Royal Canadian Hussars); Cameron Highlanders of Ottawa (machine gun); 12th, 13th, 14th Field Artillery Regiments; 3rd Anti-tank Regiment; 4th Light Anti-aircraft Regiment; 6th, 16th, 18th Field Companies, RCE; 3rd Infantry Divisional Signals, RC Sigs; 7th, 8th, 9th Infantry Brigade Workshops, RCEME; 3rd Infantry Divisional Troops Company, RCASC; 7th, 8th, 9th Infantry Brigade Companies, RCASC.

4th Canadian Armoured Division

- ### *4th Canadian Armoured Brigade*

- 21st Canadian Armoured Regiment (Governor General's Foot Guards)
- 22nd Canadian Armoured Regiment (Canadian Grenadier Guards)
- 28th Canadian Armoured Regiment (British Columbia Regiment)
- Lake Superior Regiment (Motorized)
- 4th Armoured Brigade Workshop, RCEME
- 4th Armoured Divisional Troops Company, RCASC
- 4th Armoured Brigade Company, RCASC

- **10th Canadian Infantry Brigade**
  - Lincoln and Welland Regiment
  - Algonquin Regiment
  - Argyll and Sutherland Highlanders of Canada (Princess Louise's)
  - Lake Superior Regiment (Motorized)

2nd Canadian Armoured Brigade

- 6th Armoured Regiment (1st Hussars)
- 10th Armoured Regiment (Fort Garry Horse)
- 27th Armoured Regiment (Sherbrooke Fusiliers Regiment)
- 2nd Armoured Brigade Workshop, RCEME
- 2nd Armoured Brigade Company, RCASC

The 4th Canadian Armoured Division also included the 29th Armoured Reconnaissance Regiment (South Alberta Regiment); "D" Squadron, 25th Canadian Armoured Delivery Regiment (Elgin Regiment); 15th, 23rd Field

Regiments, RCA; 5th Anti-tank Regiment, RCA; 8th Light Anti-aircraft Regiment, RCA; 1st, 10th Field Squadrons, RCE; 4th Armoured Divisional Signals, RC Sigs; 10th Infantry Brigade Workshop, RCEME; 10th Infantry Brigade Company, RCASC.

* This organization chart, for reasons of space, omits Army and Corps troops and units of the Royal Canadian Ordnance Corps, the Royal Canadian Army Medical Corps, the Canadian Provost Corps, the Canadian Dental Corps, the Canadian Postal Corps, and other units without which the army could not have functioned properly. A listing of all the units of First Canadian Army may be found in C.P. Stacey, *The Official History of the Canadian Army in the Second World War*, Vol. 3, *The Victory Campaign* (Ottawa, 1960), appendix F, pp. 657ff. This volume is freely available online at the Canadian Armed Forces' Directorate of History and Heritage website (http://www.cmp-cpm.forces.gc.ca/dhh-dhp/his/oh-ho/detail-eng.asp?BfBookLang=1&BfId=29).

A BRIEF NOTE ON SOURCES

This listing makes no attempt to be comprehensive. There is a growing bibliography on Canada and the Second World War, and the seventy-fifth anniversary commemorations will see even more. Here I list only books and primary sources that were especially useful in my research and writing.

In writing this book, I have mainly relied on the wide range of primary sources that I used in writing a number of books on the Second World War, most notably *Broken Promises: A History of Conscription in Canada* (Toronto, 1977) with J.M. Hitsman; *Canada's War: The Politics of the Mackenzie King Government, 1939–1945* (Toronto, 1990); *Canada's Army: Making War and Keeping the Peace* (Toronto, 2003); and *The Oxford Companion to Canadian Military History* (Toronto, 2010) with Dean Oliver. I also took advantage of the primary materials Norman Hillmer and I collected for two books of documents: *First Drafts: Eyewitness Accounts from Canada's Past* (Toronto, 2002) and *Battle Lines: Eyewitness Accounts from Canada's Military History* (Toronto, 2004). Peter Neary and I edited another collection, *The Good Fight: Canadians and World War II* (Toronto, 1995).

In addition I used extensively the large and searchable clippings files posted online by the Canadian War Museum as "Democracy at War: Canadian Newspapers and the Second World War." This is a splendid resource. So too is the fine collections of soldiers' letters collected and posted online by the Canadian Letters and Images Project (CLIP). Located at Vancouver Island University, CLIP has made available thousands of letters, memoirs, and diaries from all Canada's wars, and these are simply invaluable, not least for being accessible and searchable. Also very useful were the letters of Major Harry Jolley, preserved by my cousin Carol Geller and now in the Canadian War Museum, and the soldiers' letters collected by Desmond Morton and me for two popular illustrated books on the war we published in the 1980s. These letters are now in my papers in the York University archives. I also made extensive use of long interviews I conducted over many years with generals, senior staff officers, and junior officers. These interviews formed the basis for my book *The Generals: The Canadian Army's Senior Commanders in the Second World War* (Toronto, 1993), which looked at the generals' origins and training, and studied the key commanders, the militia successes, the reasons for the lack of French Canadian generals, and the senior officers who directed the home front organization. A few of the interviews have been published in *Canadian Military History*, and I hope to publish all of them in book form shortly.

There is, of course, a growing body of work on the Canadian Army's role in the Second World War. The basic texts remain the Army official histories by Charles Stacey: *Six Years of War* (Ottawa, 1955), *The Victory Campaign* (Ottawa, 1960), and *Arms, Men and Governments* (Ottawa, 1970). Stacey's colleague G.W.L. Nicholson covered *The Canadians in*

Italy (Ottawa, 1957). These are fine pieces of work with excellent maps and notes, among the best official histories by any of the combatants. So too are the official Canadian three-volume navy and air force histories.

Canada's generals have not produced much by way of memoirs. Among corps commanders, only General E.L.M. Burns wrote a memoir, *General Mud: Memoirs of Two World Wars* (Toronto, 1970), but this is focused on the Italian Campaign. Burns also wrote a good study of *Manpower in the Canadian Army, 1939–1945* (Toronto, 1956). Christopher Vokes's *Vokes: My Story* (Ottawa, 1985) is a tape-recorded, badly edited memoir that has its points but is largely an embarrassment. General Maurice Pope, who fought the war in Ottawa and Washington, produced *Soldiers and Politicians* (Toronto, 1962), which is careful, precise, and occasionally very frank. George Kitching's *Mud and Green Fields* (Langley, BC, 1986) leaves out too much, but Howard Graham's *Citizen and Soldier* (Toronto, 1987), again focused on Italy, is better. Only one wartime francophone brigadier wrote his story: *Mémoires du Général Jean V. Allard* (Boucherville, QC, 1985). The sole remaining autobiography, *The Canadian Summer* (Toronto, 1981) by Brigadier J.A. Roberts, is excellent in telling the story of an ice cream maker's rise from militia lieutenant to first-rate brigade commander.

There is more luck in finding biographies. General McNaughton is the subject of John Swettenham's three-volume biography (1968–69) and John Rickard's *The Politics of Command* (Toronto, 2010). Paul Dickson's study of Harry Crerar, *A Thoroughly Canadian General* (Toronto, 2007), is very competent and inclusive; that is not something that can be said of Peter V. Crerar's *My Father, the General* (privately published, 2001), which is another embarrassment. There is a very good chapter on

Crerar in John A. English's *Patton's Peers: The Forgotten Allied Field Army Commanders of the Western Front 1944–45* (Mechanicsburg, PA, 2009). Dominick Graham's *The Price of Command: A Biography of General Guy Simonds* (Toronto, 1993) is good on Simonds's campaigns but suffers from a lack of broad archival research. It can usefully be supplemented by the documents, memoranda, and addresses collected in Terry Copp's *Guy Simonds and the Art of Command* (Kingston, 2007). There is, unfortunately, no biography of General Charles Foulkes, though Douglas Delaney ably examines him, E.L.M. Burns, and Simonds in his *Corps Commanders: Five British and Canadian Generals at War, 1939–45* (Vancouver, 2011). The best biography of a general officer is Delaney's *The Soldiers' General: Bert Hoffmeister at War* (Vancouver, 2005). Reginald Roy wrote *For Most Conspicuous Bravery* (Vancouver, 1977), an uncritical life of General George Pearkes, VC.

There are hundreds of regimental histories and soldiers' memoirs, far too many to list. David Bercuson's *Battalion of Heroes* (Calgary, 1994) is very frank on the successes and failures of the Calgary Highlanders; so too is Gordon Brown and Terry Copp, *Look to Your Front* (Waterloo, 2001), on the Regina Rifles. No bibliography can omit George Blackburn's three volumes: *Where the Hell Are the Guns?*, *The Guns of Normandy*, and *The Guns of Victory* (Toronto, 1995–97) which are a superb account of an artillery Forward Observation Officer's war. Nor should I omit Donald Pearce's *Journal of a War* (Toronto, 1965), one junior officer's fine account. I also found good material in Donald Tansley's *Growing Up and Going to War, 1925–1945* (Waterloo, 2005), Charles Martin's *Battle Diary* (Toronto, 1994), and Gerald Levenston's *My Darling Mom* (ebook; Vancouver, 2012), the latter a collection of letters home by a staff officer at II Canadian Corps. There is much excellent material, including letters, memoirs, and battle studies, in the pages of the journal *Canadian Military History*, most especially the run of excellent letters by Captain Hal MacDonald of the North Shore Regiment, which stretch over several issues and all the war years.

If I cannot cite all the fine memoirs, neither can I detail all the excellent campaign studies. Terry Copp's books, based on detailed research into war diaries and close study of the ground, include his *The Brigade: The Fifth Canadian Infantry Brigade in WWII* (Stony Creek, ON, 1992); *Fields of Fire: The Canadians in Normandy* (Toronto, 2003); *Cinderella Army: The Canadians in Northwest Europe 1944–1945* (Toronto, 2003); and, with Bill McAndrew, *Battle Exhaustion: Soldiers and Psychiatrists in the Canadian Army, 1939–1945* (Montreal, 1990). It is clear that Copp has changed the way the Canadian soldier's war in Northwest Europe is viewed (and his *Fields of Fire* has an extensive bibliography that is especially good on regimental histories). Marc Milner's *Stopping the Panzers: The Untold Story of D-Day* (St. Lawrence, KS, 2014) is also very challenging, most valuable, and based on sound documentation and study of the terrain. This is the most revisionist account of the Canadians' role in the D-Day landings in years. Also very helpful are Bill McAndrew, et al., *Liberation: The Canadians in Europe* (Montreal, 1995) and the essays in Geoffrey Hayes, et al., *Canada and the Second World War: Essays in Honour of Terry Copp* (Waterloo, 2012).

Just as important as these studies is the very critical study by Lieutenant-Colonel John A. English, *The Canadian Army and the Normandy Campaign: A Study of Failure in High Command* (New York, 1991). English also wrote *Surrender Invites Death: Fighting the Waffen SS in*

Normandy (Mechanicsburg, PA, 2011). There are four excellent volumes by Denis Whitaker and Shelagh Whitaker on Dieppe (1992), Normandy (2000), the Scheldt (1984), and the Rhineland (1989); Denis Whitaker, as a participant and CO of the Royal Hamilton Light Infantry, offers his unique perspective. Another fine book, the very model of a battle study (not least for its superb graphics), is Brian Reid's *No Holding Back: Operation Totalize, Normandy, August 1944* (Toronto, 2005). Murray Peden's, *A Thousand Shall Fall* (Toronto, 1979) is a superb Canadian memoir of the RCAF bomber role.

Larry Rose's ably done *Mobilize! Why Canada Was Unprepared for the Second World War* (Toronto, 2013) examines the pathetic state of the military in 1939 and its consequences. Daniel Byers's *Zombie Army: Canada, the Canadian Army, and Conscription in the Second World War* (Vancouver, 2015) adds much to what we know of the NRMA men, while Dean Oliver, "When the Battle's Won: Military Demobilization in Canada, 1939–1946" (PhD dissertation, York University, 1996), explains the process of demobilization. David Halton's excellent biography of his father, CBC war correspondent Matthew Halton, *Dispatches from the Front* (Toronto, 2014), was most helpful. Volume 1 of Tim Cook's fine *The Necessary War* (Toronto, 2014) covers the period from 1939 to 1943; volume 2, which goes to the end of the war, should follow in 2015. John A. Macdonald's very good RMC 1992 MA thesis, "In Search of Veritable: Training the Canadian Army Staff Officer, 1899 to 1945," was most useful. Robert Engen used new material in his *Canadians Under Fire: Infantry Effectiveness in the Second World War* (2009). And no listing would be complete without the extraordinary Canadian Battle series by Mark Zuehlke, which includes six volumes on the campaign in Northwest Europe.

There are a number of books on the enemy in Normandy and on Kurt Meyer and the murder of POWs. On the Wehrmacht and SS, see Michael Reynolds, *Steel Inferno: I SS Panzer Corps in Normandy* (New York, 1997), Anthony Tucker-Jones, *Falaise: The Flawed Victory* (Barnsley, UK, 2008), and Richard Hargreaves, *The Germans in Normandy* (Barnsley, UK, 2006). The best book on Meyer's undoubted crimes is Howard Margolian, *Conduct Unbecoming: The Story of the Murder of Canadian Prisoners of War in Normandy* (Toronto, 1998), while the edited collection of documents by P.W. Lackenbauer and Chris Madsen, *Kurt Meyer on Trial* (Kingston, ON, 2007), is also very useful. Tony Foster wrote *Meeting of Generals* (Toronto, 1986), about his father, Major-General Harry Foster, and Meyer. Foster presided over Meyer's court martial.

For the liberation of the Netherlands, see D. Kaufman and Michiel Horn, *A Liberation Album* (Toronto, 1980); Horn's memoir, *Becoming Canadian* (Toronto, 1997); and Lance Goddard, *Canada and the Liberation of the Netherlands, May 1945* (Toronto, 2005). On veterans, see Peter Neary's fine study, *On to Civvy Street* (Montreal, 2011), and Neary's and my edited collection, *The Veterans Charter and Post–World War II Canada* (Montreal, 1998), not least the articles by Dean Oliver and Jeffrey Keshen. The very best book on life in home-front Canada is Keshen's *Saints, Sinners, and Soldiers* (Vancouver, 2004).

The international literature on the campaign of 1944–45 is vast. Books I found especially useful were Nigel Hamilton's two-volume *Monty* (London, 1987); Max Hastings, *Overlord* (London, 1984); John Buckley's *Monty's Men: The British Army and the Liberation of Europe, 1944–5* (New Haven, 2013); Russell Hart, *Clash of Arms: How the Allies Won in Normandy* (London, 2001); Richard Overy's excellent *The*

Bombing War (London, 2013); John Ellis, *Brute Force* (London, 1990); Stephen Hart, *Montgomery and "Colossal Cracks": 21st Army Group in Northwest Europe, 1944–45* (Westport, CT, 2000); Max Hastings, *Armageddon: The Battle for Germany, 1944–1945* (New York, 2004); Andrew Roberts's two volumes, *The Storm of War* (London, 2009) and *Masters and Commanders* (London, 2008); and Craig Symonds, *Neptune: The Allied Invasion of Europe and the D-Day Landings* (New York, 2014). There are many more fine books, with more being published every year. The seventy-fifth anniversary years of the Second World War will produce a print bonanza.

ACKNOWLEDGEMENTS

A s with every article and book I have ever written, my friends and colleagues have been generous with their assistance, suggestions, and sharp critiques. Lieutenant-Colonel (ret'd) Dr. Jack English in Kingston and Dr. Dean Oliver of the Canadian Museum of History offered instant suggestions and help; so too did Professors Roger Sarty, Terry Copp, Michael Bliss, Marc Milner, and Lieutenant-Colonel (ret'd) Dr. Douglas Delaney. Their writings were also of great assistance in my telling of this story. Patricia Grimshaw assisted ably with the appendices.

Books I co-authored over many years with Professors Peter Neary, Desmond Morton, David Bercuson, Dean Oliver, Norman Hillmer, and the late J. M. Hitsman remind me of the continuing and wholly positive influence such close friends have had on my work.

I am always grateful to Linda McKnight of Westwood Creative Artists, my literary agent, who protects my interests with her sharp mind and adding machine. Patrick Crean, my editor at HarperCollins, offered wise comments, almost all of which I accepted at once, not least because he was right, and Stephanie Fysh worked marvels on my prose. Thanks too to my proofreader Janice Weaver.

My wife, Linda Grayson, is my best reader, and I am enormously grateful for her support, encouragement, and sharp eye.

PHOTO CREDITS

1. Library and Archives Canada C999

2. Library and Archives Canada PA 213677

3. Library and Archives Canada 136762

4. Library and Archives Canada PA 159242

5. G.K. Bell/Public Archives Canada PA 115395

6. M.M. Dean/Library and Archives Canada PA 132732

7. Library and Archives Canada PA 132916

8. Library and Archives Canada PA 204155

9. Canadian War Museum 197301-001 P.37c and City of Toronto Archives FONDS 1266, item 61431

10. Library and Archives Canada PA 129610

11. Canadian War Museum 1980269-044 #15

12. L.A. Audrain/Library and Archives Canada PA 132786

13. The Gazette/Library and Archives Canada PA 107910

14. Canadian War Museum 19801009-001 and 19830136-001 #18

15. City of Toronto Archives SC 488

16. Ontario Archives Toronto

17. Library and Archives Canada C 87139

18. Library and Archives Canada

19. Library and Archives Canada PA 136280

20. Herbert Jessop Nott/Library and Archives Canada PA 170770/DND

21. Lt. H.G. Aikman/Library and Archives Canada PA 129128/DND

22. M.M. Dean/Library and Archives Canada PA 132726/DND

23. Library and Archives Canada PA 115567

24. Library and Archives Canada PA 146171

25. Canadian War Museum 19900198-076

26. Library and Archives Canada

27. Ken Bell/Library and Archives Canada PA 132829

28. Library and Archives Canada PA 168669

29. Library and Archives Canada PA 138429

30. Library and Archives Canada PA 151554

31. Barney J. Gloster/Library and Archives Canada PA 192022

32. Library and Archives Canada PA 140408

33. Author's collection

34. Library and Archives Canada PA 140683 and PA 134376

35. Donald I. Grant/Library and Archives Canada PA 133331

36. Daniel Gurarich/Library and Archives Canada PA 166806

37. Library and Archives Canada PA 113908

38. Library and Archives Canada 138353

39. Charles H. Richer/Library and Archives Canada PA 150930

40. Library and Archives Canada PA 114618

41. City of Toronto Archives FONDS 1266/Hem 102055

42. Library and Archives Canada PA 112367

43. City of Toronto Archives FONDS 1266/Hem 102055

44. Library and Archives Canada

45. Library and Archives Canada

INDEX

Note: Numbered units precede alphabetical listings.

3rd Canadian Infantry Division (*cont.*)
  casualties, 84, 155–56
  commanding officers, 33, 65–67, 102,
    120
  on D-Day, 65–69, 71–75
  in France, 128, 138
  in Germany, 195, 196–97, 201–2, 206
  in Netherlands, 159–62, 168, 212–13,
    219–20, 223
  in Normandy, 83–84, 85–86, 89, 91,
    99, 116
4th Canadian Armoured Division, 3,
    22–23, 121–22, 165, 271, 290–91.
    See also specific regiments
  4th Canadian Armoured Brigade, 121,
    200, 290
  10th Brigade, 290
  commanding officers, 120, 141,
    180–81
  in France, 110, 115, 128–29
  in Germany, 187, 198–99, 217–18, 220
  lack of experience, 89–90, 107
5th Canadian Armoured Division,
    205, 215, 216–17, 223, 234–37,
    287–88. *See also specific regiments*
5th Canadian Armoured Brigade, 287
11th Brigade, 224, 287
12th Brigade, 287
  in Italy, 39, 40–42, 43, 44
8th Princess Louise's (New Brunswick)
    Hussars (5th Armoured) Regi-
    ment, 224
14th Canadian Hussars (8th Reconnais-
    sance) Regiment, 220, 289
48th Highlanders of Canada, 16

A

Afrika Korps, 24
aircraft, 179
  manufacture of, 46, 47, 54
  Typhoons, 96–97, 100, 111, 127–28,
    160
airfields, 64, 86

Albert Canal, 162, 163
alcohol, 152, 245–46
Aldershot, 19–22, 253–54
HMCS *Algonquin*, 77
Algonquin Regiment, 110–11, 199, 200
Allard, Jean-Victor, 202, 203
Allen, Ralph, 210
Allied forces. *See also specific forces*
  1st Czechoslovak Independent
    Armoured Brigade, 139
  1st Polish Armoured Division, 106,
    115–16
  4th Polish Armoured Division, 106
  21st Army Group, 163, 222
  Combined Operations Headquarters
    (COHQ), 26–27, 32
  cooperation with Germans, 221, 222,
    238–40
  in Operation Totalize, 106, 107, 108,
    111
  in Operation Tractable, 113, 115–16,
    117–18
  on Rhine, 187
Alpin, Ted, 209
ammunition, 46
  supplying of, 106, 160, 168, 193, 194
Anderson, "Red" (Calgary Highlanders),
    186
Anderson, W.A.B. (Bill), 16, 17, 37, 134,
    144, 276–77
Antwerp, 139–40, 162–63, 168. *See also*
    Scheldt campaign
Apeldoorn, 213, 248–49
Argentan, 115
Argyll and Sutherland Highlanders of
    Canada (Princess Louise's), 116,
    188, 198–99, 218
Armoured Corps Reinforcement Unit,
    130
Arnold, Wayne, 86–87, 93–94
Atlantic Wall, 62
atomic bombs, 252, 254
Authie, 79, 90–91
automobile industry, 50, 55

C

Caen, 84, 90–91, 98–102

Calais, 136–37, 261

Calcar–Üdem ridge, 198

Calgary Highlanders, 59, 96, 100, 153, 183, 214–15
  in Scheldt campaign, 164, 166

Calgary (14th Armoured) Regiment, 27, 29–30

Cameron Highlanders of Ottawa, 116, 150, 290

Canada. *See also* Canada, Government of; Quebec
  during Depression, 15, 17
  economy, 45–53, 54–55
  elections, 18–19, 261–66
  employment, 46, 52–53
  in First World War, 4, 13, 14, 47, 267, 270–71
  as pro-British, 14, 57, 133
  social welfare programs, 261–62, 263
  war effort, 45–46, 52

Canada, Government of
  and Army, 7–9, 13–15, 280
  defence contracts, 46–48
  Defence Purchases, Profits Control, and Financing Act (1939), 47–48
  Department of Munitions and Supply, 49–50
  Department of National Defence, 12, 13–14, 15
  Department of Veterans Affairs, 264
  National Resources Mobilization Act (1940), 22, 24, 25, 256
  wartime pressures on, 14–15, 51–52

Canada's Jews (Tulchinsky), 260

Canadian Army, 280. *See also* First Canadian Army; *specific divisions*
  in 1939, 7, 11
  government and, 7–9, 13–15, 280
  ranks in, 283–84
  Canadian Army Occupation Force (CAOF), 249–52

Canadian Army Pacific Force, 252–53

Canadian Berlin Battalion, 249–50

Canadian Defence Quarterly, 9

Canadian Forces in the Netherlands (CFN), 255

Canadian Grenadier Guards (22nd Canadian Armoured) Regiment, 110, 117–18, 121, 216–17, 225

Canadian Postal Corps, 149

Canadian Red Cross, 148, 226

Canadian Scottish Regiment, 66, 80, 86–87, 159, 195, 223–24, 230–31

Canadian War Museum, 245

Canadian Women's Army Corps (CWAC), 53

Cape Breton Highlanders, 215, 224, 225

Caravaggio, Angelo, 121–22

Carleton and York Regiment, 16

Carmichael, Harry, 50

Carpiquet, 85–87

Cass, Sam, 209–10

cemeteries (for war dead), 119, 227–28, 255, 261

Channel ports, 127, 136–39

Chateau Beauregard (rest camp), 94

Chill, Kurt, 163–64

Christian, Jack, 236

Chrysler Corporation, 55

Churchill, Gordon, 105

Churchill, Winston, 60, 61, 169, 262

cigarettes, 149, 150, 153, 245, 251–52

Citadel Merchandising, 51

Clark, Gregory, 261

Clark, Harry, 149

Clark, Murray, 261

Clark, S.F., 88

Cleve, 209–10

Clifford, Fred, 81

Cold War, 242

Coldwell, M.J., 261

Colville, Alex, 58, 148, 255

Colville, Rhoda, 148

Commonwealth War Graves Commission, 119, 227–28

communications, 93, 107, 111, 146, 237

Compton-Lundie, Anthony, 223–24
concentration camps, 209, 210, 219
conscription, 23, 171–76
  for home defence, 22, 131–32, 169,
    253, 257–58
  King and, 24–25, 172–73, 174
  need for, 24–25, 170
  political attitudes to, 14, 18, 22, 262,
    263
  Quebec and, 13, 173, 174
Co-operative Commonwealth Federation
  (CCF), 261, 262, 265–66
Copp, Terry, 120, 201, 238, 278–79
Cosens, Aubrey, 197
Côté, Ernest, 66, 276
Courseulles-sur-Mer, 73–75
Coutts, Gilbert, 72
Crerar, Harry, 23, 103, 132–36, 151–52,
    187, 254
  before the war, 11, 14
  and commanding officers, 95, 120,
    202, 269
  as corps commander, 26, 39, 43
  as disciplinarian, 94, 204
  and German surrender, 225, 227–28,
    229
  as GOC-in-C, 4, 38, 85, 97, 191–92,
    201, 234, 270, 275–76
  Montgomery and, 132–33, 180, 278
  in Netherlands, 141, 142, 233, 244
  opinions, 27, 190, 218, 265
  and Simonds, 90, 205–6
Crocker, John, 137–38
Crown corporations, 51
Cunningham, D.G., 66, 67, 77, 82
Currie, Arthur, 4, 270
Currie, David, 116–17

D

Danson, Barney, 149, 224–25, 260
D-Day, 3, 44, 69–78. *See also* Normandy
    invasion
  air support, 64, 69–70, 74, 76

Allied advantages, 63–64, 68
  artillery support, 66, 76, 77
  Canadian role, 65–69
  German defences, 72, 73, 76
  German knowledge of, 61–62, 63
  Juno Beach, 62, 71–75
  landing sites, 64–65
  losses, 68, 77–78
  naval support, 69, 70, 76
  Omaha Beach, 78
  planning for, 60–61, 63, 64–65, 67, 68
  tank support, 72, 75–76
DeBow, "Foggy" (Calgary Highlanders),
    186
Defence Purchasing Board, 48
Delaney, Donald, 42
Delaney, Douglas, 19, 38, 94–95, 168, 236,
    238, 276
Delfzijl, 223, 224–25
Dempsey, Miles, 87, 140
Denmark, 19, 223, 251
deserters, 174–75, 240–41
Deventer, 212
Dextraze, Jacques, 182–83, 275
Dick, Clement, 88
Dickson, Brian, 109
Dieppe (town), 132, 136
Dieppe raid, 26–32, 64, 136
  air support, 27, 29
  as disaster, 2, 30–31, 271
  Germans and, 28, 31
  impact, 31–32, 37
  naval support, 27, 28
  planning for, 26–28, 30–31
  units involved, 26, 27–28
Dietrich, Sepp, 99
dikes, 142, 166–68, 187, 193
displaced persons, 250
Dives River, 116
Doakes, Lieutenant (Calgary Highland-
    ers), 153
Doggart, Sam, 216
Dorfer, Bruno, 240
Dow, Gerald, 226–27

Drury, C.M. "Bud," 95
Dunkelman, Ben, 260
Dunkirk, 139

E

Edmondson, John S., 92–93
Egypt, 24
Eisenhower, Dwight, 61, 85, 201, 208, 222
Ellis, Jean, 156
Ellis, Ross, 183
Else, Jim, 223–24
English Channel. *See* Channel ports
English, John A. (Jack), 93, 168, 265, 267–68
"Essential Qualities in the Leader" (Simonds), 237–38
Essex Scottish Regiment, 96, 129–30, 147, 163, 196, 200, 226
    at Dieppe, 27, 30
    in Normandy, 91, 92, 115
Exercise Spartan, 37–38

F

Falaise Gap, 3, 103–4, 107–12. *See also* Operation Totalize
    commentary on, 122–23, 267
    losses, 121, 264–65
First Canadian Army, 2–6, 22–23, 279–80. *See also* Canadian Army; officers; soldiers; *specific units*
    air support, 205, 270
    artillery strength, 96, 124, 275–76
    and British Army, 133–35
    British troops in, 137, 203
    commanding officers, 180–84, 201–3, 235, 238, 268–69, 276
    communication problems, 93, 111
    criticism of, 3, 31, 43, 122–23, 267–68, 270–72
    effectiveness, 120, 121–22, 123–24, 201, 267–68, 277
    failures at the top, 92–93, 267–68

field ambulance units, 216, 217, 218
French Canadian units, 129, 166, 176, 256–58
headquarters, 97, 255
improvement of, 276–80
lack of battle experience, 67, 121–22, 238, 270–72, 280
losses, 21, 171, 213, 231, 270, 280
militia units, 7–8, 9–10, 16–17, 183, 280
and Normandy invasion, 65–69, 84
as occupation force, 242–52
organization of, 144–45, 285–91
pioneer units, 130, 145
praise of, 168–69, 208
reinforcement units, 130, 202, 253–54
rest areas, 94, 251
splitting of, 39–40, 65, 271
standards, 204–5
strengths, 96–97, 124
supply problems, 163, 170
as understrength, 11, 128–29, 130–31, 139, 166
weaknesses, 122, 123–24, 267–68, 272–73
First World War, 13, 14, 47, 155
    Canadian Corps in, 4, 267, 270–71
    veterans of, 33, 36
Fitzgerald, Edmund, 248
flamethrowers, 159, 161, 166, 219–20
Fleury-sur-Orne, 91
Flushing, 143
Forbes, Charly, 166–67
Ford Motor Company, 55
Forêt de la Londe, 127, 128
Fort Cataraqui, 168
Fort Garry Horse (10th Armoured) Regiment, 67, 85, 196, 197
Foster, Harry, 20, 21, 118–19, 120, 238
    on Canadian soldiers, 122, 233
    as division commander, 180, 369
    in Normandy, 66, 83, 91
Foulkes, Charles, 122
    as corps commander, 141, 180, 203

as division commander, 89, 94–95, 120, 128, 182, 238, 269
and German surrender, 227, 228–29
in Italy, 44, 203
in Netherlands, 222, 233
France, 20. *See also specific locations*
army of, 20, 273
Resistance in (Maquis), 63, 69, 139
Frank, Anne, 220
French Canada. *See* Quebec
friendly fire incidents, 108–9, 113, 166
Friesoythe, 218–19
Frost, Sydney, 205
Fusiliers Mont-Royal, 27, 30, 91, 93, 96, 182–83, 275

G

Ganong, J.E., 33, 95
gasoline supplies, 64, 106, 192–93
General Motors, 55
Geneva Convention, 239
German Army, 124–25. *See also* Waffen-SS
2nd Panzer Division, 98, 101
Fifteenth Army, 31
21st Panzer Division, 79
64th Infantry Division, 159
81st Corps, 31
85th Infantry Division, 103–4
89th Infantry Division, 103, 108
272nd Division, 98, 101, 103
331st Division, 128
352nd Division, 62
716th Infantry Division, 62, 79
advantages, 96, 121–22, 278
Allied cooperation with, 221, 222, 238–40
atrocities, 81–83, 219
in Belgium, 140, 141
disarmed, 225, 229, 239, 241–42
horses used, 62, 63, 115, 128, 162
invasion of Europe, 19–20, 48–49
in Italy, 39, 40–42

losses, 97, 125, 127–28
in Normandy, 62–63, 79–83, 98, 99
paratroops, 41–42, 163–64, 195, 212–13
in Rhineland, 193–94
tactics, 91–92, 110
teenage soldiers, 79–83, 103, 104, 118, 212–13, 218
Volkssturm units, 193
Germany. *See also* Wehrmacht; *specific locations*
bombing of, 208
Canadian Army in, 208–9, 217–20, 249–52, 272
civilians in, 217–18, 250–51
defence of, 218, 223–25
hatred of, 18–19, 82–83, 86, 220, 223, 227–28, 241, 242
surrender of, 222–23, 225, 227, 228–29, 230, 238–39
Ghent, 168
Goch–Calcar road, 195–96
Goodman, Eddie, 149, 260
Gothic Line, 44
Governor General's Horse Guards (3rd Armoured Reconnaissance) Regiment, 204
Gray, John, 232–33
Grayson, Bill, 74
Grebbe Line, 216, 221
Gregory, Robert, 156–57
Griffin, F.P., 101
Groningen, 213–15, 219

H

Haayen, Marian, 232
Hadley, Jack, 72
Hague, The, 233
Halton, Matthew, 18, 40, 41–42, 225–26
on Normandy campaign, 85–86, 102, 114, 125–26
"Hangover Raid," 179
Harris, Stephen, 124

Harris, Walter, 101
Hastings, Max, 267, 270
Hastings and Prince Edward Regiment, 16, 245
Henry, Gordon, 81
Highland Light Infantry of Canada, 66, 71, 90, 207
Hiroshima, 252, 254
Hitler, Adolf, 97–98, 115, 136, 225
    and Normandy campaign, 62, 102, 114–15
Hitler Line, 43
Hitler Youth, 79, 83
Hochwald, 192, 196–201
Hodge, Courtney, 273
Hoffmeister, Bert, 34, 274
    as commander, 5, 180, 184, 217, 234–37, 238, 269
    in Italy, 39, 43, 44, 235, 237
    in Netherlands, 224, 225, 241
Hollen, 197
home defence forces ("Zombies"), 13, 15, 22, 253, 256. *See also* National Resources Mobilization Act
    attitudes toward, 158, 175–76, 265
    conscription for, 22, 131–32, 169, 253, 257–58
    origins, 172, 257, 260
    and overseas service, 171–72, 173, 174–75, 257–58
    as reinforcements, 171–76, 189–91, 270
Hong Kong, 2, 23–24, 136, 271
Horn, Michiel, 243, 247
Horrocks, Brian, 191–92, 201, 269, 272
hospitals, 155, 264
Howe, C.D. (Clarence Decatur), 48, 49–50, 51–52
Hughes, Sam, 12
Hürtgen Forest, 273

I

Ifs, 91
Ijssel River, 213

Ilsley, J.L., 52
Imperial Defence College, 11
Imperial Munitions Board, 47
John Inglis Co., 46
Irish Regiment of Canada, 216–17
Italy, 3, 38–45, 204. *See also specific locations*
    losses in, 39, 40, 42, 43, 45

J

Japan, 23–24, 252, 254
Jolley, Harry, 218, 230, 253
Joyce, James R., 157

K

Kan, Wim, 247
Kapelsche Veer, 187–88
Kasserine Pass, 273
Keefler, Holley, 141, 184, 202, 269
Keith, Walter, 154
Keller, Rod, 65–66, 87, 89, 109, 269
King, William Lyon Mackenzie, 22, 60
    in 1945 election, 261, 266
    and conscription, 24–25, 172–73, 174
    and defence issues, 13–15, 264–65
    and McNaughton, 17–18, 32, 38
Kitching, George, 89, 107, 112, 120
Kluge, Günther von, 108, 114, 115
Knocke, 161
Korean War, 155
Kröller-Müller Museum (Otterlo), 246

L

Laing, Darrell, 88
Laing, H.D.V., 230
Laison River, 113
Lake Superior Regiment, 110, 200, 218
landing craft (LSTs), 61, 68–69
Leese, Oliver, 43, 44, 272
Leesten, 212–13
Le Havre, 137–38, 139
Le Mesnil-Patry, 83–84

Mooshof, 197
Morgan, Frederick E., 60
Mortain, 102, 112
mortars, 92, 145
Mowat, Farley, 40, 170, 245
Moyland Wood, 194–95, 201–2
Mulberries (artificial ports), 64
munitions plants, 46–47
Murphy, William, 183–84

N

Nagasaki, 252, 254
National Resources Mobilization Act
  (NRMA), 22, 24, 256. *See also*
  home defence forces
National Selective Service system, 52
Neary, Peter, 263
Nebelwerfers, 91
Netherlands. *See also* Netherlands liberation; *specific locations*
  Canadians as occupation force, 242–49
  collaborators in, 215
  fascists in, 213–14, 221–22, 228, 229
  food relief operations, 221, 222, 244
  German evacuation, 241–42
  government-in-exile, 142, 143, 186, 221
  hunger in, 186, 221–22, 229, 232–33,
    243
  Jews in, 220–21
  men from, 243, 246
  postwar conditions, 231–33, 238–42,
    243–44
  Netherlands liberation, 3, 4, 216–17,
    220–21, 223, 233, 272, 279
  civilian response, 212–14, 232, 244,
    245, 246–48
  Dutch gratitude, 211, 228, 245, 248–49
  German resistance, 212–13, 216,
    224–25
  losses, 216, 225
Nicklin, Jeff, 206
night fighting, 35
Nijmegen, 153, 184–88

Non-Permanent Active Militia (NPAM).
  See militia
Normandy, 91, 112, 119, 123. *See also* Nor-
  mandy invasion; *specific locations*
Normandy invasion, 4. *See also* D-Day
  air support, 78, 83, 96–97, 100, 118
  Allied losses, 91, 97
  artillery support, 80–81, 83, 96
  Canadian losses, 79, 84–86, 90–92, 99,
    101, 119–20, 129
  German defence, 62–63, 78–84, 86,
    91–92, 100, 102, 117
  German losses, 79, 80–81, 83, 97, 118,
    125
  German retreat, 115–16, 118, 127–28
  naval support, 83, 85
  as success/failure, 83, 267–68
Norrey-en-Bessin, 80
North Nova Scotia Highlanders, 66,
    78–79, 161, 207, 212, 248
North Shore (New Brunswick) Regiment,
    86, 109, 138, 244
  on D-Day, 66, 71, 73, 76–77
Norway, 19–20

O

Odlum, Victor, 22
officers, 11–12, 56–57, 58–59, 202,
    274–75. *See also* staff officers
  casualties among, 121
  exhaustion and, 99–100
  First World War veterans as, 33, 36
  food and drink, 151–52, 185
  francophone, 202–3
  German, 229–30
  Jewish, 230
  from militia, 9–10, 16, 183–84
  from other ranks, 153
  from Permanent Force, 10–11, 36, 280
  ranks, 283–84
  as reinforcements, 153–54
  training of, 8–10, 100, 274
  young men as, 182–83